The Most Famous Car in the World

The Most Famous Car in the World

THE STORY OF THE FIRST E-TYPE JAGUAR

PHILIP PORTER

ORION

To the memory of my late father, Henry Porter.

CONTENTS

INTRODUCTION BY PHILIP PORTER

The title of this book is a rather pretentious one and a none-too-modest claim. How on earth can it be justified? I can imagine howls of derision in certain quarters!

I do not think that many would argue that the E-type is the most famous sports car in the world. The name Ferrari might be better known than Jaguar, but it is doubtful if many people in the street could name a Ferrari model. Even though it may not have the glamour, Ford is probably even better known than Ferrari simply because of the proliferation of examples and models. But how many people remember the Cortina?

It seems distastefully immodest to state it, as the owner, but it does appear to be true that 9600 HP is the most famous example of the most famous sports car.

Perhaps, what makes this car so different is that it has a name – 9600 HP. Not only is it universally known by this name amongst the cognoscenti, but the car even carries its name front and rear. Curiously, during my research, I learnt that in 1903 it was actually suggested that cars should display a name, like boats, instead of a combination of letters and numbers.

As a result, the car can be instantly recognised and it is amazing how people remember these things. At the time of its launch, 9600 HP was seen in most newspapers, many magazines and on television. Subsequently, it has made further appearances over the years in television programmes and magazine articles, including one newspaper colour supplement! It has even been described on TV as the most famous E-type in the world, so it must be true!

More recently, the car has been featured in international magazines, in national magazines in, for example, Denmark, in more newspaper articles and regularly on TV. It is one of the very few cars to have ever had an entire book devoted to it. I am not sure if I have proven the argument for the defence, but I will rest my case.

The whole story of 9600 HP is a complex one and the car really has had at least nine lives. It has touched the lives of many fascinating people and this is the story of those people as well as the car. Hopefully, it is no dry technical paper but rather a romance, a celebration and a detective story. The research has been intriguing, multifarious and, in itself, quite a story. I have interwoven it with the account of the challenging but brilliant resurrection of this, the oldest E-type in existence.

I have written quite a few books, but this one has been different. Like all, it has been a fresh challenge, but I have particularly enjoyed the greater breadth and, frankly, it has been enormous fun to write. I hope you can share in that fun.

One of the main reasons it has been so enjoyable is the many delightful people I have met and/or spoken to as a result. Without exception, from the world famous to more private individuals, everyone has entered into the spirit, been utterly charming and touchingly enthusiastic. As a result of my feverish research, the list of people I would like to thank would be an extremely long one – well over one hundred. May I therefore extend a very sincere thank you to all those quoted throughout the book. I have to add that John Pearson, Anne Hope, Kate Sayer and Frank Philpott have been exceptional in their assistance. Those not quoted but who have given important help behind the scenes include Maureen Partridge, Simon Taylor, Chris Adamson, Peter Hall, David Stuart Davies, Bev Goth, Martin Broomer and Ken McConomy of Jaguar and Alison Rawlings.

On the illustrative side, I would like to thank Autocar, BP, Jaguar Daimler Heritage Trust, John Pearson, Julian Ghosh, Peter Murray, Bob Blake, Bernard Cahier, John Langley, The Daily Express, Automobil Revue, Paul Skilleter, Tony Alden, Michael Tee, Peter Lockhart Smith and Kate Sayer for older material and David Parmiter, Tony Marshall, Nigel Harniman, Christian Frost and Tim Andrew for superlative recent photography. I should also like to thank the Editors of all publications quoted.

At Orion it has been a very great pleasure to work with Publishing Director Trevor Dolby, whose idea this book was and his assistant Pandora White. I greatly appreciate their advice, professionalism and support. The same goes for Leigh Jones, whose design skills have greatly enhanced this book and whose enthusiasm has been boundless.

Finally, I would like to offer my special thanks to several key people in this story – to Paul Skilleter for putting me in touch with previous owner Derek Brant, to Derek for choosing to sell the cars to me, to Norman Dewis for providing so much background information on the development of the E-type and the role 9600 HP played, and to Bob Berry for the story of his thrilling journey and much more. I shall always be indebted to the CMC team led by Andrew Tart, Nick Goldthorp and Peter Neumark for bringing the car back to life. My wife, Julie, has been wonderfully supportive and full of constructive suggestions. My great friend Steve Gilhooley – known universally as Gil – has given wise and invaluable counsel.

CHAPTER ONE

An Icon is Born

At seven o'clock on a cold winter's evening in 1961, a sleek Gunmetal Grey prototype of what is to be the most exciting production car the world has yet seen slithers out of a set of commonplace factory gates in suburban Coventry. This sleek, long, low projectile is bound for Geneva, where it is due to meet the world's press the following day, but it is late leaving.

There have been last-minute delays, inevitably. The car will need to show every ounce of its pure racing pedigree if it is to catch the night ferry from Dover and reach Geneva in time. But this car has been bred directly from a triple Le Mans-winning sports racing car. It has not only stunning good looks, but genuinely sensational performance. No thinly disguised and crude racer, this car is docile and comfortable. However, the car has more than tangible qualities; it is destined to become an icon.

The world is about to throw off the after-effects of the war, the dull uniformity of the 1950s. Fashions such as mini-skirts and outrageously long hair are about to satisfy the clamour for individuality and self-expression. It will be the era when the young break free, shock their parents and challenge the Establishment. This new sports car will shock, it will break conventions, it will make the pulse quicken, it will exude sensuality. With unintentional but perfect timing, it will be a seminal ingredient of the era popularly christened 'The Swinging Sixties'.

The night ferry safely caught, the car glides down the gangway in Calais in the small hours of the morning to begin a journey of nearly six hundred miles across France. As the driver presses on, driving flat out in this seriously fast car, the weather closes in. He encounters fog and yet the clock is ticking remorselessly. He has to balance speed with caution, the risk of being late against that of having an accident. Luckily he had raced successfully in the fifties and is considerably more capable behind the wheel than the average company executive.

The future of his company depends on this new model. The firm, which has enjoyed a glorious past, is becoming a little jaded. Having grown accustomed to leading, it is now being overtaken. The company needs a spiritual lift as well as a business boost. This car is destined to be such a success that it will not only lift the famous company, but earn immense prestige for British industry. It will achieve such notoriety and lasting fame that the car's name will become a synonym for speed.

In Reims the fog is so bad, he gets lost in the central square. As the fog finally clears south of Reims, he is once more able to use the performance. Convinced that he is going to be late and that the 200 members of the press who have been invited to a central Geneva park will have nothing to see, he has no alternative but to drive it like a racing car. This is before the age of blanket speed limits, but there are no motorways in France. He is using maximum revs in every gear between every bend. The amazing performance allows him to overtake whenever he has half a chance. He dares not take the direct route through the mountains for he fears the passes will be closed due to snow. He takes the safe option and joins all the lorries on the only route into Switzerland that he knows will be open. Accelerating, braking, accelerating, braking, he weaves in and out of the streams of heavy trucks trundling steadily along. They seem endless.

This secret new car is due to meet the press at midday. At 11.40am, the car speeds into the Geneva premises of Marcel Fleury, the local dealer. As it screeches to a halt, a team of mechanics swoop on the car and begin washing off the grime of the arduous journey and polishing its sensual, curvaceous body. Twenty minutes later, the car arrives in the Parc des Eaux Vives to meet the men who will convey their judgements to the world at large.

They are ecstatic. Their reports are eulogistic. The legend is born. The queues form. The dreams begin.

The make? Jaguar. The model? The E-type. The car? 9600 HP.

The Gunmetal Grey Jaguar E-type Fixed Head Coupé, in which Bob Berry had enjoyed the journey of his life, carried the distinctive registration 9600 HP. It was born with fame, achieved fame and had fame thrust upon it. Remarkably, this single example of the truly amazing new car has enjoyed an enduring fame from the moment of the model's dramatic launch in 1961 through into the next millennium and is generally known as the world's most famous E-type.

It had already had a very full and exciting life even before its public bow in Geneva in March 1961. As one of the very few prototypes, it had helped develop the E-type and had then been designated the Press Car. This led to it being road-tested by a number of leading magazines and distinguished journalists of various nationalities before its launch. This was the car that set the 150mph legend, but this feat was not easily achieved, and the intrepid testers had myriad adventures and many an overly exciting moment.

Still not able to rest on its laurels, 9600 HP continued as the Press Car for another year. During that time it was photographed for Jaguar brochures, used for publicity stunts and driven by such luminaries as Sir Stirling Moss. In mid-1962 it was

The Jaguar E-type caused a sensation when it was announced in 1961 and still causes a sensation today. The beautiful pure lines with minimal adornment resulted in a stunning piece of automotive sculpture. 9600 HP has had many lives and here is seen in its role as the Jaguar Press Car.

sold to a high-profile film director and in 1965 passed to a well-known racing driver. Three years later it was bought by an enthusiast who hardly used it and then was owned briefly by another enthusiast who had amassed a small collection of unique E-types. I acquired this collection in 1977 in rather unusual circumstances, after which, as I lacked the means to restore 9600 HP, it lay in one of my old rustic barns for the next 22 years.

In yet another twist in the highly involved story of this historic car, I was made an offer I could not refuse. The result would be the total, fanatical restoration by one of the top Jaguar specialists in the world, at some cost, but with the result that I would continue to own the star of my small collection and from March 2000 would be able to use and share the car with enthusiasts all over the world.

This then is the story of the car, of how it was created, what it did, who owned it and how it was restored to its former glory. It is the story of 9600 HP, but it is also the story of the many intriguing people who have played a part in the car's full and fascinating life.

But before we begin the story and the background to that story, it might be interesting to examine what made the Jaguar E-type so very special, to explain why it caused such a sensation back in 1961, and, first, to paint a brief picture of the world into which it was unleashed.

After an exciting first sixteen years of its life, 9600 HP was showing signs of its age when I bought the car in 1977. For a variety of reasons, it was destined to spend the next twenty two years in my various old outbuildings, but mainly in this C16th timber frame barn.

Sitting forlornly in the old barns, 9600 HP began to look very sad but it was not deteriorating any more and under the increasing grime was still very complete which was of vital importance as this car is so full of history.

On April 1st (yes really!), 1999 the old girl was wheeled out of the ancient barn to be taken to a firm of pre-eminent restorers who would commence a fanatical exercise in conservation as they brought the car back to life yet retaining all its many intriguing features and secrets.

The E-type became an integral part of the liberated new world that was the sixties. On 1 January 1961 another key constituent of the new liberated age arrived with the launch in Britain of the birth control pill. In world affairs, the big news was that the USA had broken off diplomatic relations with Cuba. Kennedy and Kruschev were at the head of their respective superpowers and the world was in the midst of the Cold War. Harold Macmillan was the British Prime Minister, and in mid-March, a day after the E-type had been launched, South Africa, under intense pressure, pulled out of the Commonwealth. Premier Dr Verwoerd said, 'I believe this marks the end of the Commonwealth.' *The Daily Mail*, apparently in all seriousness, reported that he made the announcement into a small black microphone! Sharing the dramatic front page were two photographs of a certain car and, announcing an exciting new competition, the words boldly displayed, 'That Jaguar Can Be Yours.'

As the Peter Kroger and Gordon Lonsdale spy case opened at the Old Bailey, miners in South Wales were striking over higher health charges and the officials of the Musicians' Union withdrew their labour! Michael Foot was expelled from the Labour Party for voting against his own Front Bench, and Dr Beeching was appointed Chairman of the Railways Board at a salary of £24,000 a year.

Four men conquered the North Face of the Eiger for the first time in winter and Floyd Patterson retained his heavyweight title by knocking out Sweden's Ingemar Johannson. The Hawker vertical take-off plane made its maiden flight, and Yuri Gagarin, a Soviet test pilot, took Russia to victory over America in the space race when he orbited the Earth in the *Vostok 1* spacecraft.

As Laurence Olivier did plight his troth with Joan Plowright, it was revealed that the 80-year-old Pablo Picasso had also married. His bride was a 34-year-old model. Susannah York was being tipped as a future star as Elizabeth Taylor was fighting for her life in hospital with pneumonia. HRH The Duke of Kent, who would be one of the very first customers for an exciting new sports car, had just become engaged to Miss Katherine Worsley.

'In France,' reported the *Sunday Express*, 'denim is picked for the big craze in holiday wear this year.'

The *Coventry Evening Telegraph* cost 2½d (1p) and a packet of Tom Thumb cigars were 4/1d (20p). Halfords were advertising oil at 10/6d (52p) a gallon and Servais silencers at 35/9d (£1.79). It was reported that a farm of 400 acres in Oxfordshire, Hampshire or Berkshire was worth £100,000 'with a really good period house'. Good farming land was realising as much as £200 an acre, but hill farmland fetched just a sixth of that.

Such was the state of Britain in early 1961. The Beatles were still a year or so off and Carnaby Street would follow. Mini-skirts did not actually arrive until 1964 and early sixties fashions perpetuated the staid fifties look. But the decade fondly recalled as the Swinging Sixties would soon be in full swing, with British pop stars, British fashions and a British sports car leading this brave new world.

Part of the reason for the E-type being so exciting was that almost every other motor car was just so mundane. In the late fifties, the Mini had arrived to stir up the dreary scene but otherwise dullness was almost deemed a virtue with every other make and model. In such an array of mediocrity, the E-type could hardly fail to be a sensation. With a top speed around double the average and a startlingly modern body, the vibrant E-type gave the dour motoring world a real kick in the pants.

To understand the impact the E-type Jaguar made on the public, it is important to appreciate something of the motoring scene in the late fifties and very early sixties and how it contrasted with the present. Today we live in an age when all production cars, however cheaply priced or modest in specification, are impressively good. They have to be because the marketplace is so competitive and the public's awareness and demands so much greater. The days of the gentlemanly motoring magazines writing charitably of absolute dross are gone. Today, if a car is not good, it is publicly crucified. The press are rapaciously analytical and not constrained about speaking their minds. In fact, it is fashionable to be outrageously critical.

Back in the fifties customers demanded solid virtues, such as interior space, comparative economy and dependability, rather than excitement. Saloon car performance was pretty feeble, the steering soggy and handling questionable, particularly in the wet. But if the car would carry sufficient persons and their luggage, the average driver would be satisfied and probably never explore even such modest limits because he drove so slowly.

That the E-type was such a contrast to this attitude, such a challenge to mediocrity, such a revelation in so many areas, is not surprising when you take a glance at the standards of the day. The most startling and obvious difference was performance. A top speed of 150mph was truly stunning when compared with 99.9 per cent of cars on the road. The Morris Oxford could manage just 80mph, the Mercedes-Benz 220 SE a fraction over the 'ton' at 105mph, one of the revolutionary new Minis ran out of steam at 72mph, the MG Magnette could manage 88mph, the Holden Special Sedan 84mph, the Singer Gazelle 80mph and the Triumph Herald Coupe 75mph. These, it should be emphasized, were top speeds, not cruising speeds, which were more modest still.

Of the sports cars on the market then, the Austin Healey Sprite achieved a maximum of 83mph, the MGA 96mph, the Sunbeam Alpine 99mph, the TR3 109mph, the Lotus Elite 111mph, the Healey 3000 115mph and the AC Ace-Bristol 116mph. Ascending to the more rarified regions, the Daimler SP250 would clock up 124mph, the 3.4 XK150 'S' FHC 132mph, the Aston Martin DB4 some 139mph and the Facel Vega a shade more at 140mph – but it required some 6.3 litres of American V8 muscle to propel its 30cwt to that velocity.

The only cars that could compete with the E-type's maximum speed were such as the Mercedes-Benz 300SL and one or two of the hottest Ferraris. But the 300SL Roadster, of which just 1858 were built between 1957 and 1963, cost £4651, and the Ferraris, which were produced in comparative handfuls, were similarly expensive with the 250 GT costing £5951. BMW charged £4201 for the very rare 507, while the DB4 Aston was priced at £3967 and the AC Greyhound at £3185. The E-type was just £2097 for the Roadster and £2196 for the Fixed Head Coupé.

Perhaps surprisingly, the E-type was bred to give effortless top gear acceleration but was still pretty quick off the line. Its 0–60mph times of 6.9 secs (Fixed Head Coupé) and 7.1 (Roadster) compared rather favourably with the Ferrari 250 GT at 6.8, Aston Martin DB4 saloon at 9.3, Triumph TR3 at 11.4, Ford Galaxie at 13.6, Morris Oxford at 24.1 and Mini-Minor 850 de luxe saloon at 28.7.

Two widely respected motoring journalists of the period were Philip Turner and Charles Bulmer, both of whom worked on *The Motor* magazine.

Around 1989 Philip Turner, told me: 'It differed so from other high-performance cars of that period in that it was so easy to drive. Things like Ferraris, and Astons to some extent, were very intolerant of town traffic. They had a light flywheel and the revs used to shoot up. Either you kept the revs up or they wouldn't pull. But this would loaf along and in that respect was more like a modern high-performance car. The roadholding was superb and it was so comfortable too.

'Even a lot of Le Mans cars weren't doing 150 in those days. It was an enormous step forward and there was no doubt it was going to be a tremendous success.'

Charles Bulmer in the early eighties: 'To put the E-type in any sort of context you need to remember what sports cars were like twenty years ago. Most of them were rough, noisy and, above all, uncomfortable. Many of them were quite slow and, even if they were not, their cruising speeds were often dictated by indifferent road-holding or human tolerance. There was, of course, a sort of hair shirt mentality which insisted that the motoring enjoyment of the real enthusiast would be ruined by comfort, weather protection and luggage space.'

As to the public reaction, 'It caused tremendous interest. It was such a striking car. Such a lot of new road test cars you drove about in before launch caused no reaction – even the Rover 2000 attracted very little attention. But the E-type nobody could possibly escape. Everybody reacted and took a second look at it. We daren't leave it in a lot of places. If you left it unattended, you had absolute swarms over it.'

Apart from performance, and value for money, the other great appeal of the E-type was its stunning good looks. When most saloons were decidedly conservative in their styling and most sports and GT cars rather traditional, the E-type bravely broke new ground and was quite simply a sensational piece of sculpture. Perhaps the best way of emphasizing that point is to look at these various cars today. Although many have become much-loved classics, all have a dated appearance. It can be argued that the E-type has remained truly timeless.

The E-type moved the goal-posts. It set a new agenda. The new Jaguar introduced levels of performance previously achieved only by racing cars and very low-volume road cars of twice and three times the price. It did so with more sophisticated suspension than even its expensive rivals, giving excellent roadholding and unparalleled ride quality for such a car. All of this was clothed in a body which would be widely

Getaway people
get Super National

Getaway people don't waste time. neither does Super National. It fires first go, warms your engine before you've pushed in the clutch! Getaway people get *go* out of life. Super National puts *go* into cars! Do you belong to the Getaway people? Get Super National at the blue and yellow National Sign.

GETAWAY PEOPLE

GET SUPER NATIONAL

SUPER
NATIONAL

National

The Jaguar E-type was very much an integral part of the vibrant 'Swinging Sixties' and advertisers, keen to cash in on the image of uninhibited speed, style and sheer sensuality, linked their names and products with this icon of the decade.

copied – Triumph GT6, Ferrari 275 GTB, Datsun 240Z, to name a few – but never remotely equalled.

That is not to say the E-type was perfect. It most certainly was not. Any balanced critique should state that the gearbox was painfully slow and archaic, the brakes could be very marginal and many found the seats to be dreadful. Most disappointingly, Jaguar durability and reliability were compromised by a policy of paying the lowest possible price for components, almost irrespective of quality. If Jaguar had charged £100 more for the car and spent it on better-quality parts, they would have saved themselves, and particularly their customers, and especially those in the States, a lot of heartache and disillusionment. Sadly an attitude of, 'We know best and we are not interested in listening to our customers and employees out in the field,' prevailed. What a tragedy. It was an attitude that would later bring Jaguar to its knees.

The impact of the XK-E, as it was called in America, in that vast country is quite impossible to quantify. That it was a sensational success is unquestionable. But this most exciting of cars, a worthy successor to the equally stunning XK120, impacted in other ways. Its magic reflected on the Jaguar sedans, and it added immensely to British prestige, with regard to engineering and in a broader sense. As stated, the XK-E was not without faults and must have driven many owners to the very edge of despair, compounded by the company's arrogant deafness to feedback. But all it took was a quick blast up the highway to restore all the good feelings, the heady excitement and rekindle the love affair. In the early sixties, the blend of sensual good looks, breathtaking performance and sheer presence was utterly intoxicating. You can forgive a mistress like the XK-E almost anything!

CHAPTER TWO

E-type Ancestry

The Jaguar story can be traced back to the early 1920s when an ambitious young motor cycle enthusiast by the name of Billy Lyons joined forces with William Walmsley to form the Swallow Sidecar Co. With an overdraft of £1000 and modest first-floor premises in Blackpool, the Northern seaside town more famous for its rock and tower, the fledgeling company was born. The Austin Seven motor car was still a couple of years away and the motor cycle and sidecar combination was a popular alternative for the working man to public transport, the bicycle or plain walking. However, the average sidecar was a very dull-looking creation that gave no thought to style.

Style is a keyword throughout the Jaguar story. Lyons always knew the importance of style. Even today, most people are more influenced by the style of a car, when considering buying one, than mere practical considerations. Walmsley had been producing a very stylish sidecar which looked like a tiny Zeppelin, and Lyons instantly saw its appeal and business potential. A sense of style and acute business acumen were his two great traits.

The Swallow sidecars were a great success, and when the revolutionary Austin Seven threatened to steal their market, Swallow started building stylish little sporty two-seater bodies on Austin Seven chassis. A meeting with Bertie Henly, a successful London car dealer, resulted in an order for 500, providing an enormous boost for the tiny company which was now rapidly expanding. The chassis were bought direct from the Austin works and delivered to the local railway station. With insufficient storage facilities, even at their larger premises, the increased quantity of chassis awaiting collection caused chaos at the station much to the considerable annoyance of the station master!

In 1928, Lyons and Walmsley decided it made good sense to move their thriving company to the more traditional motor manufacturing area of the Midlands. A run-down old munitions factory was acquired in Coventry and the range of models on which Swallow added their coachbuilt bodies expanded. Seeking greater freedom for their designs and to take another step up the ladder, Lyons did a deal with the Standard Motor Co. to produce chassis exclusively for what would henceforth be known as the products of SS Cars.

The SSI was ridiculously low and had a ludicrously long bonnet as Lyons tried to out-Bentley Bentley. The difference was that the Bentley was a true performance car and the SSI just looked it. However, as the company's adverts, which were always totally over the top, had it, the rakish new SSI had the look of a £1000 car for just £310. Though the less charitable nicknamed the cars Soda-Squirt or Super-Sexed, they caught the public imagination.

Through the 1930s the models were improved and made more practical, but still looked like a Bentley at a fraction of the price. In 1935 the new range was given the model name Jaguar and the SS Jaguar 100 sports car was added to the line-up. Particularly in its later 3½-litre form, this model was a genuine sports car and was starting to build a more serious reputation for the company when war intervened. War work consisted of producing thousands of sidecars, some 700 trailers a week, repair work on Whitley and Wellington bombers and the manufacture of aircraft parts including wings for Avro Lancasters, Spitfires and de Havilland Mosquitos. Towards the end of the war, the company was instructed to manufacture the complete centre sections for the then highly secret Gloster Meteor III jet fighter. This introduction to aircraft technology was to prove highly significant in the post-war years.

Lyons, who had bought out his less ambitious partner in 1934, realized that if he was ever to become a really serious motor manufacturer, his renamed Jaguar company had to produce its own engine. If that engine could be a technically innovative production power unit, then he could not only emulate his competitors but steal a march on them. Showing remarkable courage once again, he set his small but brilliant team of designers – William Heynes, Walter Hassan, Claude Baily and consultants Laurie Hathaway and Harry Weslake – the task of designing an engine that was powerful, practical, advanced and, just as importantly, stylish.

The resulting twin overhead cam, straight six, 3½ litre engine was named the XK. It was intended for a completely new range of large sporting saloons, but Lyons could not afford to develop the engine and the new range immediately. However, sports cars attracted plenty of good publicity and improved the image, and Jaguar had not re-introduced a sports car after the war. Also, extraordinary though it may seem in this age of zero tolerance, the sports car driver was then a forgiving enthusiast who would make a good guinea pig for developing the new engine.

Lyons had already designed a one-off sports car prototype, code-named the XL, just after hostilities ceased, and with the 1948 Motor Show fast approaching he created a masterpiece that would become one of the greatest sports cars of all time. The ultra-modern, high-performance XK120 was the sensation of the Earls Court Show.

Named for its top speed, the single bronze prototype on the stand had never actually run and when it did the maximum was initially only 104mph. However, with

The XK120, which was launched in 1948, combined great performance with glamour. Hollywood stars took the XK120 to their hearts but this brilliant sports car proved in rallying, racing and record-breaking that it was far more than just stunningly good-looking.

some development, the model was to prove more than worthy of its type name and officially became the fastest production car in the world.

The vast majority were exported and became a cult in the United States and in particular with Hollywood stars like Clark Gable, Tyrone Power, Spencer Tracy and Humphrey Bogart. A high proportion of the early examples were entered in competitions and covered themselves in glory, whether it was racing, rallying or record breaking. After victory first time out at Silverstone in 1949, three XK120s were entered at Le Mans the following year. This was purely an exploratory exercise, with no real thoughts of success, but after 21 hours the third-placed XK was averaging 8mph more than the leading Talbot and might conceivably have won had its clutch not given up the fight.

The famous Tourist Trophy race was revived the same year and held at Dundrod, Ulster. Fleet Street motoring journalist and competitor Tommy Wisdom, who would later drive 9600 HP and had been allocated one of six specially prepared semi-works 120s, wrote about the event some years later:

I was taking high octane refreshment in the Steering Wheel Club, London's mecca of motor sporting folk, when a fresh-faced, curly-haired youngster whom I already knew slightly, Stirling Moss by name, came alongside, drew up a bar stool and dropped a broad hint. He'd noticed that I'd filed two entries for the forthcoming Tourist

Trophy … what were my plans for whichever car I didn't drive myself? An hour later I found I'd accepted, subject to his father's OK, the persuasive Stirling's proposition that he should drive my XK in the TT, leaving me to handle the works-owned Jowitt Jupiter that its makers had entered.

Moss had never driven an XK120 when our TT pact was made, but the makers sportingly put one at his disposal for pre-Dundrod familiarization drives on the road. I say sportingly because I think they were beginning to kick themselves for not having offered the boy a TT drive themselves. They had turned Moss down as too young and inexperienced.

Moss himself recalled, 'You could only get Jags if you were important or press.'

Moss set fastest time in practice in dry conditions, but race day was beset with torrential rain. Nevertheless the young Moss set a cracking pace to take a famous victory that played an important part in his emerging career. 'Non-stop, gale-driven torrents of rain,' was one contemporary press description. Frank Rainbow, one of the racing mechanics, remembered the day with great merriment.

'I have never seen such rain in all my life. But it was hilarious. On the opposite side of the road to the pits was a beer tent. All the good souls were watching the race with pints in their hands – Guinness and so forth. The rain came and the wind blew. Then suddenly this marquee collapsed. It was the funniest thing in the world to see people clambering out, still clutching their pints!'

'That was my first big, big opportunity in motor racing,' says Moss, 'because I had asked a lot of people at that time if they would let me drive their cars in the TT but none of them would trust me. They thought I was going too fast for my experience, and if I was going to have an accident and kill myself, they didn't want me to do it in their car. So none of the companies, including Aston, Jaguar, MG and many of the lesser ones, would let me have one. I was very grateful to Tommy Wisdom for fixing it up so that I could borrow his. Sir William came up to me that evening and asked if I would lead the team the following year.'

Jaguar had decided to go into motor racing properly with their own factory team and specially designed sports racing cars with one single aim in mind, namely victory at Le Mans. Among European races, Le Mans was unique in that it was the only one to be reported on the front pages of newspapers across America. Lyons knew that that was where his largest potential market lay and thus victory in the 24-hour race classic would do more to establish Jaguar than any amount of costly advertising.

This car, which would initially be code-named the XK150, but later became the XK120C (C for competition), was based on the production XK120 which had done so well in 1950. However, to reduce weight a space-framed chassis was drawn up by the Project Engineer, one Bob Knight. It was also realized that a more streamlined body would help the cause, especially as the Sarthe circuit was a high-speed course with one straight of some two and a half miles length. Jaguar needed an aerodynamicist. Enter Malcolm Sayer.

No one now recalls how Sayer actually came to get the job, but in his CV he states, 'In September 1950 I started to design for Jaguar a car to resemble their XK series, and using the same mechanical components, but capable of winning the Le Mans 24-hour race. I was responsible for general layout, body and frame.'

'Lofty' England was then in charge of the Service Department, but with his motor racing background was a natural for the unofficial job of Team Manager. He stated, 'Malcolm Sayer was brought in to produce an aerodynamic shape but still keep it resembling a Jaguar in some way. This is probably why the wing line swept up and down rather than being straight.'

Famously one of the C-types, as they became known outside the factory, piloted by Peter Walker and Peter Whitehead, took a brilliant debut victory at Le Mans in 1951 after Stirling Moss, partnered by Jack Fairman (who would later own 9600 HP), had broken the opposition before retiring. In 1952, almost as famously, the hastily revised C-types failed, having been unwisely modified just before the race when Moss returned from the Mille Miglia reporting that the Mercedes-Benz 300SLs were faster.

'I was doing about 150mph on the Ravenna straight,' stated Moss of the Mille Miglia. 'It was pouring with rain, and there was a nasty cross-wind which made it very difficult to keep the car on the road. The mechanic had his head down – said he daren't look! – and as a matter of fact I was frightening myself stiff. But at least I thought I was pressing on as hard as anyone could – when a Mercedes went past me! I managed to overtake it again later, but I can tell you it shook me.' The Mercedes drivers had the advantage of being in closed cars in the shocking conditions, but this experience so concerned Moss that he telegraphed Jaguar, 'Must have more speed at Le Mans'. Incidentally, the mechanic, as Moss refers to him, was Norman Dewis, who would later conduct all the testing on 9600 HP, which Moss would also drive in the future.

Jaguar returned in 1953 without the long nose, long tail body treatment but with two important mechanical revisions. The engines were fitted with triple Webers, which increased power and more significantly torque, and more crucially the new works C-types had the revolutionary disc brakes which Dunlop had developed in conjunction with Jaguar. Larger-than-life characters Duncan Hamilton and Tony Rolt steered their works C-type to a very fine victory in Coronation year against one of the strongest fields, in terms of drivers and cars, ever seen at Le Mans.

Meanwhile in the rallying world, Ian Appleyard and his white XK120 with the distinctive registration NUB 120 had clocked up innumerable international wins to become, arguably, the most famous car and driver combination in the history of the sport.

During 1953 a prototype was constructed that was highly significant to the E-type story. Alfa Romeo had built a couple of styling exercises which were given the name disco volante (flying saucer). I discovered some years ago that Sayer had photographs of these cars, one open, one closed, in his possession, and they may well have provided the inspiration for his 1953 prototype. This mysterious car was called by a bewildering number of names. It was called the C/D, the XK120C Mark II, the XP11 but most generally at the factory it was referred to simply as the 'light alloy' car. It was a halfway house between the C-type and later D-type and introduced many of the significant features of the legendary 'D'. First and foremost, it was of (largely) monocoque construction, which was a first for a two-seater sports racing car.

This little-known one-off 1953 prototype that was generally known to the engineers at the Jaguar factory as the 'light alloy' car was a highly significant step in the evolution of the Jaguar sports car. Not only was it the first to use monocoque construction, but it introduced the elliptical mouth that would become a Jaguar hallmark. This photograph was taken by schoolboy John Pearson using his Box Brownie!

Perhaps the most exciting thing about this unique car was that it introduced the essence of the E-type shape with the distinctive elliptical mouth that has become a Jaguar sports car hallmark. If one reflects for a moment on the impact of the E-type styling in 1961, just imagine how sensational the 'light alloy' car must have seemed eight years before. However, the car was only ever seen by a very few, and little has ever been written about it. John Pearson, who is today a pre-eminent restorer of D-types and has a wealth of Jaguar knowledge accumulated over a lifetime's passion, has, as I do, a particularly soft spot for this curious prototype. He refers to it as 'our car'. John, who was at school in Silverstone village, used to play truant and walk up to the old airfield circuit. There he took photos on his Box Brownie and chatted with the drivers. Stirling Moss used to give him a lift home in his modified Standard 8 with a 10 engine – 'green with a cream roof. SFM 777, an incredible little car,' recalls John! Many years later, he would ride in 9600 HP with 'Lofty' England and during Jack Fairman's ownership. In 1973 Pearson sold me a very rare Jaguar, which is how we met.

Returning to the 'light alloy' car, Bob Berry also recalls this forgotten car. 'It was the first stab at the process that produced the D-type. I seem to remember it was used primarily to prove the method of construction of the monocoque and argon arc welding. Argon arc welding was done in the corner of the Experimental shop behind a screen which consisted of heavy sacking kept wet. Several ace welders employed by Jaguar, and particularly by Ted Loades at Abbey Panels, seemed to spend a lifetime behind this thing trying to develop the technique. If I remember correctly, the problem was not doing the welding, but doing it without distorting the panels themselves.' What added to the challenge was that this car was constructed of magnesium alloy to save weight.

Proving that he was human after all, William Lyons, the master-stylist, was responsible for this monster which became known as the Brontosaurus. Clearly it was not one of his happier creations.

'Lofty' England recalled the car and others with a touch of his famous sarcasm. 'It was made towards the end of '53 and at the same time as the Brontosaurus thing which the Old Man got built – in fact, there were cars being built all round the factory. We were a bit slow in the Engineering Dept. (!) so the Old Man decided he would push everybody along. He was a wonderful character. Therefore, he got that damn Brontosaurus thing done by Fred Gardner.' Brontosaurus was the nickname given to this especially ugly one-off sports car created by Lyons. Gardner, who ran the wood shop, had a unique relationship with Lyons, in that he was the only colleague Lyons ever addressed by his first name!

'Then,' continues 'Lofty', 'he got Bernard Hartshorn, one of the superintendents, doing one with a tubular backbone chassis with two C-type chassis back to back. I said to Sir William one day, "I don't know, Sir William, everywhere I go somebody's building a new sports car. Do you think I should start?"

'"Not a bad idea, England," he said,' recollected 'Lofty' with great amusement.

The contraption made up from the front halves of two C-type chassis mated together was probably intended for a still-born Grand Prix car project. Certainly Malcolm Sayer drew several Formula One cars and had models made for wind tunnel testing. So Jaguar's venture into Grand Prix racing in 2000 was not the first time the company had toyed with the idea of Formula One.

The 'light alloy' car was taken to Jabbeke, in Belgium, where a long, quiet stretch of motorway existed and which Jaguar and others used for high speed runs and record breaking. In spite of misfiring slightly at the top end, Norman Dewis and the prototype achieved a speed of 178mph – which sounds quite impressive but was completely overshadowed by the XK120 which Jaguar had also prepared for high-speed running and taken along. This achieved the quite remarkable speed of 172mph. Though not as fast as the 'light alloy' car, it was the more exceptional feat, for the XK120 was a modified production car with a normal top speed of around 120mph, whereas the other was a prototype sports racing car.

Back in England, the prototype was tested extensively. During December Dewis was using it to evaluate a new design of Dunlop tyre at Silverstone and on the fourth day of the new year, Stirling Moss tried it. Referring to Dewis's notes we learn, 'Chief complaints from Moss: too much understeer. Pedal layout poor. Steering wheel position needs modifying. Total number of laps by Moss 17. Best lap 1-58.'

Moss does not recall the car, but when told he complained about aspects of it, commented, 'Probably the seat. They didn't pay too much attention to the driver's comfort in those days, I'll tell you.' Looking at a photo, he volunteered, 'I must say it's a nice-looking car.'

Returning to Dewis's log: 'Continuation of tyre test by myself. Skated off circuit at Chapel Curve to the point of nearly overturning. B-fools of Dunlops swapped tyres without informing me!!!'

Meanwhile the XK120 Roadster, or Open Two-Seater Super Sports (OTS) as it was officially entitled, had been joined in 1951 by a Fixed Head Coupé (FHC) model and in 1953 by a Drop Head Coupé (DHC) version. Both these were rather more opulent than the stark wind-in-the-hair Roadster and had walnut-veneered dashboards, like the plush saloons, and wind-up windows. The marriage of the roof and the Roadster body to create the FHC was one of Lyons's great styling successes, and Stirling Moss remembers his as a fine long-distance tourer. He even used to tow his caravan around to continental race meetings during the season with his 120 FHC – until it broke loose one day! Officially the FHC was for export only, and very few right-hand-drive cars were made. The DHC had a lined, folding hood which was much more sophisticated than the Roadster's rudimentary affair.

In 1954 the XK120 range was superseded by three new XK140 models. With a little more power, enhanced brakes, improved steering and better weight distribution, the 140s updated the concept while retaining the essential XK style. The Drop Head and Fixed Head Coupé models additionally had two extra rear seats. These were ideal for small children and pygmies with no legs. The XK140s continued to sell well around the world and particularly in the USA. When the classic car boom started many years later, the poor old 140s were looked down upon by ignorant commentators but, amusingly, today they are among the most sought-after and valuable of XKs.

Also completed in 1954, the D-type sports racing car was a refinement of many of the principles first employed on the 'light alloy' car. With good reason, it has often been described as an aircraft on wheels. The fabulous D-type had many innovative features that we now take for granted, either on road cars or modern racing cars – alloy wheels, rubber bag tanks, disc brakes, monocoque construction, aerodynamic fins and, later, fuel injection.

With a body designed, like the C-type and 'light alloy car', by Malcolm Sayer, the D-type is generally regarded as the definitive sports racing car of the fifties. Created for the high speed Le Mans race, Sayer's brilliant shape allowed the D-types to be faster than the more powerful Ferraris and Mercedes-Benz and take three Le Mans victories.

After some 24 hours of flat-out racing at Le Mans in appalling weather conditions, with delays caused by blocked filters as a result of fine dust mysteriously present in the fuel and a spot of blatant cheating by Ferrari, the D-type driven by those heroes Hamilton and Rolt missed victory by a mere 105 seconds. The following year the race began with a fabulous battle between Castellotti in a Ferrari, Fangio in a 300SLR Mercedes-Benz and Mike Hawthorn in the new long-nose D-type. Then both Hawthorn and Fangio overtook Castellotti, who struggled to maintain the pace as it hotted up, the lap record falling repeatedly. On the 28th lap Hawthorn set the fastest lap of the race. Driven, on his own admission, by his anti-German prejudice, he was driving flat out with nothing in reserve. Fangio told Hawthorn afterwards that he, too, was on the absolute limit. Side by side much of the time, they sometimes even grinned at each other in enjoyment and mutual admiration.

Then, very abruptly, the wonderful duel was terminated in a sudden, sad and sobering conclusion when the worst disaster in motor racing history occurred. As usual, Malcolm Sayer was one of Jaguar's timekeepers in the pits and, according to his post-race report, the accident happened at 6.27pm.

Shortly before the accident, Hawthorn had opened up a slight lead on Fangio and had just lapped the Argentinian's team-mate, the ageing Pierre Levegh, in another Mercedes. Accelerating out of White House, the fast corner before the pits straight, Hawthorn overtook Lance Macklin in an Austin Healey, a car which had a lengthened tail for better aerodynamic efficiency, before preparing for a routine pit-stop. Hawthorn moved over to the right, with Macklin behind, and began to slow. To avoid him, Macklin swung into the middle of the very narrow track. For some reason Levegh failed to react to this and his Mercedes smote the rear of the Healey which, with its long tail, acted like a launching-ramp. The Mercedes became airborne and smashed into a concrete parapet at the side of the track, throwing Levegh out. He was killed instantly and the car exploded. As it did so, components such as the engine and front suspension scythed through the crowd. The result was 85 dead and many more injured.

We shall see how this horrific accident affected sports car racing and led directly to the conception of the E-type Jaguar. First, however, we must become better acquainted with a man who was arguably the most important figure in Jaguar's sports car history.

CHAPTER THREE

Man of Vision

Malcolm Sayer was a fascinating man – brilliant, innovative, eccentric and charming. Employing ground-breaking mathematical techniques, he created a landmark racing car and a landmark road car. The former was the curvaceous 'aircraft on wheels', the D-type, and the latter was, of course, the E-type, effectively the productionized version of the 'D'.

Sayer is often referred to as the man whose influence on Jaguar styling was second only to that of the 'Old Man' himself, Sir William Lyons. But Nick Scheele, the highly effective and hugely popular Chairman of Jaguar in the nineties, before he was promoted to be President of Ford of Europe, feels that Malcolm Sayer's influence on Jaguar styling was even more important than that of Lyons. The irony is that Sayer hated to be called a stylist. He was an aerodynamicist. However, he was far from being a blinkered boffin with narrow interests. His depth was broad, but little has ever been written about this mysterious man.

Born at Cromer in Norfolk on 21 May 1916, he gained a scholarship to Great Yarmouth Grammar School. 'As a child, he was very delicate in health, very delicate indeed,' says his sister Joan.

It was because he was born in 1916, right in the worst part of the first war. My mother had a hard job to get proper food for him as an infant. She had to show the baby before she could get a tin of condensed milk even. There was no proper rationing, we just lived from hand-to-mouth in those days – everybody did.'

An aunt took an allotment and grew vegetables for the family.

When he got to school, at the age of five, he fell prey to every disease and infection floating about. He had diphtheria very badly, and of course they hadn't the cures in those days. It took a while to diagnose them and then they had to be largely treated at home. It left

21

him very, very weak indeed. He didn't put in a proper year's schooling until he was about eight or nine, but both mother and father being teachers, they taught him a lot at home.

Of course, cars were his one object in life, right from being a very small child. We had a toy cupboard each and Malcolm's was crammed with little lead and tin models and he was very skilful himself in making Meccano models. He always loved Heath Robinson's inventions and he derived a lot of inspiration from them. He was very clever in that way.

Joan's husband, Felix Bernasconi, confirms the early interest in cars. 'He loved cars ever since he was quite small. He used to make models which he photographed and they looked quite impressive. They had cheese boxes as wheels. It was always cars he was keen on.'

'He was very, very clever at school,' states Sayer's elder daughter Kate, who is extremely proud of her father. 'I've got all these sickeningly perfect school reports. I think it was quite a burden for him being so clever. He won The Commonwealth Scholarship when he was young.' These school reports confirm that he was younger than his class's average age and this second scholarship gained him entrance to Loughborough College where, appropriately, he entered the Automobile Department in 1933. At some stage he had a motorbike, for Felix remembers he modified it to have a steering wheel instead of handlebars.

There were four halls of residence at Loughborough and Sayer lived in the most expensive, where he mixed with the sons of wealthy families. 'Father sent him there,' says Joan, 'because he wanted him to have a good chance, because they had single rooms instead of having to share, or even live in a dormitory. He got on well. He was very ambitious but he did some remarkable things. For example, he'd accept hospitality from people he'd never met and people who were obviously very wealthy or with a title, with not a hope in Hell of returning their hospitality.'

Felix remembers it well. 'The wealthy people used to invite him to their places and that used to rather worry his mother because he couldn't possibly return the compliment. We had lots of postcards from him. In one he said, "We are in this marvellous car and wherever we stop, crowds of people form round us to look at the car."'

It is amusing to reflect for a moment that the greatest 'crowd stopper' of all would be the E-type which he designed. It would be fanciful to claim that this formative experience led him to create dramatic cars. Nevertheless, it surely made an impression, and we do know he liked drama for during his time at Loughborough he revived the defunct dramatic society and stage-managed its productions.

His sister recalls his eccentric behaviour. 'He always made a terrific scene when he went in a shop. I got quite embarrassed at times. He was a showman. When he went in a shop, he never specified exactly what he wanted. He would get them to put a whole array of stuff on the counter and say, "Oh, thank you very much, there's nothing suitable" and go sweeping out of the shop in front of everybody, and I know I apologized for him more than once.

'He learnt to drive when he was at Loughborough. When he came back, he wanted a car, so we had a Ford. He didn't like that because it was a closed family saloon. Then he had a Singer and he taught me to drive that. Then he changed that. He said, "Oh, this is a common old car." He changed it for a Riley. "This is too powerful for you, you can't drive this." He had that for several years and then, "I want something better than this." So he changed the Riley for a Bentley, which simply ate up the petrol. It was a marvellous car, though. Poor old father's pocket.'

Felix recollects that they used to walk along the sea front at Yarmouth, where he was then living, and pick out all the different makes. 'In those days cars were more individual than they are today and you could tell the difference between Hispano Suizas and Bugattis.' Felix recalls that Sayer called his Bentley 'Boadicea' and had the back altered to look more like an Aston Martin with a raked petrol tank. Was it an Aston Martin that he was copying, or could it have been the sensationally good-looking SS Jaguar 100? A feature of this overtly handsome sports car was its raked petrol tank.

'He used to drive everywhere in it,' states Joan of the Bentley, 'parading up and down the sea front and that type of thing. He didn't take the Bentley away with him and it was in the garage here for years and years and years. I think the garage began to fall down round the car.' He was by all accounts a good driver and a fast one when he chose. While at Loughborough, he clearly had time for other pursuits because in addition to stage management he was Secretary of the college motor club and occupied the same post for the local branch of the Institution of Automobile Engineers. He also edited the college magazine for two years.

Kate has a number of her father's letters to his parents. They reveal that he enjoyed life to the full. 'He used to take part in all sorts of weird races. He described one race where the steering wheel wasn't working on the car and so, in order to go round the corners, he had to get out of the car and run along and kick the wheels to turn them. I don't know whether that was exaggerating for his parents' benefit or to worry his parents, but it makes a good story.

'He and two friends went to a fancy dress party in London. They sewed three boilersuits together and went as a "shapeless mass". They had rather a lot to drink and fell down the steps at the underground station. I think my dad broke his arm and somebody else broke a leg.'

In spite of the high jinks, he obviously took his work seriously because he left Loughborough in 1938 with an Hons. Diploma in Automobile Engineering. Though his first love was cars, he actually joined the Bristol Aeroplane Company, Engines Division, where, as he put it, 'pay and prospects greatly exceeded any in the car industry.' The fact that he went into the aircraft industry first would have an enduring influence on his career, his later designs and their success, and indeed the very future of Jaguar. Today we think of the automotive industry as being highly technological and Formula One being at the pinnacle of that technology. But it certainly was not so in the pre- and early post-war years. From 1939 the aircraft industry had, of course, an added impetus to develop faster, lighter and more manoeuvrable planes. Sayer's time at BAC was the perfect grounding (no pun intended) for the career that he was to follow, not that he was to know it then.

For the first few weeks he was a fitter in the Experimental Department, and was soon given top skill rating. He then joined the Experimental staff and, for about two years, supervised a small group investigating troubles in superchargers and similar components. This introduced him to realistic testing and deduction methods. Promoted to the Design Department, his first work was the recommendation of possible alternative materials or techniques for mass-producing engine parts. This study of production possibilities and limitations lasted about a year and he later considered this experience to be of great value to him.

Next he moved to the design of engine installations, and investigated interchangeable power plants for the main bomber force. Crucially, this aroused an interest in the behaviour of airflow, and gave him valuable experience in efficient structural design and user consideration.

During the next five years he was given the task of planning, assembling staff and machinery, and managing a new Project Design Department. Its brief was to design and produce practical and convincing mock-ups and models of future aircraft powerplants from fluid and imprecise design information. From this Sayer gained useful experience in drawing upon expert advice in varied fields to produce a working result and, significantly, his knowledge of aerodynamics also increased greatly.

Felix Bernasconi: 'He worked on the Blenheims a lot and I remember he said he came up with a lot of inventions. He improved the wings, that sort of thing. He was always on streamlining. Aerodynamics, that was his main thing.'

Spare time was all used in such activities as ATC, Observer corps, first aid and the extinguishing of fires and incendiary bombs.

The Bristol factory was of great strategic importance and not surprisingly was a prime target for enemy attack. During one night-bombing raid, the factory suffered a direct hit and many people were killed. Sayer was slightly injured and a photograph exists of him holding a large piece of shrapnel and with his head bandaged. He saw some horrific sights and was very traumatized. Apparently, he wandered around in a daze amid the scenes of carnage, asking, 'Is it all right if I go home?' of people who were half dead. His blood was affected and he later broke out into dreadful boils.

During this period, the drawing office was evacuated to Bristol Zoo, and he liked that because he spent his lunch-times making friends with the animals. He became particularly friendly with the bears and used to like to scratch their backs. He even trained one old bear to come and eat out of his hand.

In 1941 he married Joy Pilkington, a vicar's daughter, but they divorced four years later. In 1947 he married Pat Morgan, who was to be Kate's mother, and whom he had met on the top of a bus in Bristol during the war. When the second Mrs Sayer died many years later, Kate found in the lining of her father's wallet a little cutting

Malcolm Sayer, seen here on the day he married his second wife, was a giant in all senses of the word. He played one of the principal roles in the Jaguar success story and designed a string of brilliant sports cars. He was also a fascinating eccentric with multifarious talents.

from a newspaper announcing the engagement of Malcolm Sayer and Miss Joy Pilkington, daughter of the Revd and Mrs Pilkington, Gorleston, nr Great Yarmouth. Malcolm's parents were a little frosty with Pat to start with but it is possible they were rather embarrassed by the situation their son had placed them in. As Kate puts it, 'Imagine the shame of having to go to church when your son has been unfaithful to the vicar's daughter!'

His love of cars was not lost but merely latent, and in his spare time he designed bodies for the Gordano car project, which he later described as, 'An unsuccessful venture near Bristol'.

The Gordano was a project created by several enthusiasts from the Bristol area who were also instrumental in starting the 500cc formula for motorcycle-engined single-seaters on which several famous Grand Prix drivers cut their teeth, the most notable being Stirling Moss. Among those involved in the Gordano were designer Dick Caesar (of Freikaiserwagen fame), Dick Bickerton, R.P. Gordon Jones and 'Doc' Taylor. Finance came from Joe Fry of Fry's Chocolate (probably best remembered for their Turkish Delight) until he was killed.

It seems that myriad sports car designs were laid out on paper, but just two prototypes were assembled in the Clifton area of Bristol on the premises of Edwards Funeral Directors. They had different bodies but these were not, apparently, Sayer's work. A Cross rotary valve engine was built and briefly fitted in one prototype. Ultimately one car was powered by an MG VA 1½-litre engine and the other had a 1496cc Lea-Francis 12hp power unit. Sadly the project died with Fry.

A little later Caesar and Bickerton designed the successful Iota 500cc racing cars and also produced two motorcycle-engined small lightweight prototype sports cars known as the P2. The first of these, owned by William Mayne, an author of children's books, was quite streamlined and had a small, semi-oval grille akin to a C-type. It could easily have been done by Sayer. The second (P2-02), which had a Royal Enfield engine, was less streamlined with headlamps fronting the wings in the more traditional manner. It is not too dissimilar to an alternative early E-type design of Sayer's. Duncan Rabagliati owns the body of the second Gordano and the complete P2-02. He states that the Iotas employ monocoque construction, which is particularly interesting and pertinent to the E-type story.

The earlier project, incidentally, took its name from the Gordano Valley, which runs parallel to the modern M5 motorway from Easton-in-Gordano on the banks of the River Avon, via Clapton-in-Gordano and Weston-in-Gordano, to Walton-in-Gordano. The motorway services in this vicinity are known, and this will shock the reader, as the Gordano Services. How splendid that they should seem to have been most appropriately named after this eccentric motoring project!

In 1948 Malcolm Sayer went to Iraq, captivated by the challenge of starting a faculty of engineering at Baghdad University. His later boss at Jaguar, Bill Heynes, talking of this period in Sayer's life, said, 'He couldn't speak the language but took a book with him on the cattle boat out there and by the time he had arrived he was fluent. He was over six feet tall and the most charming man you could ever meet.'

However, on arrival he found that the university existed on paper only, that academic levels were poor, and that in fact there were few positions which a graduate could have occupied. So he planned workshops for training mechanics and fitters to repair and maintain the large stocks of state-owned transport and agricultural machinery which he found lying derelict, often for want of a small component. He also organised the testing of second-hand military and fighting vehicles bought by the Iraqi army. Constant changes of government, often by force, and general uncertainty made him leave in 1950. However, he felt that this period gave him valuable lessons in getting results from men of widely differing basic outlooks, moralities and languages. It also gave him a working knowledge of Arabic. It seems he stayed for a year or so.

'My mum brought me home earlier,' says their daughter Kate. 'He had an affair with a woman they were living with in Iraq – Molly Deakes was her name.' Meanwhile mother and daughter returned to Bristol.

As to the work, his brother-in-law Felix states, 'They learned all they could from him, and then they didn't want him.'

Then he disappeared [says his sister Joan]. Nobody knew where he was. We didn't hear from him for six months and then he suddenly appeared at Bradwell [the Sayer family home near Great Yarmouth] wearing the most extraordinary clothes. Father said, 'Where have you been?'

Malcolm said, 'I've been vagabonding in France.' What a thing. And that's all he'd say. But he was absolutely stony broke, and he had on an awful pair of shoes. We've never been a smart family, never been what you might call well-dressed, but he was absolutely beyond the pale.

We said, 'What do you mean, vagabonding?'

'I used to sing for my meals and play the guitar.' Then he fooled around at Bradwell and tried all sorts of tricks. He fancied himself as an artist. He was good at drawing but he would copy things, he was a marvellous copyist. A lot of his drawings were copies of other people's work.

In September 1950 he joined Jaguar with a brief, as quoted in the last chapter, of designing a sports racing car to win Le Mans. 'This C-type won its race in 1951,' Sayer wrote, 'and embodied several innovations copied universally by others – faired lamps, ducted radiators, simplified exhaust and a tubular chassis reinforced by sheet metal.'

Quite how he came to join Jaguar is a complete mystery. It is possible he rejoined BAC for a short while. Kate remembers living in Bristol before moving to Leamington, which is close to Coventry. Walter Hassan had left SS Cars shortly after the outbreak of war and joined BAC, where he remained until he rejoined SS in 1942. While at BAC he met Phil Weaver, who would join the renamed Jaguar company in 1946, and it is possible he met Sayer as well. Could Hassan have suggested Sayer to Heynes when Lyons finally gave the go-ahead for the XK120C (C-type) in September, 1950? An intriguing theory, but not helped by the fact that Hassan had left Jaguar the previous February to move to Coventry Climax. Was it Weaver, then, who suggested Sayer?

Leaving his wife in Bristol, he moved into digs at Mrs Blasdale's in Earlsdon, joining three other Jaguar employees. Later they were joined by Ole Sommer, the son of the Danish importer. One of the three was Alan Currie, who says that he was paid £5 a week and imagines Sayer would have been on the same. 'We were always aware that the idea was to work for the glory,' says Currie. The digs cost three guineas and Sayer travelled to work in Currie's Austin Chummy. 'He said he had a 3½ Bentley but never produced it. As time went by we graduated from "weekly" to "monthly staff" and instead of clocking in, we were allowed to sign in. We did this by writing our names in a book at the gatehouse. Malcolm would only sign "Sayer" despite being told he was not of aristocratic descent.'

Phil Weaver, who sadly died in 1999, remembered Sayer joining Jaguar. 'One day Mr Heynes phoned me and told me to come down to the office. When I walked in, Sayer was standing there. "I believe you know each other," said Heynes. I well remember Sayer drawing the C-type full-size on the floor in chalk!'

Lyons's and Sayer's method of designing a body were as different as chalk and cheese. Lyons could not draw well and used to work through a couple of trusted craftsmen – including Fred Gardner – who could translate what he wanted into full-size mock-ups, which Lyons would modify and refine. 'Sayer,' recalls Norman Dewis, Jaguar's Chief Tester, 'used to draw the contours of the whole car on one sheet of paper which went right across the wall. The wall was 20ft in length and his paper would stretch from one end to the other. He'd start from one end and it would be one mass of curves and lines. Nobody could understand it, but from that he could produce his car.'

That was the first stage in the process but the next stage was the really intriguing one. Sayer, however, kept his methods to himself. Bob Knight, who was the C-type Project Engineer and would be heavily involved in the E-type and progress through the ranks to retire in the 1980s as Managing Director, was fascinated. Sayer's closeness only served to heighten his intellectual curiosity. 'He claimed he had been taught the system of complex curved surface development in the desert in Iraq by some German as they sat in their tents!'

Basically this system was a long-hand version of what today we would call Computer Aided Design (CAD). Using complex formulae and logarithms, he could mathematically plot an entire curved shape. He produced a booklet of figures from which woodworkers could make up cross-sections of a body every few inches. By attaching these cross-sections with appropriate spacing, you had a skeleton of the body. Working with that, the skilled panel beaters could form panels to fit over the skeleton and thus make up a complete prototype body.

'He was a very able bloke,' says Knight, who is not normally generous with his praise. 'He started from sort of sketches from a notion of what he had to clothe, which is the starting point of anybody designing any body, and then he would develop the notional lines mathematically from that point onwards.'

'There was one thing in particular that everyone liked about Sayer,' according to Weaver. 'If you make drawings of some of these obtuse shapes, which were aerodynamically perfect, you could produce a drawing with dimensions on, but then a woodworker had to try and translate all those dimensions into shapes, which wasn't easy. It's a specialist job and the body makers at Jaguar, although they could make the framework of a wooden body and formers, weren't exactly slide rule experts.'

Sayer endeared himself to his colleagues because his system made it easier for them to create the required shapes and formers. Harry Rogers remembers his accuracy.

XK 120c BODY ORDINATES. SHEET 1.

STATION	₵	4	6	8	10	12	TOP 14	16	18	20	22	24	26	28	30	MAX. WIDTH	AT (INS. ABOVE DATUM)
13	20·22		17·7	17·24	17·66	18·8	19·85	20·74	21·42	21·96	22·34	22·48	22·18	20·7		29	16·5
20	25·08		23·58	22·77	21·37	22·5		24·05	24·56	25·	25·54	[25:-25·6 29:-23·65]					
30	27·5	27·35	27·1	26·7	26·18	25·7	25·62	26·05	26·54	27·00	27·34	27·6	27·75	27·2	23·5	30	
38	28·34	28·2	28·06	27·82	27·48	27·06	26·58	26·3	26·4	27·05	27·6	27·95	28·06	27·52			
46	28·92	28·84	28·78	28·66	28·42	28·02	27·44	26·86	26·76	27·05	27·4	27·8	27·96	27·5			
54	29·36	29·3	29·2	29·05	28·82	28·5	28·06	27·45	26·96	26·9	27·2	27·45	27·5	27			
62	29·64	29·58	29·46	29·3	29·06	28·76	28·32	27·68	27·06	26·7	26·75	26·9	26·85	26·2			
70	29·88	29·84	29·74	29·6	29·36	29·04	28·58	27·94	27·18	26·55	26·4	26·3	26·22	25·76			
78	30·08	30	29·88	29·75	29·52	29·2	28·68	28·04	27·24	26·44	25·96	25·66	25·45	24·9			
86	30·2	30·12	30	29·82	29·64	29·28	28·76	28·08	27·24	26·3	25·6	25·06	24·7	24·1	20		
100	30·1				29·5		28·7		27·1	26·03	25·05	24·18	23·7	22·95	19·5		
112	29·55				29·07		28·3		26·85	25·9	25·0	24·62	24·2	23·6			
DOOR REAR												24·62	24·42	23·82	20		
126	28·28	28·2	28·1	28	27·82	27·56	27·2	26·74	26·1	26·02	26·52	27·12	27·3	26·74	23		
134	26·95	26·88	26·82	26·72	26·58	26·35	26·08	25·64	25·2	25·3	26·05	26·65	26·8	26·2	20	30	
142	24·8	24·76	24·72	24·6	24·54	24·34	24	23·5	23·2	23·45	24·1	24·5	24·5	23·8		29·82	20
150	21·2	21·16	21·12	21	20·85	20·6	20·16	19·6	19·4	19·6	20·2	20·55	20·16	18·25		28·83	12
158	15·3	15·26	15·2	15·05	14·7	14·25	13·65	13·05	12·65	12·5	11·8					22·7	10

STN. 152 " 154 — 28·1 27·0

| 13 GENERAL 150. | | | ← | 2·38 | 2·39 | 246 | 2·66 | 2·98 | 3·59 ·16 | 4·45 ·75 | 5·72 1·64 | 7·58 2·98 | 17 5·16 | |
| | | | | | | | | | | | | | 6·35 | |

| 158 EXH. RECESS. | | | | | | | 4·42 3·5 | 5·6 6·55 | 7·7 7·6 | 8·26 | 9 | | | |

DIST. OUTBOARD FROM ₵ CAR, INCHES.

	0	4	6	8	10	12	14	16	18	20	22	24	26	28
FOR'D. OF STN. 13				1·47	2·18	2·88	3·48	3·92	4·21	4·26	4·05	3·46	2·06	-·066
AFT. OF STN. 160	2·48	2·43	2·33	2·15	1·90	1·56	1·16	·71	·04	-·72	-1·65	-2·83		

COCKPIT														
DIST. OUT FROM ₵	0	10	16	20	22	22	20	18	16	10	0			
STATION DIM.	89·17	89·21	89·38	90·1	98·8	103·37	117·2	119·35	120·63	121·11	121·18			

COCKPIT ½ WIDTHS.

STN.	20	24	100	112	120	102
½ WIDTH.	19·78	22·85	23·8	22·36	17·16	23·86 (≤ MAX.)

This chart of figures in Sayer's own hand is an example of how he mathematically designed car bodies. Breaking completely from tradition, he used a long-hand version of what would now be known as Computer Aided Design (CAD) decades before that became the norm.

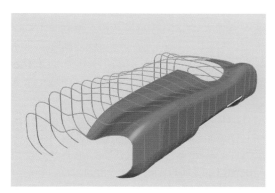

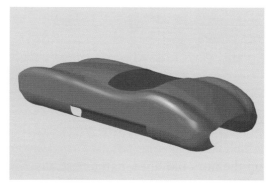

Using Sayer's co-ordinates for the C-type, his first sports racing car design for Jaguar, Peter Murray fed them into a computer programme to build up the compound shape. The individual lines indicate the various co-ordinates and the body-builders at Jaguar would have made up such cross-sections as templates.

Using the templates, spaced at intervals as in the previous illustration, the panel beaters would then have fabricated panels to fit over the templates to create the overall shape. The modern computer software can automatically 'fill in' the gaps to create a 'smooth' shape and we can see the distinctive C-type shape coming to life.

'He'd go to three figures. Working in wood, you'd be as accurate as you could.

'You wouldn't receive normal drawings from him. He did a lot of figures and you got it in book form. There were water lines and body lines, and each interception had got a dimension from a datum. He used to do them every ten inches and that's how the E-type was produced. It all seemed so complicated, but once you got the gist of it, you could work it out. We also used to make the models for him to use on smoke tests in the wind tunnel.' Body lines run from one side of the car to the other and water lines from front to rear, Harry explained to me.

Sayer's brief for the C-type had included the fact that it must bear a family resemblance to the production cars which explains the slight rise and fall of the wing line. With the D-type there were no such constraints and he was given a completely free hand to produce the very best shape he could. That he succeeded so well is proven by the fact that the Jaguars were as fast as or faster than the far more powerful Ferraris and Mercedes-Benz against which they competed on the long, ultra-fast Le Mans circuit.

'There is no doubt about it, he was a genius,' claims Felix Bernasconi. 'He came into his own at Jaguar.'

'Malcolm Sayer,' opines Bob Berry, 'was one of those very quiet, unassuming people with a very dry sense of humour. He worked solely and exclusively for Bill Heynes. He was the aerodynamicist, though he was not referred to as such. He was just a member of the design team. He had an office on the same floor as Bill Heynes, about two doors down. He worked away on his own on his projects. He produced quite a large range of shapes that he tested, mainly at Loughborough if I remember correctly. He had a very close relationship with Loughborough College. They had a wind tunnel there which he used to use. He also used to go down to Farnborough and Cranfield. He seemed to have carte blanche with these people and spent a lot of time there.

'His way of developing a body shape was a mathematical process that was time-consuming in the extreme because he had to do a calculation for each point on the bodyshell and the entire bodyshell had to be covered. So there were huge books of calculations and he'd spend months doing these things.'

Of the period following the C-type, Sayer himself wrote, 'In view of this success, I was retained and designed the various versions of the D-type. This was the first application of aerodynamic mathematics to racing car body design, and was one of the most imitated shapes ever produced. It was also the first chassis-less high-speed car. Similarly the E-type which followed was the first production car to be designed mathematically, and again it has been extensively copied. In my spare time I have designed several Grand Prix racing bodies for Stirling Moss and R.R. Walker, and improved bodies for Brabham and Cooper.'

An old friend of Sayer's, who now lives in the USA, is Fran Oldham. He worked with Sayer at Jaguar and in 1988 wrote to Kate:

No one that I know of has ever made the point that he was the first by at least 15 years to pay the slightest attention to reducing the lift that so often accompanied any reduction in drag on car bodies. The D-type bodies developed negative lift at both ends and he took a lot of trouble to make sure that they did.

I remember going to Gaydon with your father, Norman Dewis, Bob Knight and a bunch of others to run some tests. Someone wanted to try the car without the little aluminium headlamp covers that were put on until the transparent plastic covers arrived. Your father said it was a bad idea because the front end would come off the ground at about 130. Everybody pooh-poohed such a bizarre idea and Norman was duly sent out with no little aluminium covers. We heard him start to accelerate up through the gears on the long straight of the P-shaped circuit we were using, and then, when he was about two-thirds of the way to the bend at the end, we heard the engine note shut off and Norman came burbling round the end and back up to where we were all waiting, and said in his usual pungent way, 'Put the fooking things back on, yer can't steer it.'

This is not Sayer's company car. It is, in fact, one of the first D-types. It seems that in spite of his eminence and crucial role at Jaguar, he was not well paid, for it was many years before he could afford his own vehicle. His daughter Kate recalls that his Bedford van did, apparently, have an old D-type seat though!

In a talk entitled 'The Shape of Cars' Sayer spoke on the subject of designing racing cars. 'Basically the body is simply a low-drag fairing round the mechanical parts, and if this were the only problem it would be very easy. But besides being fast, it must also be stable and this is much more difficult.

'The general layout is evolved from the known data, such as power units, tyre sizes, regulation fuel capacities and so on, and at the very earliest stage compromises have to be made – for instance, the body man wants a nice narrow track and small frontal area for speed down the straight whilst the chassis man wants a wide track and fat tyres to increase the cornering force round the rest of the circuit.'

He went on to talk about the importance of avoiding lift as far as possible and ensuring that any lift acted in the right place, with the qualification that this was affected by changes in attitude due to acceleration, bumps in the road, cross-winds, roll or braking, or under different fuel loads. He also spoke of avoiding side force and commented, 'The amount of yaw which has to be catered for is quite large when you consider the case of a car overtaking a slower one and so meeting quite a violent sideways blast of air.' This last point is not something you would normally think of, but at Le Mans the speed differential could be immense between the larger-engined front runners and what Roy Salvadori calls 'the creepers'.

Sayer's designs were always very 'clean', which in part accounts for their aesthetic quality. The early E-types are a good example of his style, having little adornment to his pure body. In his talk he spoke also of another of the challenges of creating an efficient body shape. 'This has to be equipped with a series of holes to cool engine water, engine oil, brakes, sometimes the battery or generator, supply air to the carburettors and to the driver. Just as the mechanically perfect design is supposed to disintegrate just after crossing the finishing line, so these should be just big enough for the job. But once again the requirements vary not merely from day to day but as the car circulates on one lap, so a compromise is necessary. Every duct can be considered as an air pump consuming horsepower and the same applies to body leaks.'

He went on to talk about the history of car design through the pre-war years and then commented on that fickle quality, fashion.

'Fashion is also moulded from outside forces – after the war, as a reaction from angular tanks and jeeps and so on, everything became very rounded – you had larger radii on refrigerators, toasters were streamlined and cars tended to look as if they had come out of a jelly mould. Incidentally, they had lower drag than the modern, crisper angular look. The angular looks spread throughout architecture, interior design, even paintings, but it looks as if curves are coming back.' How right he was and hurrah for that!

'Aerodynamics play, I would say, a very small part in the average car design. There is quite a lot of pseudo-streamlining, with fast backs applied to slow fronts, but there are also quite a lot of advantages to be gained in economy, cooling, ventilation, stability and silence by fairly minor changes particularly at the front end. Citroën reduced their drag 17 per cent by changes to the nose which were hardly noticeable. Odd fittings can cost a lot in drag too – the average roof rack can increase drag 10 or 15 per cent even when empty.' Sayer's successors would, some years hence, give much more consideration to efficient shapes for production cars as the successive fuel crises pushed economy to the top of the agenda.

Sayer had clearly retained his sense of fun from his student days and used to play practical jokes on people he didn't like. There was one chap with whom he worked who had his own special mug and was very possessive about it. So on one occasion Sayer put the mug on a high shelf, having first filled it with water so that when the chap retrieved it, he got drenched!

'He got his wicked sense of humour from his mother,' Kate reckons. 'He made all sorts of awful puns. He always had a writing pad by his chair and he would do vile cartoons of people on television. For some reason he took a dislike to Long John Baldry. He also used to get cross when people played the wrong chords. He had a well above average ear. He played the piano extremely well. He wasn't so good on the guitar. He used to lie on his back and play it on his chest. He reckoned he could get a tune out of anything. Somebody challenged him and gave him a little one string fiddle at a party. It was only about a foot long. He played Humoresque.

'He loved his work but everything else went by the board,' recalled his sister. 'He was very practical when it came to his work, but impractical with ordinary things.' His daughter Kate, on the other hand, remembers that he liked to improvize to make things:

He used to make furniture out of rubbish and very cheap things. He bought a huge amount of orange paint – enormous amount. Everything was painted orange. I had a little go-kart that was painted orange, and a lamp. It must have been a cheap job lot. He liked using hardboard – all the kitchen cupboards were made of hardboard.

I've still got some quite big shelves which are made out of old bits of chests of drawers and hardboard. I think he got it from his dad because he was a brilliant carpenter. His dad was also very artistic and taught art and maths. As far as water-colours are concerned, Grandfather was better than Dad. They were both interested in mechanical things.

A man called Harry Wilson used to give him a lift to Jaguar every morning. We didn't actually have a car of our own until the sixties and then we had a broken, beat-up old Bedford van that had belonged to a chimney sweep and been burnt out. He re-fitted it out himself but he got all the parts free – Lucas gave him the headlights and the driver's seat was one of the ones that came in first in one of the Le Mans races. He had a D-type seat for the driver! It also had a bench seat in the front and it was red, and Dad didn't like this red. So he got some leather stain and stained it blue, and everyone who sat in it got blue all over their back and their legs!

We were pretty broke. Presumably he wasn't paid very well. I can remember my mum going and asking about council houses.

These two men formed an important partnership. While Malcolm Sayer (left) created the shapes on paper, brilliant panel beater Bob Blake translated them into metal. Blake was an American who had joined Jaguar in the fifties after Briggs Cunningham gave up building his own sports racing cars.

The Sayers had a dog and always had cats, but he was not awfully keen on cats, which is rather ironic. 'He liked to draw them. He made a beautiful wooden cat out of mahogany for my cousin. He used to draw loads and loads of cartoons to amuse us, and write silly poems as well.'

Alan Currie, with whom he had shared digs, recalls that Sayer designed a cross-Channel rowing skiff for a competition and even designed candelabras! He also states that a great personal friend of Sayer's was Roland Emmett, the cartoonist. 'My wife tells me that Pat wanted some indoor plants to liven the place up. Malcolm stepped in and made them – so much easier than growing them and they lasted better. They were in fact the first artificial pot plants any of us had seen.'

Tragically prematurely, Malcolm Sayer died in 1970. For many, his pièce de résistance was the one-off mid-engined sports racing car known as the XJ13 which was built in the mid sixties but never raced. Although probably only Bill Heynes knew about it, he had actually suggested a mid-engined G-type to succeed the 'D' in 1959. It is rather a shame that the XJ13 was not logically called the G-type, for it completes the progression of his classic designs and influenced another car that would be built some 29 years later. Jim Randle, Jaguar Engineering Director in the 1980s and the father of the XJ220 supercar, says, 'You can see the 13 in the 220. That was what I wanted in the styling.'

That styling was the work of Keith Helfet who, from the 1980s onwards, has carried on the traditions created by Lyons and Sayer. Helfet's work includes the still-born eighties F-type, which style later saw the light of day in slightly modified form as the XK8, the XJ220 supercar, the XK180 prototype and the 2000 F-type concept car. Keith is not afraid to say whom he admires most and where his inspiration was derived. In his last years Sir William Lyons used to visit the Styling Department regularly after the BL debacle was finally put out of its misery and Jaguar became once more independent.

So I had the benefit of five years of support and input. He was a very important influence in my design career. I am also one of Malcolm Sayer's most devoted fans. He was an unsung hero, and certainly one of my heroes.

I think when you analyse a lot of Malcolm Sayer's designs, and this is what I appreciated and liked about them, there were features that could be seen on many other cars, but he could instinctively create beautiful surfaces. I felt that that was what was important – that was the essence of Jaguar.

One can be modern as long as the shapes one creates are lovely shapes in themselves. Fluid shapes tend to be aesthetically pleasing; one therefore takes the functional elements and wraps them up in lovely shapes. They tend to work, I believe, aerodynamically very well. Sayer was an aerodynamicist, and there is therefore a natural tie-up. [As Helfet says, you do not have square fish or square birds.]

I was acutely aware when I was doing both the F-type, which was to be the E-type successor, and the 220, when I was aiming at an XJ13 successor, that not only were these very hard acts to follow, and it was an exciting design challenge, but also it was something quite daunting.

Keith Helfet readily acknowledges Sayer's genius and every single contemporary speaks highly of him, both for his ability and as a delightful person. Yet it seems he never received the acclaim he deserved at the time. It is only in more recent times that history has plucked him out of relative obscurity and placed him upon the pedestal which he should have occupied long ago.

'I think this is what he died of,' states his daughter Kate. 'I am convinced he died of a broken heart. He died of a massive heart attack but he didn't get the acknowledgement that he deserved. And I think that's what eventually killed him.'

It is particularly ironic that he hated to be called a stylist because his designs were automotive sculpture. If proof be needed, a 3.8 E-type is a permanent exhibit at the

New York Museum of Modern Art. Sayer uniquely blended science and art to produce timeless shapes of exceptional and enduring beauty. He brought science to the art of car design; and scientifically produced works of art.

Moving on to the mid-sixties, Sayer created his ultimate sports racing car, the fabulous mid-engined XJ13. Tragically, it was never raced but the XJ13 was to prove the inspiration for the nineties super-car, the XJ220 and still thrills many a Jaguar enthusiast to the core.

CHAPTER FOUR

Creating a Legend

The world, and particularly the motor racing world, was rocked by the awful accident at Le Mans in 1955. As is often the case when a catastrophe happens, there was an over-reaction to the tragedy. In France the motor racing officials needed to be seen to be taking the accident and resultant death toll seriously and be reacting to it. There were, therefore, various suggestions flying around about how to make the race safer and, as ever, one of them was to make the cars slower. The obvious and easiest way to do this was to restrict the engine size of cars allowed to compete. Some of the proposed changes and aspects of the new regulations were actually adopted and some turned out to be rumour only, and it is now somewhat difficult all these years later to distinguish between the two.

At Le Mans cars were categorized as either prototypes or production cars. Prototypes were cars of which less than 50 would be built. To qualify as a production car, the manufacturer was supposed to have produced, or laid down, 100 replicas. In practice few, if any, of the manufacturers honoured this ruling, although Jaguar came nearest with their intention of building 100 D-types.

In November 1955 the British magazine *The Motor* reported that in future there was to be a ban on Prototypes of more than 2½ litres. The D-types still qualified as 'standard production cars, unlimited capacity'. With their genuine intention to build 100 D-types, this was of less immediate concern to Jaguar, but any future competition car would have to be built with these new regulations in mind, or so it seemed. As a consequence, on 1 December Competition Department Superintendent Phil Weaver sent engineering chief Bill Heynes a highly significant memo outlining his thoughts for a new model.

2½ litre prototype

Two courses are open to us on this car – one is to design a prototype as small and light as practicably as possible and run it purely for one season as a prototype only.

On the other hand, it is likely that next year we shall be faced with a proposition which permits only cars of 2½-litre capacity in all categories. This would mean we could possibly run the 2½-litre car as a prototype, as I feel we would not want to put through another 100 cars, with such limited use, as the present D-type in production to make the car valid for the production car race, in which case it might be advisable to consider making the prototype car in such a manner that it would have at least a limited demand in a better equipped version, such as the Porsche, for purposes other than racing. In this case the closed type body would seem to be the most satisfactory answer.

To enable the D-type Jaguar to compete in SCCA racing in the USA, some sixteen were converted into the road-going XK-SS model (left). Though the D-type shown has one or two non-standard features, this shot serves to illustrate the main differences between the models. The XK-SS was a step towards the E-type.

This was the beginning of the E-type. It was conceived with the new Le Mans regulations, actual and expected, in mind. There would be many changes in direction over the next five years, but this is undoubtedly the start of the E-type's birth.

The reference to not wanting to build 100 cars needs some explanation. Believe it or not, Jaguar could not sell all the D-types they had built, which seems somewhat ironic today when they are so sought after and examples change hands for £1m plus. The D-type was not accepted by the Sports Car Club of America (SCCA) as a production road car, which is curious because they were driven on the road, and so Jaguar converted a number of remaining D-types into the model known as the XK-SS. With a full-width screen, a door for the passenger and a rudimentary soft-top added and the head fairing behind the driver removed, the XK-SS was mechanically unchanged but visually rather altered. The delicate headlamp rims and small bumpers were a foretaste of the items to appear later on the E-type. Just 16 examples of the XK-SS were completed before a massive fire at the factory in February 1957 destroyed all the tooling and put paid to any further D-type or XK-SS production.

Meanwhile, a meeting of top engineers was held at Jaguar in the New Year, on 30 January to be precise, and the resulting report states, '2½-litre engine in D-type car'. By this Bob Blake pencilled on his copy, '200hp for 180mph, 7,500rpm, aluminium block, use lighter brakes and wheels'. Furthermore he wrote and underlined three times, 'NEW BODY – W.B. is 6in longer'. Blake was an American who had built every Cunningham sports racing car before millionaire sportsman Briggs Cunningham gave up his ambition to see one of his cars triumph at Le Mans and started running Jaguars. Bob, who had met his wife while he was stationed in Britain during the war, moved to England and joined Jaguar. He was a brilliant panel-beater and artist in metal, who would play a leading role in creating the E-type prototypes in conjunction with Sayer.

Was this the inspiration for the E-type Fixed Head Coupé? It is a closed version of the 1950s Alfa Romeo Disco Volante (flying saucer) and I found this shot among a collection of Sayer's photographs.

Another report, dated 5 March 1956 and headed '1956 Competition Cars', ran as follows: 'NEW CAR 2½ LITRE – Layout to be done using as much existing chassis components as possible'. In other words, the plan was to use D-type parts wherever possible. On the engine front, apart from the wet sump, iron block 2½ litre, which was being tested with triple valve springs, nimonic valves and titanium con rods, another power unit with an aluminium block and dry sump was being built up.

Malcolm Sayer began work on designing the body and structure for this new

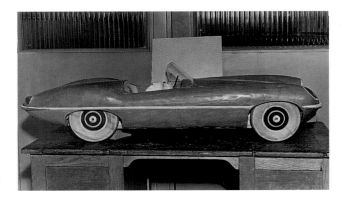

In reaching his final E-type design, Sayer had several models made during the fifties. On this model you can see the alternative front wing treatments that he was considering – the faired-in headlamp and the more conventional exposed headlamp.

2½-litre sports car during 1956, though progress does not seem to have been all that swift. With the D-types still acceptable and performing very adequately, and the emotive reaction to the accident calming down with the passage of time, there was probably little need for urgency. Furthermore, with Jaguar announcing at the end of the year that they were retiring from racing for (supposedly) one year, the deadline became the 1958 season.

The name E-type was logically adopted and applied very early on. Sayer in his early paperwork referred to it as the 'E-type Prototype' and others termed it simply 'E-type No. 1 car'. I believe Phil Weaver may have christened the first prototype 'E1A' and that has stuck with more recent commentators, the 'A' standing for aluminium of which it was indeed constructed.

There is absolutely no doubt as to who designed the shape, and thereafter a number of gentlemen played a part in bringing this car and subsequent offerings to reality. Inevitably there was a certain amount of crossover as the small team worked together. As Bob Knight says, 'Design at Jaguar was invariably development led.' In other words the item was created and then drawn rather than the more conventional converse procedure. Cyril Crouch, whose area of expertise was body construction, mentions that the C-type, D-type and prototype E-type, 'were what we called "fag packet jobs" in that they were done in the shop and drawn afterwards'.

Phil Weaver describes the set-up. 'They very sensibly, I think, decided not to disband the Competition Department. I think that was very wise because we had a very skilled nucleus of people. There were only about ten of us and nine had been either in the RAF or in the aircraft industry.

'When we finished racing in 1956 the firm decided to call us the Prototype Shop and we continued with the E-type, which is what they thought was going to succeed the D-type. The first car we built was done more or less by word of mouth between Sayer and Bob Knight in the Drawing Office, and that was E1A. It was a lovely little car, about a two-thirds scale model of the eventual E-type with a 2.4 litre engine.'

Richard Hassan, son of Walter, was just commencing his apprenticeship and acquired great respect for Tom Jones, for whom he worked for a period in the Drawing Office. 'Tom Jones was responsible for laying out the E. Tom was one of the unsung heroes. Mr Heynes, and my father when he was with the company, could not have done what they did without the practical ability of someone like Tom Jones, who put across what they wanted to the likes of us. He was also very popular down in Experimental, which was even more important, and he had a great relationship with the people in there.'

Both Tom Jones and Cyril Crouch would play a part in the restoration of 9600 HP more than 40 years later.

Meanwhile, though, work was progressing with E1A and it was ready to run by mid 1957. Bill Heynes told me that on 15 May, 'we took it down to the test track with Lyons, "Lofty" and the drivers and I said to Dewis, "Come on and drive it" and he said, "I'm not driving it". Nobody would drive it, so I drove it and did over

100mph. After that they all wanted to drive it. It was a good little car.'

After the first runs, Sayer drew up an airflow test programme and Norman Dewis began testing the car in earnest. Over the next few months a debate took place between Lyons and Heynes, with 'Lofty' England joining in later. Several memos flew between them as Heynes and England argued for a return to racing with Lyons cynical and not convinced of the merits at this stage. Ted Brookes was in the Experimental Department, and remembers the pride in the company in those days. 'You could walk down the machine shop and be stopped twenty times by men asking how the car was going on.' Around this time a second, larger car began to take shape in Phil Weaver's shop. This would become known as the Pop Rivet Special. Phil explains the curious tale of how this second prototype came into existence:

We did a mock-up in wood and metal with all the bits held together on wooden blocks. Sayer had had the panels made and then the whole of the car was fitted up out of plywood and things like that, so that the Old Man could come in and see the shape. He could then say, I want this altered here a bit and that altered there a bit. But everything underneath was held together by wood nailed on a plywood base.

You could actually fit the wheels in position and hold the steering column in the right place so that, when you looked at the car, it looked as though it was driveable but, of course, it wasn't.

I will never forget Mr Heynes coming down to see me one day. They'd obviously decided that that was the E-type. That was what they wanted. I can see it there standing in our little prototype shop nailed to the floor. Anyway, Mr Heynes came down into my office one day and he said, 'Phil, I want Norman to try that car.'

So I said, 'What?'

'Oh, yes,' he said, 'I want him to try it. It's no good having a car like that and not knowing how it goes.'

So we had the job of pop-riveting it as best we could and brazing it where we could, so as to make it a one-piece car and bolt all the bits on to it. We had to make the inner structure with good stiffness so that Norman could see how it handled. With the help of the Drawing Office, Bob Knight, Tommy Jones and my gang of blokes working virtually non-stop for a week, we had that car running within a week so that Norman could drive it. The Pop-Rivet Special – I shall never forget it!

On 10 February 1958 Lyons inspected the new body, which was much more akin in size to the eventual production car, and a day later Heynes issued a report of their meeting entitled 'E-type Body'. This report confirms to us that while the basic shape was undoubtedly Sayer's, nevertheless the master stylist, Lyons, had a hand in finalizing important details.

Around this period, Doug Thorpe, who was then with Lucas but would later join Jaguar to look after the Styling Department, saw the E-type prototype. 'I couldn't believe it. I didn't think people were brave enough in this country to do such a car!'

However, in May not only did an outsider see the first car but he drove it, and on the public roads as well. That man was Christopher Jennings, who at the time was Editor of *The Motor*. He had a country retreat in South Wales and he and his wife, a splendid lady of the old school who as Miss Margaret Allen had driven in rallies for SS before the war and raced at Brooklands, drove the car around the area for the weekend.

Bill Heynes recalls, 'I worked with Jennings on this and that, and wanted him to try it. However, I got a lot of opposition from the Old Man even though he thought a good deal of Jennings.'

Christopher Jennings was seriously impressed and conveyed his views forcefully in a memo on the subject to his Managing Director at Temple Press:

> I spent the past weekend in a car of such sensational potential that I feel that you might wish to know about it. The car is a Jaguar, known at the moment as the E-type. I visualize a road test speed not very far short of 150mph which is going to make us think. On Sunday morning soon after 7am in perfect conditions we made a 20-mile warming-up and then 'had a go'. The result was almost fantastic. The first 20 miles from Carmarthen to Llandovery was covered at an average of just over 70mph and Brecon was reached in 43 minutes, giving an overall average for the 48 miles of 67.7mph.

There is no question this makes fascinating reading but Bill Heynes explained to me the added significance and importance of it.

The first prototype to be built was made in aluminium and was smaller than the eventual production E-type. Known as E1A it was lent to Christopher Jennings, who was Editor of *The Motor*, for his assessment. Margaret Jennings, who had raced at Brooklands pre-war, also drove it and is seen here in South Wales.

42

'After Christopher Jennings had had the car, we got permission to build the E-type. He had a lot of influence with Lyons, and Lyons let us get on with it.'

On one occasion Sir William took the Pop Rivet Special home for the weekend. He was going up the Coventry bypass when he pulled up at some traffic lights behind a couple of apprentices in an Austin Seven. They had been looking at the prototype, trying to figure out what it was. One of them leapt out and bent down to look at the trade plates to read the company name.

'Oh,' he called out, 'it's a Jaguar.' He then looked up and saw Sir William glaring at him!

In June Bill Heynes re-opened the racing debate with his Managing Director. From his memo, entitled 'Competition Cars for 1959', we gain a fascinating insight into the thinking at that time plus initial thoughts on a very exciting new model. We learn that Heynes was thinking of no less than 10 or 12 racing E-types and the proposed mid-engined G-type.

During July works team drivers Mike Hawthorn and Ivor Bueb tried E1A but 'Lofty' England recalled that 'they were not very quick'. Nor was progress, and it seems that other work generally took precedence with the very small team of engineers. Curiously there did not seem to be any great sense of urgency, or maybe the team was just overstretched with parallel work on the smaller saloons and the XK150. With the tiny team so involved in the racing side, production car development had suffered and there was a good deal of catching up to do, as Tom Jones explains: 'We had launched the 2.4 [saloon] and it wasn't a very good motor car. We had a lot of trouble with the car and, because all the engineering resources for that period went into racing, it didn't get developed to the extent that it should have been. So it didn't really become a motor car until late 1959 when we launched the Mark 2 version.' It seems possible that the E-type development was delayed by Lyons.

Sir William's involvement with the E-type [states Bob Berry] was very limited. It was largely a Heynes/Sayer design with Sir William saying, 'If that is what you want to do then fine, I like the idea.' Sir William got involved because he couldn't stand the back end of the E-type. He always had a fetish about concealing all the mechanical components. If you look at the back of any of the Jaguar saloons, they all have a skirt which hides the rear suspension, which hides the exhaust pipes. If you look at the rear end of an E-type, you've got the drain tube sticking down, the bottom links of the suspension hanging down, the whole of the exhaust system in full view. It really offended him and quite a lot of time was spent by Lyons and Fred Gardner in trying to come up with an alternative rear end style which concealed all this. If they increased the depth of the back of the car, it destroyed the aerodynamics. If you put on a skirt, it clearly looked like an add-on and therefore offended Lyons from an aesthetic point of view. He finally conceded that it was not capable of being done without destroying the purity of the original design.

A lot of tooling time was taken up in fiddling around with the rear end and he finally let it go, but he did so with great reluctance. He was not happy about it at all.

He also felt the wheel arches were too big for the size of the wheels. That was because Sayer wanted to conceal the wheels within the wheel arch, and so the wheel arch had to be big enough to allow the car to go on full lock. But in a straight ahead position, which Lyons argued was how people always saw it, the wheels were never sufficiently far out for him. One of the features of Jaguar styling is that the wheels always fill the wheel arches.

So he had a number of aesthetic objections to the E-type that he was persuaded had to be because that was what the aerodynamics required.

Meanwhile Bill Wilkinson of the Engine Experimental Department, was evaluating an engine fitted with the new shallow sump required for the E-type and comparing it with a similar unit in 150 'S' specification. Initially the shallow sump engine gave a loss in performance and oil pressure above 4500rpm, but various small modifications overcame these problems. His engine report makes interesting reading, especially when you consider Jaguar would claim 265bhp for this engine!

Engine Report

	E-type				XK150			
RPM	BHP	BMEP	Torque	pts/bhp/hr	BHP	BMEP	Torque	pts/bhp/hr
4000	180.2	170.0	237.0	.510	182.5	172.0	239.5	.516
4500	204.5	171.5	238.5	.496	204.5	171.6	239.2	.498
5000	219.0	165.1	230.0	.510	221.9	167.2	232.6	.507
5500	226.5	155.6	217.0	.519	230.3	158.0	220.0	.528
5750	225.0	147.8	205.9	.547	228.0	149.7	208.0	.558

Bob Knight had only been spasmodically involved with the E-type up till now and dismisses E1A as an adventure. He feels strongly that this little car had little to do with later developments, but one of those later developments which was very definitely significant was the designing of the independent rear suspension which was to be so widely and highly acclaimed.

There is an amusing story behind the creation of the Jaguar's new independent rear suspension, as Bob Knight explained to me.

'The IRS used on the E1 was clearly not a production proposition. There had been a good deal of casual discussion as to what should be done and I had something in mind. In the course of one such conversation with Sir William Lyons on the first Monday in October 1958, I outlined this and said that I believed that the new one could be designed and made, and running on a car in a month, if all the stops were pulled out.

'He said, "I bet it couldn't."'

'I said, "I bet it could!" Whereupon bets were placed. As he walked away, I realized that I had been had. He would either get my money or the new IRS in 28 days.' The new suspension would be used on all new Jaguars for the next 25 years.

Gradual progress was being made with finalizing the body construction and, interestingly, fibreglass or aluminium was being considered for the bonnet. Welding techniques were progressing and would play a significant role in the body design of the E-type.

'I had a tremendous amount of help at that time,' states Cyril Crouch, 'from our welding engineer, Bernard Nicholls. In parallel, he was looking into CO_2 welding with BOC and I was making use of this process. Also he had a tremendous knowledge of the capabilities of spot welding, way beyond that of Pressed Steel Fisher. He designed all our spot welders and advised on all welding. As a result of him, CO_2 welding techniques and the E-type were developed hand-in-hand. Rather than have to find access for spot welding guns, we could use this process, which was also much cleaner than the old oxy-acetylene welding or the argon arc.'

As we have seen, the original intention was that the E-type would be a dual purpose road and competition car, and if Heynes had had his way the racing car would have been on the world's tracks for the 1958 season. However, as the project progressed, it diverged and a separate car was designed purely with racing in mind. This design remained on paper for some time and actual building of the single Competition E-type did not commence until late 1959, with more earnest progress starting in early January 1960. This car was known as E2A and the story goes that Briggs Cunningham, by now an important Jaguar dealer, was over at the factory, spotted it being built and persuaded Sir William to have it made ready for Le Mans

Original thoughts were that the E-type would double as both a sports racing car and low production ultra high performance road car, but then the project diverged and a dedicated racing version was designed. Christened E2A it was a halfway house between the 'D' and 'E' and raced unsuccessfully at Le Mans in 1960.

that year. The race proved to be a disappointment and, though E2A set fastest time in practice, its 3-litre engine let the side down. Following the Le Mans foray, E2A was fitted with a 3.8-litre carburettor engine and shipped to the US, where Cunningham's team ran it with mixed success.

By this stage Jaguar had only built prototypes of what would become known as the Roadster. Bob Blake played a part in the creation of the Fixed Head Coupé model and worked closely with Sir William on this.

I had a body in the Comp. Shop up the top near Len Hayden's old bench. I took a whole mess of $^3/_{16}$in steel rods and did a profile, a side elevation of the screen and the roof, flowing into the tail. I'd got this all tacked up and Sir William walked in the door.

The Old Man looked at it and, boy, he liked it. He fell in love with it the minute he walked in the shop. He wouldn't say a word. He put his hand to his mouth, the way he did. He just walked round and round it, and looked at it from this way and that way, and the front. He couldn't see much of the back because it was close to the benches, therefore I opened the shop door so he could look at it from the other side of Experimental where the lathes were.

He said to me, 'Did you do this, Blake?'

I said, 'Yep.'

'It's good. We'll make that.' And we did!

To my question, 'Sayer did the Roadster but you did the Fixed Head?', Blake replies, 'Yes, completely. Malcolm drew it afterwards and corrected all the errors, but I did the basic shape and the big back bootlid.'

They wanted one that would open, I guess [Blake continues]. So I said, 'We'll do it this way' and I had a helluva time getting a strong enough hinge support to take care of the weight of that door and the glass.

The very shape of the back of that car told you where the aperture was going to be. That meant that the hinge pins would not be parallel to centre but tapered to the back and they had to be cranked from the underside of the roof skin to get clearance. So we had to get some strength in there. The first ones I made worked all right but had to be beefed up. It proved the principle. Then it was drawn up and stiffened, but even then it had to be stiffened a second time.

It could have been done in fibreglass or aluminium and saved some weight, but that hunk of glass was so heavy. Some aluminium tailgates were made off production tools and that's what they should have done in production, but I think the boys with the hammers and the lead [filler] on the [production] line couldn't handle aluminium. They'd have messed up more than they could produce but they could correct steel.

Uniquely, 9600 HP was much later discovered to have an aluminium tailgate.

It might be amusing to reflect on the opening tailgate for a moment longer. Traditionally, tailgates on European cars were hinged at the top, whereas American practice was to hinge the rear door at the side like the other car doors. Bob, being American, may have intuitively adopted US practice. Also, some years later, the Reliant Scimitar GTE would be hailed as a new concept – the sporting car that doubled as a semi-estate car. Today, they are called hatchbacks and are everywhere. Arguably, 9600 HP pioneered this concept, although the more you study automotive history, the more you learn that everything has been done before!

One of the curious paradoxes of Jaguar history is the subject of brakes. In conjunction with Jaguar, Dunlop had developed the disc brake for cars and, as we have seen, superiority in the braking field helped Jaguar achieve much of its great success at Le Mans and elsewhere. You would, therefore, expect the E-type to have been preeminent in the braking department. It was not. Much development time was taken up, even in the late fifties and early sixties, with brake problems, and the brakes on the 3.8 production E-types were barely adequate for a car of such sparkling performance.

Bob Berry states that Bill Heynes had ambitions of using the power-operated servo system as used on the D-types and scoring a first for production cars. In the end, he had to give up this dream for reasons of cost and Jaguar substituted the much-criticized Kelsey-Hayes vacuum booster. This bellows device, that looked more like a musical instrument from the music hall, had the virtue of being small and the vice of failing when most needed. Sudden, hearty application of the brakes could beat the servo entirely, leaving the poor old driver to pump the pedal and pray. One or other usually did the trick, but not before the heart had stopped for the odd nano-second.

Until quite late in the day, Sayer was continuing to conduct a series of aerodynamic tests on the prototypes, as Norman Dewis recalls:

The airflow tests were done with tufts of wool. We used to buy a ball at the wool shop in Nuneaton and cut it into four-inch pieces and then with Sellotape stick them all over the car. I would just follow Malcolm's instructions.

Then I would drive on the circuit at given speeds, up to say 130mph, or as fast as they could keep up with me in a car at the side. Malcolm would observe the side. His car would get in front of me and he would get in the back and look through the back window and observe the front. Then he would follow the Competition car and watch the rear. From that, he got a very good idea of the airflow and he could change it if necessary.

In fact very few changes were made. He used to do wind tunnel tests first on a model and then later we could have a complete car in the tunnel at MIRA.

We used to have to do this work at ten o'clock at night because we wanted the maximum air pressure through the tunnel, because of our speeds, and the electricity board wouldn't allow us to do it in the day because it took all the power from the village of Higham-on-the-Hill, and all their lights used to go out! So we had to wait until after ten o'clock, till most of the people had gone to bed and we could have the full power.

We used to go down the pub and have a few drinks and wait till the pub closed. Then when they'd all gone home, we'd look around Higham village and see all the lights going out. Then we'd say to MIRA, come on, we can do the test now and that would go on till two in the morning sometimes.

Malcolm felt that although the wind tunnel was an excellent facility for giving you the lift and yaw, and all that, it still did not relate to a car actually moving on an open-air circuit. So whatever figures he got at MIRA, he always allowed about 8 per cent discrepancy between the car on the circuit and what it was in the wind tunnel.

He did the wool tuft tests on the circuit just to check his work in the tunnel. You could see a higher drag on the circuit, which is why he allowed the 8 per cent difference. He was right every time, there was no question about that. He really knew his stuff.

Meanwhile XK150 sales were tailing off pretty dramatically and the pressure for a replacement was mounting. 'The desperate need,' says Bob Berry, 'for something new in the sports car field was paramount. There was no project in the company with a higher priority than the E-type, both as a Roadster and a Coupé. The only reason the Roadster was done first was because it was quicker to build. Manufacture of part of the coupé was taking longer than had been thought, and no doubt Ted Loades knows more about that.'

Of the prototypes, by July 1960 E1A had sadly been scrapped (though some parts of the body structure do remain in existence) and the Pop-Rivet Special had met the same fate, as had No. 3, which was simply an unpainted body. Most of the development testing through 1959–60 was done by a blue Roadster (No. 4) and a red Roadster (No. 5). In mid 1960 the first prototype Fixed Head (No. 6) was built and just used for durability work on the car-breaking Belgian *pavé*. It was said that 1000 miles on the *pavé* equated to 100,000 on the road, and by the end of this a car was good for nothing but the scrapyard, the eventual fate of No. 6.

Shortly after No. 6 came, not too surprisingly, Prototype Number 7, another Fixed Head Coupé. This one would have no less than nine lives. Luckily, it escaped the fate of its brethren and would shortly be hogging the limelight, but not before it had first done its fair share of development work.

CHAPTER FIVE

From Design to Reality

I have never been able to pin down exactly when Prototype No. 7, which would later be registered 9600 HP, was completed but it was certainly during the second half of 1960. Of one thing there is no doubt: for the first couple of years of its existence, the car would lead a very active, full and intriguing life.

Ted Loades, a fit 90-year-old now living on the Isle of Man, ran Abbey Panels, who made prototype bodies and production panels for Jaguar. He recalls that in production the FHC roof was made by Pressed Steel, but as for 9600 HP, 'We made it by hand.' He does not remember any particular difficulties but recollects 'having long chats with Lyons. He was a very hard man but brilliant.'

In the intervening forty years, a substantial proportion of Jaguar's records have sadly been destroyed. Until comparatively recently, no sense of history prevailed within the company and often when people retired or moved offices, their paperwork was lost or binned. When the engineering department moved to their smart refurbished site at Whitley, instructions were actually issued to dispose of older records. I even have records of the unique XJ13 mid-engined prototype that an employee, who thankfully was an enthusiast, rescued from a skip.

Luckily, many former employees were rightly proud of their work at Jaguar and took a smattering of their records home with them upon their retirement. Over a period of something like twenty years of writing about Jaguars, I have amassed quite an archive myself, based on items given to me by former employees or lent to me for copying. Piecing together Jaguar history has been a case of trawling the paperwork and interviewing literally hundreds of people, including managers, engineers, designers, testers, drivers, entrants, customers, team managers, mechanics, dealers, importers, suppliers, ad agency personnel, competitors, journalists, restorers and enthusiasts. Memories though, with all due respect, are not always reliable and it is a case of comparing many recollections with the scant paperwork and reconstructing as far as possible.

Thank goodness, Norman Dewis kept some of his daily testing logs and kindly gave me access to his notebooks when I was researching for my hefty tome on the E-type and these proved invaluable. Norman joined Jaguar in 1952 and had a fascinating career with the company until he retired in 1986. His initial project, when he moved from Lea-Francis to Jaguar, was to work closely with Dunlop to develop the disc brake. As recounted earlier, he rode with Moss in the Mille Miglia and was Jaguar's reserve driver at Le Mans on several occasions. In 1955 he got his chance when Desmond Titterington was unwell and Dewis was paired with Don Beauman, a protégé of team leader Mike Hawthorn.

They had been lying as high as fourth when at midnight they had a misfortune which 'Lofty' later recalled with great amusement. 'Beauman went into the sand at Arnage. He'd just about dug out the car, after working for about an hour, when somebody [Colin Chapman's Lotus] hit him and pushed him back again! He arrived back at the pits with sand everywhere – in his eyes, ears, mouth, all his clothes, chok-a-blok with sand, poor sod!'

Dewis would have liked to race more for the works team, but he was considered too valuable as Jaguar's Chief Tester to be exposed to the risks of the circuit. He had the title of Chief Tester, but in truth he was virtually Jaguar's only test driver as Bob Berry, with whom Norman also shared a privately entered D-type, explains: 'Norman Dewis did a very substantial mileage on the E-types, as he did on all the cars. It was such a small team but that was the story of Jaguar. Norman did 95 per cent of all the testing and was often out in the E-type from crack of dawn to dead of night, Saturdays as well. That was the only way the programme got done. Jaguar listened to what Norman had to say. He was not the most popular guy in Jaguar, but

This is the earliest known reference to 9600 HP. It is Norman Dewis's daily testing log and, as we can see, on 4th November, 1960 he noted that he had inspected what he termed, the '2nd Hard top E-type'. The first example of a Fixed Head Coupé barely saw the light of day and was simply used for destruction testing before being scrapped.

he told it like it was and he had a good relationship with Bill Heynes.'

The very first reference to 9600 HP in any paperwork yet unearthed appears in Dewis's log in which he notes he spent Friday 4 November 'Inspecting 2nd Hard top E type'. Until it was registered in early 1961, the car was generally known at the factory as the 'Second Fixed Head Coupé' (FHC) or 'Second Hard Top'. Both the first and second FHCs, which were respectively given chassis numbers 885001 and

885002, were built in left-hand-drive form (in fact the first seven FHCs were all LHD). The respective Body Nos. of the first two were V1001 and V1002. As mentioned, the first FHC was used on the car-breaking Belgian *pavé* and scrapped.

Prototypes

No. 1 Open	Pastel Green	E1A, reg. VKV 752	Scrapped
No. 2 Open	Pearl Grey	Pop Rivet Special	Scrapped
No. 3 Open	Unpainted	Body only	Scrapped
No. 4 Open	Cotswold Blue		Scrapped
	Cream & Blue E2A, Competition car		
No. 5 Open	Carmen Red	1st Production type	Scrapped
No. 6 FHC	Met. Grey	Used on *pavé* testing	Scrapped
No. 7 FHC	Met. Grey	9600 HP, Press Car	—
No. 8 FHC	B.R.G.	Body only	Later built up

The various early cars and the specifications to which they had been built, or would be built, were detailed in a document entitled 'E-type Schedule No. 1' dated 18 November 1960. This lists the two hard-working Roadsters and four Fixed Heads. The first FHC was Dark Metallic Grey with Grey upholstery and was to USA spec. The second was to be identical, bar its Black interior. The third and fourth FHCs, which would be completed later, were destined for the New York Show and would be shipped in three and a half months time. All these cars were to be built by the Experimental Department, and two more Roadsters were to be built, obviously as a pilot exercise, largely by the Production Department. The first of these would be the open Press Car and become known by its distinctive registration 77 RW. The other Roadster would join the two FHCs and another open car on a ship to the States.

On 22 November Dewis wrote out a long list of items that he felt needed attention or improvement on what he titled, 'E-Type. HARD TOP. No. 2'. As one's eye meanders down the page, it is intriguing to attempt to deduce whether he had driven it by this stage or whether he had purely examined it. Searching for any clue, one reads, 'Channel supporting radiator has no rigidity' – not conclusive. 'Bleed nipples on rear calipers almost inaccessible' – examination only. 'Will the rubber hoses that feed off the fluid bottles have retaining clips' – not promising. Looks unlikely car had run. On the other hand – 'Bonnet locks inadequate to hold bonnet firm' – more positive, but not conclusive. 'Rear edge of the N/S door fouls wheel-arch post.' Oh dear, sounding as though he is merely reporting a visual examination. Aha! 'N/S Splash guard rattles on sub-frame' – sounding more like a problem detected while driving. Yes! 'Both doors have vertical shake.' Surely proven! Dewis had driven the car by 22 November.

E. TYPE. HARD TOP. Nº2.   22-11-60.

Channel supporting radiator has no rigidity.

Retaining clips required for front roll bar bearing rubbers.

Insufficient clearance between exhaust downpipes & sump.

Center exhaust pipe close to floor stiffener.

Exhaust silencer mountings feel too rigid.

Bleed nipples on rear calipers almost inaccessible.

Re-position exhaust tail pipes, ie move pipes outboard.

Rear brake pipe fouling sharp corner of floor & scuttle. o/s.

Could not the brake & petrol pipes have better retaining clips?

Several bolts on rear suspension V mountings inaccessible.

Brake pipe fouls centre scuttle mounting stiffener plate.

Speedo cable requires better & neater run around scuttle.

Have the rear suspension link arm bushes been modified? Bolts have been found a loose fit in bushes on previous assemblies.

Will the rubber hoses that feed off the fluid bottles have retaining clips?

Bonnet locks inadequate to hold bonnet firm.

N/S Splash guard rattles on sub frame.

o/s   "   " clip fixing loose on sub frame.

Petrol tank drain plug not centralised with hole in body.

Both doors have vertical shake – door edges will foul scuttle panel when fully open, are check straps correctly set.?

Rear edge of N/S door fouls wheel-arch post.

Door clearances vary around scuttle.

Rear lid release catch difficult to operate, lid will rattle on lock fixing.

Roof drip channel badly finished.

Left: Having examined and probably driven 9600 HP, Dewis drew up a comprehensive list of items that he considered needed attention. Norman's blunt comments did not always endear him to his colleagues but he had their respect. It was a fundamental part of his job to be highly critical.

Such a momentous revelation is not going to shake the world or rewrite the history of the universe, but it is all part of the fun of gradually unravelling the story.

Another snippet to be gained from this most historic document and which may amuse enthusiasts with experience of E-type shortcomings is: 'Sealing of headlamp glasses inadequate.' Other interesting or amusing comments included 'Where will the jacking points be installed?' and 'Rear lid release catch difficult to operate, lid will rattle on lock fixing.'

The first actual records so far traced of 9600 HP testing are dated 24 November when Norman Dewis noted, 'MIRA Testing E type hard top No. 2. Report issued to RJK'. RJK was Bob Knight. On the last day of the month, Dewis was bedding in the brakes and recorded that the car had covered just 194 miles. A few days later, on 6 December, he collected his boss Bill Heynes from Heynes's home at Wolverton. Next day Norman was out in the car with Bob Knight conducting a 'Short road test with RJK assessing different hardness of rack mounting and rear "V" mounting rubbers'.

A number of former Jaguar personnel recall seeing the car around. 'I came into contact with it not much earlier than the beginning of '61,' says Bob Berry. 'Obviously I had seen it around as Experimental were using it as a development car. My recall is that it was used very extensively as a development car. It wasn't used as a back-up. I seem to recall it was Bill Heynes who kept pushing to put a coupé into the development programme on the basis that the coupé shell, being more complex, might need more development time than simply putting a top on a roadster.'

Snow, ice and fog interrupted all testing in mid-December, though Dewis delivered the car to Birmingham on Monday 12th, and then things halted for a day or so over Christmas. On 28 December he was out again in 9600 HP trying it on the road. 'Rear link bottom pivots stiffened to floor panel, harder rubber "V" mountings,' he noted. Busy with other work, he was not out in 9600 HP again until Friday 13th! In spite of the date, the handbrake tests went satisfactorily and he was able to report, 'Both wheels lock – 9 notches on handbrake'.

It seems strange today that, with the E-type launch only a couple of months away, there was not more intensive testing being done. Apart from work on petrol injection with the blue open prototype, there was no other E-type testing being carried out.

Things started to hot up a little in later January. On Sunday 22nd Dewis was out with 9600 HP testing 'on the M1 for maximum speed. Weather foggy and wet surface. 7 runs made from Northampton to Newport Pagnell. Maximum speed recorded 143mph on speedo. 5600 RPM on Rev Counter. Tyres; R.S.5, pressures 35psi front, 40psi rear.' The maximum speed was not enough!

Next day he was doing more maximum speed tests at MIRA and compiled a chart of readings on the speedometer against the true speed calculated by the timing equipment. The speedo was found to be reading slightly fast and was indicating 140mph when the true speed was 135.7. With trade plates fitted, which must have interrupted the air flow over the nose very considerably, a true maximum 135.7mph at 5400rpm was achieved through the timing lights. The wheels were swapped for some fitted with racing R.5 tyres. They had a slightly larger rolling radius and the speed, not surprisingly, increased marginally to 137.8 with a speedo reading of 142mph at 5600rpm by the end of the straight. The day after, he tried the car again with trumpets in place of air cleaners. The results on the road tyres were just fractionally improved, with a best of 136.2 through the timing lights.

This early shot of 9600 HP was taken in the Experimental Dept. where the car was built, originally in left-hand drive form. We can see various differences from production cars in the radio console area and the profile of the facia top. During the restoration, it was discovered that the glove box on this car was made of fibre glass.

Though it was pretty late in the day, on 24 January Malcolm Sayer issued a report entitled 'Programme of Stability Tests on E-types'. Clearly they were looking for ways of increasing the speed, including removing the front bumpers which, though delightfully delicate, nevertheless broke up the clean flow of air over the nose of the car. He suggested that photographs be taken of the car stationary, at speed in standard form and at speed with the front bumpers removed. He also wanted the handling to be assessed in a cross-wind without front bumpers and with the quarterlights open.

He suggested adjusting the suspension to give a nose-down attitude and then photographing the car as before and checking the handling. If the nose-down attitude proved to have beneficial affects, he proposed decreasing this nose-down attitude until the best compromise between appearance and stability was reached.

'If none of the above shows any improvement, test fitted with a vestigial fin such as might be acceptable aesthetically.' Remembering the racing D-types had a fin on the headrest fairing, it is fascinating to see that Sayer was considering a 'vestigial fin' for the road cars. Obviously the maximum speed was causing concern as the magic 150mph, though unlikely ever to be used by the vast majority of owners, nevertheless was of tremendous publicity value. Furthermore, by this stage the advertising and promotional literature would be well on its way to being printed. It was essential for the cars, or at least the Press Cars, to achieve this figure. The pressure really was on.

On Wednesday 25th, given over to Sayer's tests, photographs were taken at 140mph and Dewis reported that the 'front of the car lifts about 2in and the rear about 1in'. Similar tests followed next day and the car was fitted with narrower racing tyres on the front. 'This condition gave a much better, stable straight line run. More understeer. Possible to attain higher speed round banking.' With these tyres pumped up to 40/45 and the trade plates removed, the car managed 143.2mph through the timing lights and an indicated 147 at 5,800 by the end of the straight. Lunch that day for Sayer, photographer Bill Large, colleague F. Merrill and Dewis cost 15/- (75p).

Friday was spent writing reports and on Monday, after the red prototype Roadster had been photographed for Road & Track, Dewis was again out in No. 2 Fixed Head in search of those few more elusive mph.

A run on the same tyres as the last tests, but with front bumpers removed, yielded 145.6, but this was through the timing lights which, though accurate, did not represent an absolute maximum due to their position on the relatively short straight at MIRA. With the number plate off the maximum improved to 146.8 and then the red 'E' was tried. With the hood up, and number plates and bumpers on, the car managed 142.6. Without overriders and number plate, this improved marginally to 143.8.

On Tuesday, the FHC speeds were actually lower and the next day a Performance Test report was compiled on the car's acceleration figures with the following results – 10–110mph 28.4 secs, 0–100mph 16.5 secs, and the standing quarter mile took 14.8 secs. The same day Dewis measured turning circles, noting a 4ft ½in difference between left and right-hand locks. Clearly the top speed figures were causing concern and this probably explains why the 'production engine' (1001-9) was about to be changed, having clocked up 1,414 miles. On Thursday, 2 February Sayer issued a memo to Heynes, with copies to Knight and Dewis, summarizing the work done and his thoughts on maximum speeds.

He noted that 'each of the following caused loss of speed, in order of magnitude – air cleaner, trade plate taped to nose of car & over-riders. Together they are probably worth at least 7mph.' Under 'Handling', he stated, 'As would be expected, a noticeable improvement in cross-wind running resulted from removing the over-riders.' With the benefit of a 10½mph following wind, Dewis wound No.2 Gunmetal, as Sayer termed it, above 6000rpm and to no less than 156mph, minus air cleaner, bumper, overriders and trade plates.

Dewis then issued a report detailing more than 98 items that needed attention on the car. These ranged from the first, and most fundamental, that the engine should be 'changed for one of known performance' to 'fit exhaust heat shields' – obviously Norman's feet were getting a trifle too warm. Other comments included, under 'Brakes', 'Investigate long pedal travel, during test brakes failed due to pedal reaching toe board.' 'Inspect frame member and welded joints for cracks.' 'Make provision on body for jacking and supply jack.' 'Fit front bumpers less over-riders.' Significantly, as we will learn later, 'New type lock & safety catch to be introduced on rear lid of F/H models.'

Shortly after, Dewis issued a further list entitled 'Preparation of Fixed Head E-type No. 2 Car For Road Test'. Progress was being made as this one only had 45 items listed.

Clearly good progress was being made on achieving the desired top speed which did not seem possible within the constraints of MIRA, as Norman Dewis explains. 'We used to use the M1 for doing the maximum speed test. Very often we would be doing 150 and other cars were there as well doing very high speeds, Aston Martin and other firms. It was a very useful place to do maximum speeds.'

The late Roger Woodley was an apprentice at the time. 'The prototypes had been creeping around the factory, everybody had glimpsed them,' he stated. 'But there was a general veil of secrecy over any new car and this made it all the more exciting. The M1 motorway had recently been opened and the rumour was always, "Norman has just done 150mph on the motorway" or "Norman has just got from London in 40 minutes" and it all built up to be something really rather special.'

In early 1961 Norman Milne was working on the commercial vehicle side at BMC, having just finished his apprenticeship a year or so before. He was given the exciting task of driving a 7-ton truck around the high-speed circuit at MIRA.

I was testing for maximum speed – 50mph – and fuel consumption at 10mph increments – constant 40mph, 30mph and ultimately 20mph. At the time, these tests were conducted on the inside lane of the high-speed circuit, and the low-speed consumption tests were boring to say the least …

Every few seconds, this grey car flashed by me. It was Norman Dewis in 9600 HP and he was doing about seven laps to my one. There weren't many closed cars that could travel at such a rate of knots and I was impressed. After lunch in the MIRA mess, I was walking back out to the vehicle park when Jaguar's chief test driver sauntered alongside.

'My, that's some job you've got,' I ventured. 'I'll swap places with you anytime!'

'Are you the chap in the BMC 7-tonner?' asked Dewis.

'That's me. Must be great up there, travelling at those speeds all the time,' said I.

'To tell the truth, it's much the same and just as boring as your 20mph circuits in the wagon,' claimed Dewis. And I obviously didn't believe him.

'Tell you what; are you doing anything special for the next hour?' he asked.

'Well, no,' I replied, hopefully not too eagerly. 'I'm well ahead of schedule, plenty of time in hand.'

'Fine,' said Norman. 'Hop in and you can sample the high-speed circuit from the comfort of the passenger seat.' And with that we were smoothly, almost silently off round and on to MIRA's banked circuit. Accelerating steadily, we were soon past 100, 120, 130mph and on to 140mph where this prototype settled down nicely, effortlessly and quite quietly at 142mph. I remarked that it felt like low-speed flying.

After several laps of this, I asked Norman if the speedo was accurate. 'Pretty well spot-on,' he claimed. 'Is 142mph the genuine top speed?' I enquired. 'Yes, that's it,' he replied, no-nonsense like. 'Would she do 150, if really pushed?' I persevered. 'No, I doubt it,' responded the very matter-of-fact Dewis, who truly regarded 140mph as of no greater significance than my ultra-modest 20mph.

Over an hour later we cruised back into the vehicle park with more than 150 miles on the clock. For the latter half of the run, as we lapped at a consistent 140–142mph, we had the radio playing; the reproduction was superb!'

Through a friend at Jaguar Milne later learnt that, 'The Press demonstrator had been tweaked quite a bit.'

We can deduce that this is 9600 HP in the Experimental Dept. because at this stage only the two Fixed Head Coupés had been completed and the other one had light grey upholstery. Note the non-production ashtray, elasticated door pocket and the lack of anything other than a rudimentary pillar between the door and quarterlight glasses, to say nothing of the prototype Mark X saloon behind.

Between his high-speed running, Dewis was also compiling a number of Performance Test Reports. It is notable that these did not concentrate on acceleration times from rest but acceleration times from one speed to another in top gear. The virtues of flexibility and torque were of obvious importance with the saloons, but it is significant that Jaguar considered them to be important with the sports cars as well. It is proof that Jaguar were trying to produce a thoroughly civilized car of good all-round performance.

The purpose of all our power units,' states Norman Dewis, 'was to try and achieve this very good performance in top gear which was a selling feature of the car. The figures were very good considering they were smooth, with no snatch, and you could do a 10–30mph time.'

Most of these tests were carried out on the Fixed Head and from such a report dated Sunday, 5 February we learn that it had now been designated the 'Press Car'. The car had also been fitted with 'experimental engine E 5020-9' and the tests were mainly devoted to trying to find the best carburettor needles, air cleaners, exhaust systems and suchlike. With no bumpers and an engine 'of known performance' the figures improved marginally – 10–110mph in 27.2 secs (previously 28.4), 0–100 in 16.0 secs (16.5), and the standing quarter mile in 14.8 secs (same).

Fitted with racing tyres at 25/30psi, an air cleaner but no number plate, the car could only record 139.6, though the track was 'rain soaked'. With road tyres fitted and pumped up to 35/40 and the track drying out, the best speed improved fractionally to 140.8. Trumpets then replaced the air cleaners, and the bumpers and trade plates were removed and this time 143.16 was the best after some eleven attempts. The replacement engine was revving a little higher at 5800rpm. All these speeds were measured by the timing lights.

Incidentally, the 'E' prefix to the engine number denotes that it was an engine in the charge of the Experimental Department, and not necessarily that it was of itself experimental. However, this power unit moved in distinguished circles, for a lot of the engines fitted to the D-types and racing Listers of the period were 'E' prefix engines. As to its actual specification, there has been much speculation over many years and there continues to be. There are many people from the period, journalists and Jaguar personnel from other departments, who subscribe to the theory that it must have been a higher-performance engine.

Equally, there are others who were in the Engine Experimental Department and the publicity office who still maintain that it was simply a well run-in, carefully put together power unit with well-polished ports. They contend that the phrase 'engine of known performance' meant nothing underhand but was to be taken literally. Today we would describe the engine as 'blue-printed'.

Some years ago, I questioned Charles Bulmer of *The Motor* as to whether he felt 77 RW had a specially prepared engine. 'Undoubtedly, yes. I asked Bob Berry about this some years later. He said it wasn't a specially tuned engine but what they had done was to go through their stocks of used development engines, put them on the bed and chosen the best one. It was fairly obvious, driving the car, that it wasn't a new engine and it was undoubtedly faster than the later production cars.'

This engine actually started life in September 1959, described in period records as 'First assembly of 3.8 PI engine'. It had a restless life, for it spent the whole of 1960 and early 1961 being installed, removed and refitted to the test beds developing petrol injection. On 2 February it was 'prepared for chassis installation as carburetted engine'. It was then 'handed over to Mr Knight's section for installation in E-type Coupé No. 2'.

Dewis had a meeting with Gregor Grant, the founding Editor of *Autosport*, on Wednesday 8th. His magazine was going to be one of the chosen few who would be entrusted with the highly secret car before the launch at Geneva, which was now just five short weeks away. The pressure was mounting and it was all hands to the pump. The indefatigable Dewis spent part of Thursday actually working on the car, but at least the hitherto anonymous car was about to acquire a name.

From the black interior trim, we can assume again that this is 9600 HP. Curious features visible include the side window arrangement, the odd-looking tailgate hinges and the alternative over-riders. At this stage, the car had not yet been registered.

THE MOST FAMOUS CAR IN THE WORLD

On Friday 10 February the car was registered and became 9600 HP.

Pat Smart explains how it came to have this number. Pat, who joined the company as an apprentice in 1953, has stayed with Jaguar through thick and thin and is one of the few diehard enthusiasts left within the company. Today his responsibility is to look after special sales, including to the Royal Family, but he was then working for Home Sales.

In those days I used to register all the company cars and we used to have a friendly person at the Council House, because we did registrations in Coventry in those days. Now we have to go to Northampton. I used to speak nicely to the person in charge and say, 'We would like a nice number.' This is something you can't do now. I got some super numbers in the past, like 77 RW, for example.

I'd say, 'What's the next nice number?' and they'd show me a sheet. We used to try and get double '0's or 0. 9600 HP just happened to be the next round number, there's nothing more mystical than that. You couldn't go more than a week ahead. You couldn't reserve them in advance. You just had to be there when the book was opened, so the secret was to know the person who had the book to know when they were going to open the next series. [HP denotes the car's Coventry origins.] I remember seeing the car. We all fancied it. I remember seeing Norman and Bob Berry in it. It was *the Fixed Head* – not *the* Fixed Head, but *the Fixed Head*. It was the only one around.

With no time for weekends off, Dewis spent Saturday and Sunday 'testing and preparing E-type Fixed Head No. 2. Brake failure occurred.'! This was not to be the last drama. Monday, Tuesday and Wednesday of the next week were spent 'finalizing' this Gunmetal Grey prototype and 'delivering the car to Maurice Smith of *The Autocar*'.

CHAPTER SIX

150 or Bust

To maximize the impact on launch, it was essential to Jaguar that several leading journalists should have driven the car before its introduction so that their road tests, or at least driving impressions, could appear at the time of its public unveiling in mid-March.

'There were only two full-scale road tests done,' Bob Berry told me. '*Motor* did 77 RW and *Autocar* did 9600 and they were, in our book, the two most important journals by miles. Gregor Grant and John Bolster [of *Autosport*] would have been third on our list, and then *Motor Sport* and a series of one-day stands for other people.'

Of the select band of journalists who did sample 9600 HP prior to launch, the honour of being the very first fell to the late Maurice Smith, then Editor of *The Autocar*, and concurrently of *Flight*. He was actually Wing-Commander Maurice A. Smith, DFC & Bar, to give him his full title.

His secretary at *The Autocar* was Elizabeth Hussey, whose uncle, Fred Connolly, was a friend of Sir William's and ran the famous company that provided all the leather hides for Jaguar and other prestigious makes, and continues to do so to this day. 'Maurice was not just a pilot,' states Elizabeth, 'but he was a Master Bomber in the war. He was actually the Master Bomber at the Dresden raids. He used to look down and organize the bombing while it was going on.

'Somebody was once saying, how terrible, that he must feel dreadful about it, and he said, "Well, I was a young man and this is what I was told to do to win the war."'

It seems rather appropriate that a man who was used to flying should conduct the first E-type road test. Sadly, Maurice Smith died in February 1987, but the previous year I had interviewed him for an article I was asked to write for his old magazine to celebrate 25 years of the E-type. Very helpfully, as it turns out, he himself had written a very detailed piece for the magazine four years earlier [1982] for the 21st anniversary. I propose to quote extensively from his article and our interview, plus more recent interviews with the elusive Peter Riviere, Miss Elizabeth Hussey and Bob Berry, who as head of PR organized it all. The road test, which took place on 16 and 17 February and was reported in the 24th March issue, was quite an adventure, to judge by Smith's 1982 account:

> Jaguar may agree that they were not always the easiest people to work with over road test arrangements. They seldom knew when a test car would be available, which made it difficult to plan printing schedules and book channel crossings. Maximum speed runs exceeding about 120mph usually had to be done on the continent.
>
> Word had been put about and publicity material prepared to the effect that E-types would do 150mph, so the claimed top speed already wagged the car, so to speak. The actual car chosen for our test was the very well loosened up LHD second prototype coupé, as indicated by the famous chassis number 885002. Chosen may not be the right word since Jaguar used to develop on a shoestring and it was probably the only coupé. The registration number 9600 HP, painted at an illegal angle on the nose, was worth 2 or 3mph as compared with a separate number plate.
>
> To achieve 150mph maximum, the 3.8 engine had to be a very good one. The necessary power was conjured up during prolonged work on the test beds, the engine being pulled out and reinstalled more than once. For the specification provided at the time, we dutifully wrote of the engine, 'The version used in the test car is basically the same as that fitted in the XK150 'S' (265bhp at 5,500rpm).' As an afterthought in rounding off the report, we pointed out that some 40 more bhp could be found in highly developed versions of the 3.8 engine. Perhaps the original test bed figures still survive. It would be interesting to know what they really were.
>
> We – that is Peter Riviere and me – were told officially not to exceed 6000rpm on pain of death to the engine. Conversely, we were told not to lift under 150mph on pain of death to us as journalists/testers. In the event we were compelled to use our judgement because calculations showed that 150mph in top on Dunlop R.5 tyres at 40psi required (from memory) 6130rpm. But more about tyres and rpm later; in any case Harry Mundy, who knows about such things, mentioned that he doubted whether valves and pistons would meet under 6300rpm.

Harry Mundy was Technical Editor of *The Autocar* and would later join Coventry Climax. When Jaguar acquired Climax, he moved over to Jaguar and had a major hand in designing the V12 engine.

Bob Berry explains the thinking behind the choice of racing tyres. 'We wanted to make absolutely sure the integrity of the tyres would remain. We delivered it on R.5s, there's no doubt about that. It was a fairly last-minute switch. Norman Dewis wasn't happy about the amount of running at maximum speeds that we'd done on the RS.5s and he was pushing very hard that it was run on racing tyres just to make sure that no matter how much running they did at maximum speeds, the integrity of the tyres was absolute. All they did was to inflate the tyres to the higher pressures that

Dunlops had recommended. I think the spare wheel was also a R.5 and it wouldn't fit in the bloody wheel well!'

The afternoon the car was due to be handed over to *The Autocar*, 'Norman fitted a set of brand new R.5s,' wrote Smith, 'and took those to MIRA to bed them in. So he took the surface off them. There was some discussion as to whether we should reduce the tread depth but it was finally decided to leave them as standard.'

The R.5s were hard-riding tyres and did nothing to improve the general acceptability of the car [Smith's account continues] and I seem to recall that we fitted a set of RS.5s after the maximum runs were taken so that we could experience the car in a standard form.

As the proposed day of delivery approached (to be closely followed by the printer's deadline for the report), Jaguar remained equivocal. Minor details to complete, they reported. Trim and paintwork inspection. In fact much time was being absorbed by Norman Dewis testing on road and track emerging, returning then re-emerging through the factory gates at Browns Lane, trying to coax the obligatory figures out of the car. In between times, now legendary chiefs of engineering, development and production were insisting on wind and mechanical noise levels being just so, doors shutting with the correct clunk, gears changing like ... and time had almost run out.

Norman was making a final evening check run at maximum speed (where I wonder?) when the rear hatch window sprung open, jumped its safety catch and slammed round. Back at the works which, being Jaguar, had all the trades and skills under adjacent roofs, late night repairs were started – dents to knock out, frames to straighten, hinges and catches to replace. Some say that Bob Berry personally sprayed in the Gunmetal Grey and polished it up. Then there had to be more checks of seals, wind noise, latch, etc.

The scene changes to my home in Surrey, since *Autocar*'s offices and garage, then situated near Waterloo Station, closed around 10.30pm and, more important, so did the Brunswick Arms. It seemed best therefore to go home and await delivery of the E-type while getting a few hours sleep. Bags and test gear were packed, the papers were in order, £7 a day expenses had been collected and we were booked out of Southend Airport intending to report at 10.55am for 11.30am take-off. (Ah, happy memories of Silver City and their successors.)

About 5.00am a cheerful, if red-eyed pair, arrived at my home bringing the E-type and another Jag in convoy for the drive back to Coventry. Bob Berry and Norman Dewis joined me in eggs and bacon as a grey and foggy dawn broke outside, and it was then that I learned of the rear hatch mishap.

Bob Berry now takes up the story:

We delivered it to his house, which was near Egham. It was a very nice house way out in the country and it was a helluva job to find the goddam place. We did sit down and have bacon and eggs and left it with him.

The problem with 9600, and I remember this very vividly, was the difficulty of keeping the rear boot lid shut. That was the sole cause of the delay. Keeping the lid shut of the third door proved to be little short of a nightmare, and this was precisely why Heynes had been so desperate to get a coupé into the test programme. In this respect his suspicions were correct. The locking mechanism was less than satisfactory. Because it was such a big door, resting on a relatively small surround, it used to chatter and a combination of the high internal pressure and the chattering would mean that the door would jump off the catch and on to the retainer.

If you were travelling quickly and it went on to the second catch, the explosion was rather like a paper bag bursting. There was the de-pressurization of the interior and then there was all the wind noise. It really was a very disconcerting experience. Funnily enough it was not something that showed up on the *pavé*. It was only when we started running 9600 on the roads that the problem arose. It certainly took two or three days of intense work to try and come up with a solution.

Bob recalls that the tighter the lid was pulled down on to the aperture, the greater was the problem. He states that the respective profiles did not match well, the panels touching each other in some places and not in others, which is what caused the chattering. After much experimenting, they decided to use a bigger, softer rubber seal round the aperture and not to have the lid pulled down quite as tightly when shut. The *cushion* effect of this new softer seal damped out the problem.

'Throughout the whole of the Geneva process, it never once came off the catch, which I thought was extraordinary. Having experienced it three or four times when I was running it myself on the motorway, it was really most unnerving, to put it mildly.'

As to his own role in readying the car, Bob states, 'There was some effort put in, but it was really a minor one to bring it up to what I thought was a test car standard. There was the usual conflict. Some people were trying to solve the problem with the door, other people were trying to uprate the interior from bits that simply didn't exist. Odd trim panels were being made. If I remember correctly the boot lid had a Perspex screen and the panel was aluminium. I think Bill Heynes's view was that the lid lacked rigidity, (a) because it didn't have the proper glass in it, and (b) because it was not made of the correct material and the welded frame wasn't, to quote, "the correct specification" – which, in my experience, is an engineer's way of saying, "I don't really know what the answer is"!'

Maurice Smith: 'Travel plans included picking up a member of *Autocar*'s staff who, having enjoyed the ride, would then go on to a skiing holiday from Antwerp, our first night base, where my co-tester Peter Riviere was already doing some preparatory work. Antwerp came into the picture because the E-type needed what was then known as super premium fuel (100 octane) for the maximum performance testing. Belgium and Holland could offer only lower octane super or normale, therefore a special fuel supply had been laid on at the docks.'

The member of staff to whom Smith is referring was none other than his secretary, Elizabeth Hussey. Elizabeth would leave *The Autocar* in 1963 and proceeded to have a most distinguished journalistic career in the skiing world. On this occasion, Elizabeth says, 'I probably had my flight booked anyway for the next day. I should think it was Thursday, February 16th.' This was presumably in case the car was not delivered in time. Miss Hussey was then living with her parents, sister and brother Anthony, who is a present-day director of Connollys. Anthony, whom I have known for many years, says, 'I remember the car very well because Maurice Smith called at my parents' house to collect my sister. The address was High Banks, Coombe Park, Kingston Hill, Surrey – now flattened with two houses built on the land.' He remembers it so well because it fired his enthusiasm for cars. 'It was how I got interested in cars. I had come out of the army where I had been driving heavy lorries on ice and, as a result of 9600 HP and writers like "Steady" Barker in *The Autocar*, the car bug bit.'

'He came round to us,' continues Elizabeth, 'and it wasn't certain until he saw the car whether my skis would fit in it or not. So we didn't make an absolute decision until he'd got the length of the car inside and he could see that I could fit my skis in. I don't think he telephoned me during the night, I think I was just going to be ready to go if he turned up.

'We were very excited about it when it came for road test. We felt that this was a milestone.'

There was no speed limit [continues Maurice Smith] on most of the continental motorways at the time but they were often two-laners and traffic could be patchy. We had previously used the legendary Jabbeke road between Ostend and Brussels, stretches of which, at a price, could be closed for testing. Otherwise you tried to out-guess the farmers who crossed it with their animals and wagons. This was acceptable at the right times of day and up to about 120mph, but it could be fraught at any time. The E-type test was different and was likely to require at least twice as long a clear stretch to gain the extra 30mph to 150. Therefore a new stretch of motorway had been chosen which, being only part completed, led nowhere and was virtually deserted, they said. Today it is a 14km stretch of the E39 from the outskirts of Antwerp to Herentals – almost straight, mostly level and frequently flanked by pine woods. This, it was felt, would give proper two-way runs to cancel out any wind or gradient. The speed was to be read on a carefully calibrated car speedo. Our test fifth wheel with its accurate electric head went with us but was not suitable for towing above 130mph because it was apt to take off from the road surface and occasionally from the car! A cross-check was made with a Jaguar-approved formula based on rpm, gearing and R5 rolling radius which, at 40psi, was said to have no appreciable growth at 150mph.

Luggage, test gear and a pair of skis fitted inside without too much trouble, good wishes were exchanged and in the first light we set off to check in at Southend Airport – a tedious, traffic-clogged journey across the Greater London area. The car behaved well in traffic, remaining docile with no fuss or plug trouble but needed clearing out

The E-type Fixed Head Coupé was to prove a superb long distance performance car, a true Grand Tourer. The first to venture abroad with the car were *The Autocar* who travelled through France to conduct their high speed runs in Belgium.

occasionally to regain full response. The mist was thicker near the Thames and, at Southend, clearly too thick for take-off. We sat and waited, wondering whether to phone Peter at Antwerp. The hoped-for midday clearance did not happen and by afternoon was obviously not going to. Flying was cancelled for the day, the weather forecast – little change.

We needed those performance figures without delay, so the one chance was the night boat from Dover. I made my first crossing on the Tilbury ferry and motored on, still in fog, to the Channel port. We booked and waited. Finally, the ship crept from its moorings in sea mist to fog-horn accompaniment which, from the noise and vibration, seemed to originate beside my bunk.

At some ghastly wee hour we were unshipped, still in fog and darkness. Do you remember those first E-type headlights? Nicely faired-in with 45 deg sloping Perspex enclosures defracting half the beam vertically upwards to produce a wall of bright fog. This, a misted-up car interior (ventilation was poor), and unfamiliar minor roads, made the prospects unpropitious, to say the least. We crawled away from the docks on dipped headlamps, crossed a canal, turned left and aimed for where we thought Belgium should be.

Smith elaborated to me how he modified the headlights: 'We gave up trying to drive on headlamps but, as you know, in effect, they have no sidelights. So we got out and taped paper over the headlamp glasses. I think we used the bags we had had our sandwiches in! Anyway, we taped over most of the lamp, except for a slit, to try and stop the upward rays shining back from the fog.'

'There were always problems with test cars,' recalls Elizabeth Hussey, 'because naturally they weren't always ready to be launched even. They were still perfecting them.'

Smith takes up the story again in his article.

After perhaps two hours, we stopped to rest smarting eyes. With the engine off we could suddenly hear waves, which seemed promising as far as direction to Ostend was concerned. Then as first light showed, we heard a tram. Having travelled on the only tram track in the area on an earlier visit, we knew roughly where we were, and that we must have left France and entered Belgium without the aid of customs. Petit déjeuner at Middlekerke was very welcome and it was not long before we were on route to Ghent and Antwerp on a now clear morning.

Peter was waiting at the Dock Hotel and arrangements were in hand – 100 octane, racing tyres and the rest – for an early morning test session next day. My passenger, having unloaded her skis and kit and stoked up with a good meal, departed for Switzerland from the station across the road.

Six o'clock the next morning, out on the unfinished autoroute brought the start of a bright day with some mist patches and a dazzling orange sun ahead for the outward run. We had a good look at the road and checked that it was possible to turn and cross on to the return carriageway. First, we ran off the high-speed acceleration figures with the fifth wheel attached: 90–100mph in third (6 secs); 100–120mph then 110–130 in top (only 8.5 secs). We confirmed that the car's generally accurate speedo was in fact reading slow when running on racing tyres: 130mph indicated was 135mph true.

With the car now hot and eager, we took turns solo at the maximum speed runs. It was relatively easy to wind up to 145mph – in under a minute – but the extra 5mph took a long time to show. At first, we were getting up to 149mph outwards and 147 on the parallel stretch back. The mist patches had gone, there were still no other vehicles and the sun was beginning to warm the atmosphere. Soon an occasional VW Beetle appeared - in fact there seemed to be little else in Belgium at that time. We found that if a Beetle was just going out of sight on the horizon as we set off, the Jaguar could catch and have to pass it on the two-lane speed stretch that followed, with a differential speed of at least 110 – not something we would do by choice.

By February 1961, 9600 HP had been fitted with an engine built by the Experimental Dept., as opposed to a production engine. This second power unit can be easily identified by its cam breather pipes on top, akin to the racing D-types. But how modified was this engine? That is the $64,000 question!

To get to 150 we had to approach that chosen straight at not less than 135mph. My rather cramped right leg quivered with the pressure to hold the pedal flat on the floor, and as the Beetle came backwards towards me, as it seemed, my toes instinctively curled up, trying to ease off the pedal, and disobeying my instructions. The car felt stable and safe. In these days of air dams and wings it seems surprising that the long curving nose did not lift and make the front end too light, nor the short tail allow the car to wander.

After two or three runs each we had a roadside conference. The car was shimmering with heat, the exhaust pipes ticking and all around a smell of hot tyres and oil. We had both just topped 150 on the outward run but were sticking around 148 on the return. Conditions were improving, so we would have one or two more runs.

Maurice described to me what happened next. 'Two things happened on the runs which were terrifying, both to me actually. We were beginning to despair and literally had foot hard down, almost bending the floorboards. Having passed the inevitable Volkswagen with a speed differential of about 120mph, the passenger door sprung open on to its safety catch. The body had flexed and there was a tremendous outside reduction of pressure round the outside of the doors, together with interior pressure – you could actually see the windows pulling outwards if you left them ajar. Anyway, it either flexed or was pulled open and it sounded like a rifle shot, it went with such a bang on to its safety catch.

'It was fairly terrifying when you're concentrating and wondering what's going to happen next. My fear had been a burst tyre.'

Our scares were not quite over [Smith's written account continues]. On the return run, again in the high 140s, came a banshee wail accompanied by a burst of machine-gun fire. Could the natives so resent our activities? This time it was the bright metal trim strip around the windscreen seal which had torn adrift and was holding only on a screw at one end. Its edges played like a reed in the slipstream and the loose end had been beating on the roof.

My final and best run showed 151.5 out and 148.5 back. The waiting Peter had in the meantime been entertained by a kindly and solicitous Belgian chap who, seeing him sitting by the roadside with a fifth wheel and forks, felt sure he must have had a dreadful accident with his bicycle.

The car now seemed to be using nearly as much oil as petrol and both were getting low. More vehicles were appearing and we were beginning to feel conspicuous. Peter's last run was happily his best at almost 152 outwards and about 149 back, so we called it a day. The mean top speed worked out at fractionally over 150mph, and we were satisfied that the figure was fair. We should not have to resign after all.

The precise figures, according to their subsequent report, were a best run of 151.7mph and a mean of 150.4mph. It was mighty close!

As we toured back to Antwerp the car cooled and settled down again being the gentle, flexible sports coupé we arrived in.

'This was,' Maurice told me, 'one of the outstanding tests that I had anything to do with. It was also terrifying!'

I have long wanted to meet Peter Riviere and eventually, by circuitous means as recounted in Chapter 11, I did so near the end of the last century.

'For the more high speed vehicles in those days,' he told me, 'we used to go to Ostend and do the runs on the Ostend/Brussels road, which was far from ideal because it wasn't motorway, and hay carts and suchlike, I seem to remember, could rumble across, even if we did them early in the morning. I think I was there for something else as well. I think I had gone over earlier to cover a record attempt by the Forrest Lycett Bentley. I think I might have had a lift out in another road test car with Philip Turner from *The Motor*.'

I suggested to Riviere that they had been put under some pressure to come back with the right figures.

'Yes, we had indeed! I remember that only too well. We also wondered whether or not it was going to melt before it got there. The road test, I see, notes the fantastic oil consumption but what I remember was that the whole thing was close to melting point. All the needles were going straight off the end.

'I think we actually decided the thing was a bit touch and go, to be absolutely honest,' recalled Riviere with great amusement. 'I don't think we even tried doing the high speed runs with two up.'

'You didn't fudge it, did you?' I asked.

'No, we didn't fudge it. It was genuine, as far as you can do it off the rev. counter and speedo, and the degree to which you have got the right pressure in the tyres and the tyres haven't expanded and a few other sorts of things. Given all those factors, what we would have had with modern radar, I am not certain. If one was absolutely honest, one couldn't say you had a 150mph motor car. Under extreme conditions, it would go at 150mph but that doesn't make it a 150mph motor car.

'It was, I remember, quite exciting and there was quite a lot of noise going on, and quite a smell. I think after the final run, we just jacked it in and decided it wasn't going to go any faster.

'It [the road] was remarkably empty and it didn't go to anywhere from anywhere. Its only one slight disadvantage was that it did have a slight curve through it. No one was expecting anybody to be travelling at those sort of speeds in those days. I think I ran a 1.6 Porsche at the time and that would do 105mph, or just over,' recalled Riviere laughing. 'The Jaguar was certainly the fastest I had ever been.'

I enquired how he had felt about doing this speed.

'I suppose I was just 27 at the time, that's what it comes down to. You didn't think so much about it.'

Maurice Smith was the Editor and rather older. I wondered how Peter came to be chosen and suggested it was quite an honour in those days for such a young man to be chosen.

'*Autocar* staff was terribly small. I suppose "Steady" [Barker] might have been the one. Peter [Garnier] and Harry [Mundy] were married with children so I may have been the obvious person!' he said chuckling.

'I suspect that all this happened before eight o'clock in the morning and we were back down in Ostend for lunch and back in the office by that afternoon.'

Riviere would soon move on from the motoring scene and change direction fundamentally. 'I left journalism and did what I think I always intended to do and became an academic. I left *The Autocar* in September '62 and returned to academia and did a doctorate, and stayed in the academic world ever since.' For many years he has been a Professor of Anthropology at Oxford University.

Looking back to 1961, I asked finally, 'Was this a landmark test for you? Was it one of the ones you particularly remember?'

'Yes, very much so. I am afraid one or two of the others that stand out are for opposite reasons because they were so horrible. I remember an early Corvair which was quite unbelievable. Trying to keep it in a straight line at MIRA was absolutely terrifying.

'In terms of a really great car to drive and great fun, the E-type was an outstanding experience.

'He was a very good young driver,' maintains Miss Hussey. 'I remember him going off on a rally, which he was covering, and there was a very good German driver competing in the rally who was following him for some time and who said it was amazing that he managed to go so fast and yet never needed to touch his brakes.

'He was a lot of fun. He was always thinking of good things to write about. I went with him on a great trip following Cobbett's rides [Cobbett's *Rural Rides*, published 1821]. William Cobbett did his rides on two horses, so we did the same trip in a 2CV. Peter wanted to follow the route as accurately as possible. It meant going down through ditches and all sorts. We went past somebody's garden somewhere down in Hampshire and the chap was mowing his grass. This was excellent because when Cobbett had ridden past, the chap had been mowing his hay!'

Elizabeth Hussey, a spirited lady, remembers the *Autocar* team of those days with great fondness. 'They persuaded me to buy a Mini-Cooper. I had three Mini-Coopers in succession. In fact I had one when I was in Rome and it was great because the Italians all thought it was just like a Fiat 500 or something. Of course, it had a lot more power and so Italians would always follow any girl in a car but I could just sprint away. It was also a very good car to have in ski resorts because you could do hand-brake turns and things. It was very good going up the last hairpins to a resort, which are always difficult. I discovered that the car parks at the bottom of cable cars are very good places for practising hand-brake turns late at night!'

Piecing together the happenings of February 1961, it seems that if Smith and Miss Hussey left in the early morning on Thursday 16th, crossed that night, rendezvoused with Riviere next day and did the runs early the next morning, that that was Saturday 18th. They returned to the UK later that day and their colleagues, Ron "Steady" Barker and Stuart Bladon, took up the reins on the Monday for other aspects of the test.

'I did the road test with "Steady",' recalls Bladon. 'I remember we met at the Berwick Road junction near Watford and I left my car on the grass by a garage, not something you would do today. We drove up the M1 in the E-type and did a lot of the figures on the motorway. When we had a very fast car, we used to do the maximum speeds overseas. Everything else above 90mph would be done on the M1, for example 90–110 in third … We would knock these off in a series, timing at 10mph stages and then work out the individual figures later. We then drove up to MIRA and did the rest of the figures there.

'I found it fascinating and was tremendously excited. "Steady" drove up there and I drove back after lunch. Ron Barker wrote the road test.'

The accuracy of Stuart's recollections is verified by an entry in Norman Dewis's log for Monday, 20 February. 'MIRA. Meeting with *Autocar* in connection with E type F/H No. 2 on press test. Clutch adjusted, rear exhaust manifold nuts tightened.'

'I never doubted the speed,' states Stuart Bladon. 'It had the power and a lovely smooth body. For the high-speed runs, it was fitted with different tyres. Being racing tyres, they would have had less rolling resistance which would have helped the top speed. They also had great conditions – you can tell from the road test.' Good point! Turning up the original report, it states under Test Conditions: 'Weather: Dry, sunny, still air for maximum speed runs. Air temperature, 41.7 deg. F.'

I asked Stuart how his Editor worked. 'Maurice Smith never wrote an article at the time and never used a tape recorder. He used to scribble in a notebook.'

I mentioned to him the Great Engine Debate and the suggestion by some that the engine was a little special. 'Jaguar did go to tremendous lengths. It wouldn't surprise me. They had polished heads for the test cars.'

It might be interesting to look at the 9600 HP performance comparisons between the three engines, as tested by Jaguar, plus the *Autocar* figures.

9600 HP performance comparisons

	1/2/61 Prod. Engine No. R1001–9 3.31:1 axle ratio 6.00 x 16 R.5s Dry	5/2/61 Exp. Engine No. E5020-9 3.31:1 axle ratio 6.40 x 15 R.S.5s Wet	18/2/61 Exp. Engine. No. E5020-9 3.31:1 axle ratio 6.00 x 15 R.5s Dry	1/3/61 Prod. Engine No. R1019–9 3.31:1 axle ratio 6.40 x 15 RS.5s Dry
Standing1/4	14.8	14.8	14.7	n/a
50–70	5.5	5.4	5.4	5.76
90–110	6.4	6.3	6.3	7.39
0–100	16.5	16.0	16.2	16.0
10–110	28.4	27.2	n/a	30.5
Max	n/a	n/a	Best 151.7 Mean 150.4	n/a

With under three weeks to go to the launch in Geneva, the action became more and more frenetic. After the chaps at *The Autocar* had had first crack, several other journalists drove the car pre-Geneva, but it isn't easy to work out when. The distinguished journalists included John Langley of the *Daily Telegraph*, Bill Boddy and Michael Tee of *Motor Sport*, John Bolster of *Autosport*, Raymond Baxter of the BBC, Basil Cardew of the *Daily Express* and Bernard Cahier of *Sports Car Graphic*, plus a correspondent (probably Harold Nockolds) from *The Times*. All were lent 9600 HP before it had to be readied for its eventful journey and big day.

A third engine (R1019-9) was fitted by 1 March, when a further Performance Test was conducted. It was actually slower than the previous one, which may tell us something. However, recently discovered period paperwork states that R1001-9, which was the first engine to be fitted, had been re-numbered R1019-9. Very confusingly, it also states that there was another R1001-9, which would be known as No. 2 R1001-9, but later it was re-stamped E5019-9. So, to summarize, the first engine, which was the very first E-type engine, had been refitted in 9600 HP. I risk being labelled an anorak but I find this all rather exciting!

We now see the car with its third engine, although very recent research suggests the first and third were actually one and the same! Note the lack of cam breather pipes on this engine.

Next day, Dewis issued a third report on 9600 HP. The Fixed Head list was getting shorter, though the brakes were displaying roughness, the oil pressure was reading low, the handbrake warning light was permanently on, the speedometer was inoperative and the chassis plate needed changing as a different engine from that stated was now fitted. Norman volunteered to adjust the carburettors.

We are now faced with a puzzle. By various means we have determined that the representatives of at least seven publications drove the car between *The Autocar* 150mph runs and 14 March, when the car left for Geneva. This period is punctuated by several days when the car was worked upon and is split into two windows by the fitting of the R1019-9 engine. Reference to the attached chart of dates will probably make the following rather easier to understand.

One way of determining which window each of the gentlemen sampled the car within is by any under-bonnet photos, if taken. We know that engine number E5020-9 had a D-type cam breather arrangement, with flexible hoses routed over the top of the engine. From his own photo taken while he borrowed the car, we can tell that Bernard Cahier fell into the earlier, 5020 window. He also said in one of his articles that he drove the car 'towards the end of February'. Curiously, he also states that he 'tested the maximum speed on a motorway' another day. However, he does thank *The Autocar* for their assistance and it is likely he tried it whilst they had it on test.

The face of a 150mph car. Pre-launch the car was lent to a carefully selected band of trusted motoring journalists. The unusually long nose caught out one or two as we can see.

John Langley mentions in a more recent article that his drive took place one February morning, so he too comes into the earlier group. The *Autosport* engine shot indicates the second period. Unfortunately, we do not, as yet, have any under-bonnet shots taken when the other gents tried the car, and with no further data we are stumped. As Sherlock Holmes said, 'It is a capital mistake to theorize before you have all the evidence.' As a long-standing member of The Sherlock Holmes Society of London, I am sure Bill Boddy would agree.

Assuming 1019 was fitted on 28 February and that *The Autocar* had handed the car back on Tuesday 21 or Wednesday 22 February, the first window was about four days including the weekend, because Dewis mentions 'Preparation of E-types', plural, on both Friday 24 and Monday 27 February. On 2 March Dewis noted, 'Preparing both E-types for press'. It seems that the second window, therefore, fell between 3 March and, say, 10 March. Bill Boddy in his *Motor Sport* article stated he borrowed the car just over a week before the announcement. That suggests he had it on either Monday or Tuesday, 6 or 7 March.

February

5	Sun	Perf. Test, now Press Car, E5020 fitted
7	Tues	
8	Wed	Meeting with Gregor Grant
9	Thu	Dewis working on 9600 HP
10	Fri	Car registered 9600 HP
11	Sat	Testing & preparing. Brake failure
12	Sun	Testing & preparing.
13	Mon	Finalizing car
14	Tues	ditto
15	Wed	ditto, delivering (or next morning)
16	Thu	Smith & Miss Hussey set off, drove in fog across London to Southend, Tilbury ferry, Dover, overnight crossing
17	Fri	Docked early hours, drove up coast to Belgium, breakfast, drove to Antwerp, met Riviere, Miss Hussey caught train
18	Sat	150mph runs, returned to UK
19	Sun	
20	Mon	Dewis MIRA met up with Autocar, made adjustments
21	Tues	Autocar/Cahier?
22	Wed	Autocar/Cahier?
23	Thu	Dewis running-in 77 RW
24	Fri	Dewis – preparation of E-types
25	Sat	Lumsden pranged 77 RW
26	Sun	
27	Mon	Dewis – preparation of E-types
28	Tues	Engine R1019-9 fitted in 9600 HP

March

1	Wed	Perf. Test MIRA, now fitted with R1019–9
2	Thu	Dewis report on work needed, preparing both E-types for press
3	Fri	
4	Sat	
5	Sun	
6	Mon	
7	Tues	
8	Wed	
9	Thu	E-type Performance Tests mentioned by Dewis in log
10	Fri	Dewis – preparation of 77 RW
11	Sat	
12	Sun	
13	Mon	
14	Tues	Bob Berry departed

To throw a spanner completely into all these hypotheses, *The Autocar* gents in their 17 March launch issue wrote, 'For the past three weeks we have had a coupé undergoing road test.' With respect to these gentleman, I cannot see how this can be possible and, as Holmes memorably told Watson, 'When you have eliminated the impossible, whatever remains, *however improbable*, must be the truth.'

Bernard Cahier is a French journalist who contributed to publications around the world. He was the European Editor of the US magazine *Sports Car Graphic* and also did a short piece covering his driving impressions for *Motor Racing*, the official organ of the British Racing & Sports Car Club.

'I thought the car was superb,' he told me. 'It was a great experience. It was terribly exciting, you know, for those days, really fast. Handling was good. Brakes were OK. Gearbox was no good – typical Jaguar 'box. And the seats! The car looked lovely but the seats were uncomfortable and the gearbox was not very good. You couldn't rush it.'

I asked Bernard if he knew about the car in advance. 'I was always in touch with them. I had very close relations with Bob Berry. I was one of the very first to drive it, I really was, before the main core of the press drove it. I had it all day and drove quite a bit, mostly country roads. Well, the traffic was OK in those days.

'It was so beautiful, it is still beautiful. That car has not aged.'

One of Cahier's photographs shows 9600 HP with him (so obviously he did not actually press the shutter for this one), Harry Mundy of *The Autocar* and top Grand Prix driver Tony Brooks. I was eager to know whether Brooks drove the car. He did not recall it so I sent him a copy of the photo. We spoke again.

'We have solved the mystery,' he said. 'From the photograph it is obviously on the forecourt of my garage at Weybridge which had recently opened. My memory is terrible but my wife is my memory and she remembers it. Harry Mundy and Bernard

Above: While the car was with the chaps from *The Autocar*, they allowed their continental colleague, Frenchman Bernard Cahier, to sample the car. Cahier (left) and Harry Mundy, Technical Editor of *The Autocar*, called on Grand Prix driver Tony Brooks (right), who also tried 9600 HP.

Below: The car was photographed by Cahier on the forecourt of Tony Brooks's recently-opened Weybridge garage. At various times during February and March 1961 the car had no over-riders and no motif bar bisecting the mouth, or the combination seen here, or the full complement.

Cahier called on spec and said, "What you think? Give it a try?" There wasn't much traffic around there in those days and I gave it a good try. My wife recalls that I said it was "very good". I was obviously impressed because I was not given to making such statements lightly.' I am indebted to Pina Brooks for her fine memory.

Bill Boddy, the famous WB of *Motor Sport*, is virtually an institution and worshipped by many of the older school. Apprenticed to Kings Autocars, he began freelancing at 17 and was Assistant Editor of *Brooklands Track and Air*, ran *Motor Sport* throughout the war and became Editor in 1945. He continues to contribute over fifty years on. For a very long time, he had to cope with his publisher, the unpredictable and irascible Mr Tee.

'*The Autocar* and *The Motor* always got road test cars before us and I used to complain to the SMMT. Our circulation was double that of *The Autocar*, or so old Mr Tee used to tell me. We probably made such a fuss that they [Jaguar] said, "Come up here and have it for half a day."

'They said, "Be careful, it does 150mph." But it handled so well. You got into it thinking, "Well, it is a bit of an exciting motor car" – long bonnet, you know and I thought, "I must be a little careful", but it was so docile. I thought it was going to be a sideways car all the time.' He shared the experience with one of Mr Tee's three sons, Michael. I read Bill a quote from his article about the frustration of traffic crawling along in the outside lane at 90 to 100. 'Michael must have been driving then. He was braver than me and a very good driver.'

Michael Tee takes up the story and corroborates Bill Boddy's account:

We picked the car up and, the thing I remember most, was that Mr Boddy was driving, and we were doing 110mph and he said, 'I can't go any faster.' He said, 'You had better have a go.' I always did the high-speed runs.

So I had a go and did 135mph and I said to him, 'This feels a hell of a lot faster than 135.' In those days on the M1 they had posts [at regular distances] so we timed it using the posts. The speedo was way out. It was 20mph out.

It was unusual for the speedo to be 'slow'. Most manufacturers claimed 100mph and you timed the car and found you were only doing 90mph!

Such a beautiful car and a delight to drive. They let us have it for the day. Took it down the M1 and then across country. We timed everything. The mid-range acceleration was so very good and that particularly impressed Mr Boddy.

There was much less traffic in those days and I don't remember anyone getting in the way. The M1 was known in those days as 'The Murder Road' and you could hold it at peak revs for several miles.

Another comment made by Michael Tee: 'The seats really did grip you.' Tee felt this was a beneficial result of Jaguar having 'a racing stable. They actually held you when driving fast. I actually remember the comfort.

'They said, "This is not a pre-production prototype. It is a pre-production model."' Yes, well. Not quite strictly true. Let's be charitable and say that by this stage, the car had completed its prototype role and was now a pre-production car!

I asked Michael Tee about the reaction from people as they drove past. 'When we drove through towns, people's heads turned. The old fingers were pointing. We drove a lot of pre-production prototypes but this was more of an attention-catcher than any of them. A lot of people did turn and look.

'The Bod loved that! I said, "You're going to have to wind the window down soon and start waving."' We touched on the subject of whether the car was modified from standard. 'I do remember when, later, we did a full road test on an E-type, the Bod said to me, "It is not as fast as the original one." They denied the car [9600 HP] was as fast as we said it was! The later car was quite a lot slower.'

Talking of maximum speed, he said, 'I was always careful about going into the red. The speeds we got were on the flat and not taking a long run down hill.'

Michael Tee confirmed the speed quoted in the article Bill Boddy subsequently wrote for *Motor Sport*, namely, 155mph, and that this was a timed calculation.

I asked Bill Boddy if he felt Jaguar cheated, and he told me a splendid story about what the MG company got up to before the war:

When they came out with the J2, they wanted to be able to say it was a 70mph car. Sammy Davis [the journalist and racing motorist] had the car on the road and they said, 'Sammy, you'll come down to Brooklands, won't you? We'll lay on lunch for you at the Aero Club. You'd like to take it on the track and time it over the half mile, wouldn't you?'

So Sammy said, 'Of course, yes. I can't say it does 70mph without timing it over the half mile. We always do that.' He drove it down and they said, 'We'll just put it in the MG sheds. Lunch is laid on at the Aero Club.' And they chatted till about three in the afternoon and Sammy said, 'I'd better get cracking now and do the half mile test.' It came out at 72, or whatever.

Then people started buying them and they had difficulty getting more than about 63. MG got masses of letters and people calling at their service stations saying. 'Look, *The Autocar* says it does 72, ours staggers up to 63, what's wrong with it?'

Of course they'd got a special engine prepared for Sammy and he didn't know. They changed the engine very quickly over lunch. They kept him as long as possible over lunch – 'Another glass of wine, Mr Davis?'

An RAF fighter pilot during the war, Raymond Baxter then joined the BBC and became the Motoring Correspondent. During the fifties and sixties he used to commentate on Grand Prix racing although, sadly, there was not the same level of coverage in those days as we enjoy today. More recently, he will be remembered as the long-running presenter of the *Tomorrow's World* programme. He also did a few international rallies during the fifties and sixties.

There was not much that did not open on the E-type. The excellent access to the engine was a stark contrast to the inaccessibility of the previous XK models. The rear lid was an early form of what today would be called a 'tailgate'. Although a vast number of unique features would later be found by the restorers, which is hardly surprising of a hand-built prototype, the car now resembled the later production cars in most external respects.

I very well remember driving the 'prototype E-type' several weeks prior to the Geneva Show [Baxter recalls], while the car was still embargoed.

I was invited to the factory by Bob Berry who accompanied me on the short drive to MIRA. After watching Norman Dewis do a couple of high-speed laps, I was given the same pleasure, allowing myself to go higher and higher up the banking until it was 'flat out' all the way.

On the way back, on a cross-country route, we encountered a pack of hounds who crossed the road in front of me – all except one, which ran the wrong way. I just bumped her bottom and bowled her over, but before I could reach her she had got up and followed the pack. At that point I became aware of a beautiful girl on a superb hunter peering at me over the hedge. She cut short my profuse apology saying, 'Stupid little bitch. It was her fault anyway and she'll be fine.'

Arrived back at the factory. 'Lofty' came out to meet us and asked me what I thought of the car. 'World beater,' I said, 'but I can't get my feet really comfortable on the pedals. Looking down on me from his great height, 'Lofty' said, 'I don't know what you are talking about.' The 'trough' for one's heels was [later] incorporated into the production car.

One of the first to drive 9600 HP was John Langley, then a young reporter on *The Daily Telegraph*. He has never forgotten the experience and has often written about it over the years. For him, like all the motoring journalists and broadcasters, it was an absolute landmark.

Of the other members of the exclusive 'Pre-Geneva Drivers' Club', John Bolster and Harold Nockolds are sadly long gone. John Langley, however, is happily still very much with us and has written in more recent times on several occasions in his old paper about his first acquaintance with 9600 HP.

When the Jaguar XK8 was launched in 1996, *The Daily Telegraph* devoted the front page to an early assessment of the car. The main feature shared the page with a smaller piece by John under the title of 'The E-type Is Still My Type'.

In the piece, which began, 'John Langley casts his mind back 35 years, when he drove the world's most exciting supercar at 149mph down a half empty M1,' he wrote:

For one impressionable young reporter, 1961 was a vintage year. In the space of nine months, I joined the world's best newspaper, married the loveliest girl in the world and drove the world's most exciting car at 149mph on the M1. (I was also carried out of a Fleet Street pub on a stretcher, but that's another story.)

The car was the then still-secret E-type Jaguar. My motoring colleague on *The Daily Telegraph*, W.A. (Bill) McKenzie was away, so when the chance came to drive the new Jaguar some weeks before its launch at Geneva, they asked me to try it.

It is difficult now, when high-performance cars are commonplace, to realize what a sensation the E-type caused. It wasn't just its sheer effortless speed, but its stunning looks, all with complete docility and at a price that made its few foreign competitors look absurdly expensive.

The view down that long, sleek bonnet is still one of the great motoring experiences. To an astonished world, here was a reasonably priced supercar that looked as if it had just spent a night at Le Mans with a D-type.

One who was clearly interested was the driver of a Jaguar saloon which came rushing up behind us as I eased the dark grey sports car on to the Coventry by-pass on that dry February morning. Within a few seconds, we had left our pursuer far behind, without really trying.

This was the very car – 9600 HP – that Jaguar's PR man and racing driver, Bob Berry, later drove through the night to get to the Geneva Motor Show in time, after being held up by some last-minute problems. I learnt afterwards that one of my senior colleagues had managed to clobber a bollard just after leaving the factory on a trial run, fortunately without much damage except to his self-esteem. [It seems that this was a journalist from one of the London evening papers. Apparently, he misjudged the length of the bonnet and it happened in Coventry, just as he was leaving the factory. How embarrassing for the poor chap!]

Anyway, we were cruising very easily along the M1 when a clear stretch of road gave me the chance to see what it could do. Within a few seconds, the needle was nudging an indicated 149mph before a distant glimpse of traffic made it advisable to lift off.

Although I had driven a few fast cars before, I still remember being startled at how quickly one catches up with slower traffic from such high speeds. By today's standards, the M1 that morning was half-empty, and it was of course some time before the imposition of the blanket 70mph speed limit. It was said later that the test cars had been specially tweaked to go a bit faster than the standard models, but I still regretted that I did not quite make 150mph.

We returned on the A5, where the E-type's ability to leap past groups of cars and lorries with a deep-throated growl in second or third gear was, if anything, even more impressive. The car's only real flaw was the ponderously slow, though tough and reliable, four-speed gearchange, but with so much power on tap from the smooth six-cylinder XK engine, that was not too much of a handicap.

It's all very well for Jaguar to describe the new XK8 as the E-type's spiritual successor but, fine car though the XK8 undoubtedly is, nothing could quite match the impact that original E-type had on at least one driver.

Up till now everything had been done under a cloak of secrecy. But that was all about to change. Secrecy and anonymity were about to be exchanged for mega-stardom.

CHAPTER SEVEN

Public Unveiling

In this age of scoops and spy photography, it is hard to imagine that a car as dramatic as the E-type could have been kept secret from the public. To maximize the impact when Jaguar did finally unveil the new model, they needed an event of suitable international stature. They also needed an example of this sensational new sports car to show the world.

Difficult as it may now be to believe, the car *was* a well-kept secret and hence a total surprise to the public in March 1961. But then this was a different age, an age when all journalists, or at least their editors, would toe the line and advertising revenue influenced decisions. The aura of secrecy that surrounded the car and the standards of the day are well illustrated by two incidents in late 1960.

Anthony Marshall has been one of Fleet Street's leading photographers for over forty years, working for *The Daily Telegraph* until his retirement in 1999.

I met him in 1987 in Switzerland when I was taking the role of Sherlock Holmes for ten days of festivities to celebrate the

Jaguar chose to launch their ultra-exciting new sports car at the Geneva Salon (Motor Show) in March 1961. The E-type was intended, and would prove to be, a truly international motor car and Switzerland was a suitably international country in which to unleash the new Jaguar.

centenary of the publication of the first Holmes adventure. My first recollection of Marshall was of him, dressed in Victorian garb, as all the press had to be, walking backwards in the middle of a band in Montreux photographing us. As a former News Photographer of the Year, Sports Photographer of the Year and Royal Photographer of the Year, he was the natural leader of the international press corps who dogged our every footstep, and Tony and I became firm friends. Typical of Marshall, he tried to calm my nerves when I had to make a speech *en français* to the Swiss President (who looked remarkably like Jimmy Carter) with a few kind, thoughtful words: 'Don't worry, he's only their equivalent of The Queen!'

Back in 1961 Tony Marshall was with the old *Sunday Despatch*.

I'd been up to Birmingham and coming back down the motorway, I pulled in at the Newport Pagnell services and saw this incredibly wonderful car, with a bicycle wheel on the back which I discovered was the fifth wheel [used for accurate speed measurement by road testers]. There were two chaps in caps – serious looking professional motorists – but they had pulled up right by the entrance. They hadn't gone round the back of the car park, so they were obviously quite proud of what they were doing.

I didn't know anything about the E-type, but I thought, 'that really looks something.' In those days we used big Rolleiflexes and I remember putting a flash on, because it was dark, and taking a photograph. I showed it to one or two people and they said, 'Oh, that must be the new Jaguar sports car.' I gave it to our motoring correspondent but he failed to use it. Some months later, I asked why not and he said that he had had a word with Jaguar and they had asked for it not to be used. There was a suggestion that if it were used there would be no more information forthcoming and the advertising would stop.

Michael MacDowel, who had joined the company in June 1960 and worked in the Service Department under 'Lofty' England, remembers that Peter Berry, who owned a racing Jaguar Mark II saloon, was 'very pushy to see an E-type. It was before the launch and it was totally and utterly *verboten* that we showed anybody an E-type'.

Peter came up to the factory, and he was a persuasive man, and somehow or other, he persuaded me to show him the E-type, which was somewhere near Experimental. I thought, 'Well, we can slip in and slip out again.' Went in the door, showed him the E-type, another door opened and in walked Sir William. I could have just died. I thought, 'That's it, I've had it'.

'England had me up and gave me such a dressing down. Sir William didn't send for me – that would have been the end, I think. 'Lofty' gave me a hard time, but that was typically 'Lofty'. He was always very, very hard, totally demanding but utterly fair. His sarcasm was just unreal!

Obviously they didn't want anybody to see it because they didn't want it to leak press-wise or detract from the magic of the Geneva Motor Show launch. That's why that was such an embarrassing incident, but 'Lofty' realized that it was just one of those stupid mistakes that people make.

A few trusted journalists, such as Philip Turner of *The Motor*, knew of the E-type's existence in advance and would have seen the prototypes testing at MIRA.

'You had far more entrée in those days before the PR people got involved', says Turner. 'I used to wander in and out of Experimental and have coffee with the designers. Bill Heynes used to do little sketches for me on the backs of envelopes. Nowadays you have to set it up with a PR man, who sits there looking very agitated.'

On the decision as to where to launch the car, Bob Berry has this to say:

Jaguar were under a lot of pressure to take it [the E-type] to the New York Show which was in April. There was a lot of pressure from the North American part of the company to launch there, because they said they would be the biggest market and therefore ought to have first crack at it. The company's view at Browns Lane was that we were looking for a world-wide launch for this and since Geneva, and to a lesser extent Paris, were *the* two major shows on the European scene, Geneva was suitably international. We finally decided it would go to Geneva, which of course collapsed the timescales very substantially.

The company was operating on a very, very limited timescale anyhow. I seem to remember Norman Dewis doing nothing but drive E-types at that stage. He had three cars, of which the coupé was one, and most of the development was done on those three cars. The coupé was what today would be called a mule and it got a good hammering. When it was a decided this car would go to Geneva, and it was a last-minute decision, 9600 went through a very rapid updating to get it into a condition where it was capable of being shown with some confidence to the press. It wasn't battered but it was well-used and had to be brought up to date and, quote, re-furbished.

Actually it was virtually *Hobson's Choice*, for Jaguar had so few cars completed. Having decided upon a US launch in April, the four cars for the show stand had to be shipped on 28 February. The two original prototype Roadsters were hardly representative of production cars and probably not in a fit state to be displayed. The first LHD FHC and Roadster were both being used on the pavé and so that only left the two Press Cars, 9600 HP and, in principle, 77 RW available. Another FHC was completed on 6 March, so that Jaguar would have a pristine example for the show stand, and this was sent down to Geneva on a lorry operated by a transport company called MAT.

The Geneva Motor Show was due to open its doors on Thursday 16 March. The day before was Press Day and the 'E' was to be shown to the press that day enabling the world's newspapers to report the launch on the day the show opened. Bob Berry, who had carved out an amateur but very successful motor racing career driving a highly modified XK120 and the famous ex-Works D-type OKV 2 during the fifties, was given the task of taking 9600 HP down to Geneva for the press launch on the Wednesday. As it turned out, he was going to need every ounce of his ability and experience if he was going to get the car there in time. 'It was the most incredible journey and I've never forgotten it.'

Berry joined Jaguar in rather an unusual way, as he explains:

I was a student at Cambridge reading Modern Languages and had an interest in motoring and motor sport. I was going on holiday in July [1951] on a summer university course in Grenoble and so I wrote to 'Lofty' England and said I had noticed they were going to Le Mans, and could I do anything to help. I was just fishing, as many hundreds of people had done before, and have done since.

To my absolute astonishment, he wrote back and said, 'If you're passing through Coventry, pop in.' So I found an occasion to go down there, needless to say, and the upshot of the conversation was, 'If you are going to be there, come along and I'm sure we can make use of you.'

I duly presented myself at the Hôtel du Paris in Le Mans on the Monday before the race, and I don't think I went to bed until the following Sunday night. I shall never forget the sight of people like Bill Heynes, who hadn't wielded a tinsmith's hammer in centuries, trying to shape a rear cover for the headlights, as they decided to try Marchal lights instead of Lucas and the backing plates wouldn't fit.

There was one mechanic per car, and then there was Jack Emerson, the engine specialist. The amount of work that had to be done in the period was just unbelievable, and I was the gofer as I spoke French. I spent all my time fetching and carrying. It had the right sort of effect, as a combined effort, because they won. As a way of saying 'thank you' they said, 'When you have finished your course in France, if you would like to spend the remainder of your holiday working at Jaguar, we would be very happy to have you.' I went there for about two months, at the end of which 'Lofty' England said to me, 'Why don't you come and work for us permanently?' – which is what I did.

Berry worked in the PR Department under the legendary Ernest 'Bill' Rankin, who did so much to build up the image of first SS Cars and then Jaguar. Bob succeeded Rankin as PR supremo, before being seconded to Leyland International in the late sixties when Jaguar had been tragically gobbled up into the catastrophic British Leyland adventure. He returned for further spells as a director under first Geoffrey Robinson (who later entered politics!) and then Sir John Egan, before deciding to move on to fresh challenges.

Understandably, as it is such a long time ago, memories of the Geneva launch are now a little clouded in the mists of time for most people. Indeed, it has proved surprisingly hard to find anyone who was there. Yet, as Berry explains, it was an unusually large event for Jaguar.

'I think it was a general invitation put out by the SMMT [the representative body of the British motor industry] because I don't think we had anything like the statistical information and the background to run the sort of press launch that the E-type became.' Jaguar invited all their usual contacts from the UK and European press, but Berry is of the opinion that the SMMT supplemented the Jaguar list:

How it became such a jamboree, which in fact it was, I think was largely because of the publicity put out by the SMMT through their very well-organized Press Office.

We had one car for the stand and one for the reveal at the Parc des Eaux Vives, and I can't recall why the last-minute panic set in. This car [9600 HP] was due to go anyhow as the car outside that people could get into and sit in, and then we were going to use it on the test circuit. Norman Dewis and the other guys were desperately trying to get 77 RW ready and it was agreed that Norman would bring out 77 RW for the second week.

There was uncertainty as to whether in fact the car that was scheduled to go on display at the press launch was going to be ready in time. Press Day was Wednesday and the show opened on the Thursday. Therefore it was a scramble to get it ready. It was always the intention to get it there but it suddenly became an imperative because we were staring at a situation where a group of invited press – as well as an unknown number, amounting to something like 150 or 200 other press people – would actually go to Geneva and not find anything there. And that's what changed the whole 9600 story from a drive out to Geneva and, as long as it was there some time during the day, that was all that was needed, to saying, 'The bloody thing's got to be there because it could be the only car we've got.'

There was a sudden conviction that the show car was not going to make it and therefore 9600 might well have made it to the Motor Show. Now whether that's got something to do with the vehicle being lost in transit by MAT, I really can't tell you. The show car was a typical 11th hour, 59th minute [job] and I suspect that it might well have left beyond the deadline set by MAT.

I can remember it happening. I was all set to go out in the normal way, nothing very special about it, and then this bloody great panic started.

It wasn't finished until the night before, and I crossed on the midnight Dover – Calais ferry. I had the job of getting it there on time and it was an incredible run down.

Before Bob describes his journey of a lifetime, let us just consider his challenge. The Browns Lane factory, which we estimate he left at about 7pm, was close to the main A45. As he turned left out of the factory gates, Browns Lane quickly became The Windmill Hill. Turning right at the 'T' junction, very briefly on to the Birmingham Road, he would have then turned left on to the Dunchurch Highway. He would have reached this dual carriageway in a couple of minutes. The old Fletchamstead Highway, as it became after about a mile, skirted Coventry but to this day consists of a tedious succession of traffic lights and islands. Though the M1 was trumpeted as the London to Birmingham motorway, in those days it petered out somewhere near Rugby. However, with Coventry behind it, the A45 became a quiet, fast stretch of dual carriageway that connected to the M1. Barbara Castle had not yet imposed her 70mph speed limit and so Berry was free to use the car's performance and the traffic would have been very light by today's standards. He could have hit the outskirts of London by around 8pm, but then his journey would have slowed very considerably.

This was well before the M25 orbital motorway, and the North Circular and South Circular ring roads were dreadful, congested roads, punctuated by frequent bottle-necks. Straight through the middle and out the other side on the slow crawling Old Kent Road was the better way, and is confirmed by Bob as his route that evening. This could have taken a good couple of hours, even in the evening. The main roads from London to Dover would have probably taken at least another hour and a half, which adds up to arrival at the docks at around 11.30, just in time to board the midnight ferry. Berry takes up the story from docking at Calais.

None of the autoroutes was there of course. So it was Calais, St Omer, Béthune, Arras, Cambrai, St Quentin, Laon, Reims, Châlons-sur-Marne, Vitry, St Dizier, Chaumont, Langres, Dijon, down to Chalon-sur-Saône, which used to be the old milk run. From Châlon you could go to Tournus, down to Bourg and then Nantua, Bellegarde and so into Geneva, which I did, as despite the fact that it's the longer way, I was fairly confident the road would be open. The alternative is to go down from Dijon across to Dole, Champagnole and then St Claude and Col de la Faucille and into Geneva that way. But that's often shut and I decided I didn't want to go there and have to turn straight back.

My chief recollection was the very poor weather. It was quite foggy, in fact it was very foggy from leaving the port as far as Reims. I remember arriving in the centre of Reims in that huge square and really not being very certain where the hell I was. It was as bad as that. I wrong-slotted it on two or three occasions simply not being able to pick up the route in the fog. Just south of Reims, the sun started to come up and heading south across the flat plains of Reims through the vineyard area the fog quite rapidly lifted and, not to put too fine a point on it, I just drove it flat out.

I was so far behind schedule as not to be possible. But on the basis that if you don't try, you're not going to achieve it, I simply drove it as if it was a race. It's the only description I can give you. I drove it flat out between the corners and all that sort of thing. It sounds likes Biggles but that, in fact, is what happened.

It was a case of balancing speed with getting there in one piece. I was going as fast as I possibly dared – sort of torn between being late and shunting it. On the long straight roads of northern France it was running at 120s, 130s, 140s – it ran at whatever speed I could get between the corners. So I really did drive it flat out all the way there, and because the weather reports were so poor in the Geneva area, instead of going the short route over the top, over the St Cergue Pass, and down into Geneva on the north side of the lake, I opted to go the long way round through Nantua and Bellegarde, which I knew would be open because it was the main route for trucks into Switzerland, and sure enough it was. And it was nose-to-tail trucks!

In those days it was a very steep and very twisty run, and the most nerve-wracking part of that was doing the 'slotting' bit [overtaking] at every possible opportunity. That was pretty tense stuff because time was really running out and it really looked impossible. I just kept forcing on and forcing on and forcing on.

It was not a ride I relished in retrospect. I didn't relish it at the time really. I suppose 'foolhardy' is the best description of it. Youth often makes you do things that you wouldn't have done normally.

It was a great ride and the car really went well. If anyone doubted it was a 150mph motor car, they couldn't talk to me about it, because it demonstrably was – no question about that. It just went bloody well.

It poured with rain and it was unpleasant and cold, and there was a lot of traffic. The ability to accelerate on relatively short straights, overtaking vehicles, was really quite amazing. It was the first time I had really driven it in other than controlled conditions on the motorway or in testing. It was the first time I had really driven it hard under normal road conditions. I don't think there are many cars, even today, that would reproduce that. I felt enormously safe. The suspension, I used to think, was exceptionally good, particularly the original cars which were so light. The original E-types were really very well put together – certainly 9600 was great.

A bag of apples and two pints of milk sustained me for the whole run down. I only stopped for fuel. I think I stopped once in Reims and I think the second time was south of Chalon. The second time I really thought I had run out of fuel because I was trying to stretch it as far as I could. But I was surprised just how much fuel it used. In retrospect, it wasn't surprising. I had a large sum of French francs for such an eventuality. So it was a case of stopping, throwing in the fuel and just going on again. I really didn't feel very hungry until I got there. It really was a great experience.

I'd done the route before and I was familiar with Geneva and where the dealership was. At that stage it was in the basement of a huge block of flats. The showroom was a very small one in the old part of the town. The whole of the service department and parts, etc., was in the basement. So you had to know how to get to it, otherwise you'd spend quite a lot of time looking for it. I'd been there quite a few times on business, so I knew my way around the place. It was a fairly easy drop from there to the Parc, because both were on the south side of the lake.

I arrived in a great big heap at the premises of Marcel Fleury, who was the Jaguar distributor then for the French-speaking part of Switzerland. They were all standing around waiting for the thing to arrive and, literally, I was hardly out of the car before they were cleaning it, because there was twenty minutes to clean it and get it down to the venue, the Parc des Eaux Vives.

The launch was to happen in the Parc des Eaux Vives in the restaurant and everyone was milling outside. I turned up with 9600 HP literally just as it was about to start.

I think it's the only car I actually drove flat out from one end to the other of a journey, simply to get there on time.

Lyons, though, was furious. 'Good God, Berry, I thought you weren't going to get here.' He also had some comments to make about leaving things to the last minute, though that was hardly Bob's fault.

Patrick Mennem, who had previously been with the *Coventry Evening Telegraph*, was Motoring Correspondent of the *Daily Mirror* and recalls: 'There were 150 to 200

As Bob Berry was driving flat out to reach Geneva just in time, Sir William Lyons was growing increasingly anxious and angry as he waited, not knowing Berry had been held up by last minute delays and fog en route. The massed ranks of Press, seen here, give some idea of the vast number present and the impact the launch caused. Note the restaurant to the left.

The Press, who ringed the car in the *Parc des Eaux Vives*, were awestruck. They had never seen a production car quite like this. The styling was not a copy of the trend-setting Italians, it was not essentially British – it was Jaguar's own unique style. Add to the style the promised performance and it was a truly stunning concept.

While an anonymous car had been unveiled inside, this car became the public face of the new E-type. Following its pre-launch work, 9600 HP was not allowed to rest but would have a busy life ahead. Compare the photo on the following pages with the recreation thirty-nine years later on pages 236–238.

people there, which in those days was enormous. There was a gasp when it was unveiled, which was very unusual for the press. I have never heard it since.' He still recalls Bob Berry being delayed by 'problems at the last minute, crossing by the night ferry and meeting fog en route'. He thinks he averaged 62mph on the drive from Calais.

In 1966 Douglas Armstrong took a similar length route from Calais to Geneva in a 4.2 E-type. He stated that it was 578 miles (930 kms). Assuming Berry did cover this distance at an average of 62mph, that equates to 9 hours, 20 minutes. If he arrived in Geneva at 11.40am, leaving 20 minutes, as he says, to clean the car, and be at the Parc for midday, that suggests he left Calais at 2.20am. This allows just over two hours for the crossing, assuming there was no hour difference between the UK and mainland Europe at that time! If all our deductions are sound, it appears that Bob Berry and 9600 HP travelled about 800 miles in around 17 hours, including crossing the pond.

Press photographers ringed the car as Sir William Lyons proudly stood alongside 9600 HP. The fabulous E-type, an icon of the Swinging Sixties, a car that distilled all Jaguar's Le Mans experience into a road car clothed with a stunning, sensual body, had arrived. For Lyons and Jaguar, it was another international triumph.

The press reports were eulogistic. 9600 HP was featured, illustrated or mentioned in *The Autocar*, *The Motor*, *Autosport*, *Motor Racing*, *The Daily Telegraph*, *The Times*, the *Daily Express*, the *Daily Mirror* and many other publications right around the world.

With the benefit of their pre-launch run in 9600 HP, *The Daily Telegraph*, *The Times* and the *Daily Express* had announced the car in their Wednesday editions. John Langley wrote in *The Daily Telegraph*, 'Driving the car is more like flying than motoring. On the M1 I found the car would cruise smoothly and quietly at 110–120mph. Bursts of acceleration rushed it up to just over 140mph on two occasions.'

The man from *The Times* wrote in his piece, 'Your correspondent drove the E-type coupé recently and found the most remarkable quality, apart from performance, was the flexibility which the car displayed. It is easy to drive in traffic and will pull away smoothly in top gear from walking pace. When the tremendous power is used the steering, roadholding and braking all give confidence. The E-type is claimed to have a maximum speed of about 150mph and will accelerate from a standstill to 100mph in 16 seconds.'

Basil Cardew waxed lyrical in the *Daily Express*. Under the headline 'NEW JAGUAR CAN BEAT THE WORLD' there were two photos of 9600 HP. 'A so smooth drive at 140mph and not a rival anywhere,' he wrote.

'It is the first of the E-type range – and it is about the most docile top-performance car I have driven in years.

'As I drove the car effortlessly at 140mph, a Jaguar spokesman explained that the complete freedom from vibration was derived from mounting the whole suspension and drive units on rubber blocks.

'As we sped through the countryside we knew we were the speedmaster of every car we met.

'Yet the Jag man told me that with altered axle ratios the car would do 165mph, "So at 150 there is no strain whatever".

'He said it had taken two or three years to bring out the new models and their concept was derived directly from the famous Jaguar D-type sports cars which have won Le Mans.'

A tempting hint of the new car shared the front page of the *Daily Mail* with news of an American cargo airline requesting permission to carry passengers with its cargo on a 'no glamour deal' to London for £47 10s. (£47.50) single fare compared with the then lowest tourist rate of £86 10s. (£86.50). It was also reported that President Kennedy would 'put new proposals to Russia when the atom test ban conference starts in Geneva next Tuesday'. It was stated that he hoped this would lead to 'the first international arms control agreement in the nuclear age.' Alongside was a box containing the words, 'VISION – LIFTS THE DUSTSHEET', under which was the photo of a Fixed Head under a sheet, and the further words, 'and reveals the year's most exciting new car. See Page 7.'

Page 7 included a large advert which stated, 'You can't beat BURTON tailoring', and a smaller one for Bile Beans which stated, 'She doesn't let constipation ruin her complexion – do you?'. Dominating the page, however was an article under the headline, 'THE PEDIGREE OF POWER'.

'VISION presents the background story of the year's most exciting new car, the thoroughbred with the promise of a champion.' Wrote Denis Holmes from Geneva, 'From zero to 100mph in 16 seconds flat – every inch of this sleek Jaguar is a winner.

'It will do 150mph straight from the showroom – yet cruise in traffic at 10mph in top gear. Fit competition gearing and it will do 170mph. This is the car whose sleek lines raised cheers when Jaguar chief Sir William Lyons ripped the dust-sheets from it here tonight.

'This is the two-seater E-type grand touring Jaguar, the first new car offered for sale this year, and a powerful shot in the arm for the motor industry's 1961 export drive.'

He concluded, 'It will be a winner everywhere, I am convinced. If ever there is a model which can persuade Jaguars back to racing, this is it.'

The *Daily Mirror* entitled their piece, 'ENTER – THE 150mph JAG' and went on to say 'Here is a new British sports car, so fast that when it takes the road most drivers will get only a REAR view.

'It is the Jaguar E-type … and it is capable of 150 miles an hour, say the makers.

'The Jaguar E will be put on the American market soon. It will be the fastest mass-produced sports car ever offered for sale in America.'

The matter of the launch, or launches, and which car did what on which day is now thoroughly confusing. *The Daily Express* and the *Daily Mail* both printed their reports on the Wednesday and referred to events on Tuesday. The former referred to

THE SUNDAY EXPRESS LONDON APRIL 30 1961

THIS IS THE FINEST OF A LEGENDARY BREED—A SUPERB ADVENTURE FOR THE EXPERT DRIVER

WHAM!—And you are doing 150 miles an hour

ROBERT GLENTON puts the fabulous new E-type Jaguar through its paces

DO you know what 150 miles an hour is like? I do. I have been testing the new E-type Jaguar.

Odd how the Jaguar has become a legend in our time. Not just in this country but all over the world.

Small boys turn pale with anticipation, pretty girls smile immodestly, and jealous men turn racing green. I deplore motoring legends. A name is not enough. Succeeding models too often turn out to be as unimpressive as some children of famous men.

But not the E-type Jaguar. It will be the Pitt the Younger, the David, son of Jesse, of the family tree.

It is the best, the finest, and the most superb Jaguar of them all. I am delighted to rave over it.

On so many counts. It is well over £1,000 cheaper than any car even approaching its class in Britain, France, Germany, or even Italy. The Americans have nothing even vaguely like it at any price.

For the expert driver it is a superb adventure.

It travels at speeds higher than those with which Grand Prix champions made their names only a few post-war years ago.

And it is remarkably safe. There is nothing of the wing-and-a-prayer and blind faith in the top speeds of this car.

TELL-TALE CLUES

Come with me on the fastest road test I have ever done for the Sunday Express.

The car is low and sleek and beautiful. Its lines are as clean as a jet fighter, for it is meant to slice through wind resistance like a stiletto between the second and third ribs.

When you first see it, three tell-tale clues give you a flutter in your tummy.

The obvious one is the speedometer. It says bleakly "140 150 160."

Secondly, look for the front number plate. There isn't one. This is the first British production car ever made which has them painted on the bonnet. And why? This car goes so fast that the drag of such a small oblong of metal would ruin its top speed.

Thirdly, take an apprehensive peer at the padding. Not just on the dashboard, but round the windscreen, above the windscreen, and even lining the roof.

After all this it comes as a shock to discover that the E-type moves without a single racing mechanic in sight.

Turn the key, press the starter and it rolls away with only the slightest throatiness that the saloon Jaguars haven't got.

Press the throttle pedal gently, then firmer, then hard. Forty miles an hour, change into second: 75 miles an hour, make a quick change into third ... cursing a little as you do so.

The Jaguar gear change was never its best point. The E-type hasn't altered. In contrast to the urgency of the car, a noiseless change must be made with the solemnity of a beadle's stride ... 100 miles an hour. 110 ... 115 ... The wind noise grows, there is the sweet scent of high speed, an almost imperceptible whiff of warm clean oil. Already your eyes are searching the distance like a home-hungry sailor.

Change pedantically into top 120 ... 130 ... 140. The noise rises, the road ahead is a mesmeric ribbon growing whiter and whiter and the world around blurs greyly.

This is the time one thinks. Nearly every car, when it reaches absolute top speed, becomes a little unstable. It lifts a little, the steering grows light and the limit of endurance is very obvious.

What about the Jaguar? Feel the steering as softly as if you were picking up a fledgling, check the instruments, study the roadholding.

The E-type could be motoring in town traffic for all the alarm there is. Down goes your foot, down goes that little fraction of pedal movement that's left ... 150 miles an hour.

A RARE WORLD

You have to raise your voice only a little to talk about as loud as a long-distance call would need.

At 150 miles an hour you are in the rare world of Fangio, Jack Brabham, and Moss.

And now the Jaguar is snarling.

Brake. There's no danger, no pulling, no instability. With discs at back and front, the Jaguar slows down fast and precisely.

At 110 crawling miles an hour, your passenger lights a cigarette.

He's a rare man. A lifetime of speed in an afternoon.

An afternoon? It has taken less than a minute from a press, on the starter button.

FOR THE SKILFUL

What else is there about the E-type that makes it the most sensational sports car of our time?

I've used it for Saturday morning shopping. My wife has driven it. It will drift through London in top gear at about 15 miles an hour.

It has the pokiest ashtray of all time.

It does 18 miles per gallon and is an uncompromising two-seater.

The E-type is a car for the skilful and enthusiastic minority. But the best thing about it, the reason it is undoubtedly unique is a small thing.

After its announcement, after the fabulous overseas orders, certain that he could sell every one he made at twice the price.

Bill Lyons, the head of Jaguars took another look at the car, at its triple windscreen wipers, and its superb visibility, and decided he wasn't content.

He had door handles altered and fittings rearranged.

For the time being he is satisfied.

Now for performance—
GEAR SPEEDS : Top. 152 m.p.h.; third, 115 m.p.h.; second, 78 m.p.h.
ACCELERATION : 0-30 m.p.h., 2.7sec.; 0-100 m.p.h., 16sec. The speedometer was 3 m.p.h. SLOW at 100 m.p.h.
FUEL CONSUMPTION : 18 m.p.g.
FOR THE TECHNICAL : Engine, six cylinder, twin overhead camshafts ... capacity 3,781 c.c. B.H.P. 265 at 5,500 r.p.m. Suspension : Independent front and rear.
PRICE : £1,550. Total (with tax), £2,196 19s. 3d.
WILL IT FIT YOUR STATUS ? Length, 14ft. 7½in.; width, 5ft. 2¼in.; height, 4ft.

WHAT IS YOUR VERDICT?

How much power has a policeman?
by FENTON BRESLER

NO one except a German likes being ordered around. The British have a particular objection to it—even when done by a policeman. They always want to know: "Why? What is your authority?"

That is exactly what London business man Charles Henderson wanted to know a few months ago.

Charles had garaged his car and was strolling languidly home along the Embankment. It was two in the morning and he paused for a moment to peer meditatively into the glistening waters of the Thames.

"What have you got in that briefcase?" asked a voice—and Charles turned round to see a uniformed constable eyeing him suspiciously.

"Some documents from the office," replied Charles. "But what's it got to do with you?"

"Would you mind opening it, please," said the policeman.

"I most certainly would!" retorted Charles. "It contains some highly confidential documents."

And so they went on, the constable asking Charles to open the case and Charles more determinedly refusing. It ended with an extremely indignant Charles being "escorted" to a police station—where reluctantly he allowed the case to be opened.

The sequel

It contained — confidential documents.

The sequel : Charles sued the policeman for false imprisonment—for wrongfully "imprisoning" his movements during the period of questioning.

"This is an entirely misconceived action," said the policeman's counsel. "Ever since two Acts of 1839, the Metropolitan and City of London Police have been empowered to stop, search, and detain persons reasonably suspected of having or conveying anything stolen or unlawfully obtained. This constable was only doing his duty."

"He was exceeding it," retorted Charles's counsel. "As you say, the Acts grant this power only where persons are reasonably suspected of having or carrying stolen property. There was nothing reasonably suspicious about my client. Surely a respectable business man is still entitled to carry a briefcase in the street at night?"

WHAT IS YOUR VERDICT? Was the policeman within his rights?

More trousers! More trousers! More trousers—with 'TERYLENE'

This dramatic headline in *The Daily Express* was typical of the unrestrained fervour among the national Press. Even the normally reserved British expressed views in unambiguous, blatant language. In this way 9600 HP introduced the E-type to the world.

a preview 'today' and the latter mentioned the car 'raised cheers when Jaguar chief Sir William Lyons ripped the dust-sheets from it here tonight'. At that time John Coombs was one of Jaguar's main dealers and motorsport entrants and 9600 HP would later pass through his hands. 'I was at Geneva and Lyons gave a party. There was great excitement. It really was the most astounding sports car that has ever been produced.' Was this party on the Tuesday, Wednesday or Thursday night? Was it at the party that the car was unveiled, as the *Mail* suggested? Was it in the restaurant at the Parc des Eaux Vives?

Patrick Mennem thinks it happened in the restaurant and is convinced the car unveiled was a non-runner. 'We were not allowed to take it out.' On the other hand, it is possible that car was just being kept clean, ready for its transfer to the Show hall that night. Bob Berry thinks it happened in the restaurant too. Bernard Cahier says it did not and there was no way you could get a car inside. Dougie Armstrong says that in all his years of attending launches there, he never saw a car inside the restaurant. From a visual inspection today of what looks to be a totally unchanged building, it does appear tricky.

Thursday's *Telegraph* followed up its initial piece with a report from Geneva, dated Wednesday. 'The new Jaguar E-type Grand Touring model, having its world premiere, was unveiled today in a Geneva lakeside restaurant.' So, that is another vote for the restaurant!

Thursday's *Daily Mirror* carried a photograph of a Fixed Head and a stylish French gent leaning nonchalantly against the side of the car. It was captioned: 'Jacques Charrier, estranged husband of film star Brigitte Bardot, yesterday went home with a new star – the E-type Jaguar car, smash hit of the Geneva Motor Show.'

The same day's edition of *The Coventry Evening Telegraph* reported, 'The first personal sale was to Brigitte Bardot's husband, the French film actor Jacques Charrier, who flew to Geneva from Rome yesterday to test the 150mph car. The Jaguar was hailed as the sensation of the show by the Geneva Press today, and when the doors of the show opened, large crowds flocked to the stand and deluged the salesmen with enquiries about the car's performance.' The same page carried an advert for suits at eight guineas!

From this article we learn that Charrier was in Geneva on Wednesday and he is photographed outside in the Parc with what must be the Show FHC, as it has no registration. So we know the Show car was in the vicinity. Incidentally, it is complete rot to say he took it home with him! If he drove a car, 'It would have to have been 9600,' states Bob Berry.

The 17 March issue of *The Autocar* included an article headed, 'Exciting New E-type'. After briefly setting the scene and whetting the appetite, the piece concluded, 'This is certainly the fastest car ever tested by this journal; its maximum speed is – see next week!'

On the same date, *Autosport* appeared with a splendid shot of 9600 HP on the front cover with John Bolster in the driving seat. Inside a dramatic low-level, front-on photo of 9600 HP headed Bolster's highly enthusiastic piece which began: 'If Les Vingt Quatre Heures du Mans has been responsible for the new E-type, then that Homeric contest on the Sarthe circuit has been abundantly justified.

> Here we have one of the quietest and most flexible cars on the market [he went on], capable of whispering along in top gear at 10mph or leaping into its 150mph stride on the brief depression of a pedal. A practical touring car, this, with its wide doors and capacious luggage space, yet it has a sheer beauty of line which easily beats the Italians at their own particular game.
>
> 'All this, and 20mpg economy too, comes at a price which is about half that of the current crop of glamour-wagons.
>
> 'To give some idea of the potential performance, let us try to imagine an even lighter XK150S with a greatly improved aerodynamic penetration. Let us then envisage the virtual elimination of wheelspin by virtue of the IRS [Independent Rear Suspension]. The result, of course, is something out of this world, as the performance figures prove.
>
> 'Figures are all very well, but these almost incredible times are recorded in a silky silence that has hitherto been utterly foreign to the sports car.
>
> 'Well, that is the new Jaguar, [Bolster concluded], and it is certainly the most important machine that has been introduced for a long time. *Autosport* has always championed the independent rear suspension of the rear wheels, and we have often wondered what a Jaguar would be like with this desirable feature. Now we know, and the answer is – it's a winner.

The *Daily Mail* had been continuing to publicize on the front page its competition for two E-types. 'That Jaguar Can Be Yours' it stated one day. 'The Most Wanted Car In The World', it enthused the next day. In the *Sunday Telegraph* Nigel Lawson, a future Chancellor of the Exchequer, recommended Jaguar shares. The following Monday's edition of the *Mail* carried an article entitled, '150 MPH JAGUAR STARTS AN EXPORT BOOM'.

'Worldwide orders for the new 150mph-plus E-type Jaguar have created a fantastic export boom for Britain. Firm orders from Europe alone in the three days that the Geneva Motor Show has been open have topped the £500,000 mark – a staggering piece of salesmanship in a vital export market. It will be years before Jaguars can even keep abreast of world demand.' Jaguar shares gained 2s 6d (12p).

Apart from this initial gain, it seems the rise was not sustained, much to the disappointment of one investor. 'I was in America,' says Stirling Moss, 'when they showed the car to the dealers. I can't remember why. But there was one thing that really surprised me. Here was this stunning looking car, and all the dealers said, "God. This is fantastic. We're gonna sell a lotta these." I bought some Jaguar shares. This was insider-dealing really! I'd heard the reaction. Didn't make a blind bit of difference to the share price. I was so disappointed. I thought, "Here is a real success

MARCH 17, 1961

AUTOSPORT

1/6

EVERY FRIDAY

Vol. 22   No. 11

BRITAIN'S   MOTOR   SPORTING   WEEKLY

Registered at the G.P.O. as a Newspaper

9600 HP

IN THIS ISSUE
THE NEW JAGUAR – SIX PAGE SPECIAL FEATURE
TRACK IMPRESSIONS OF THE KIEFT F.J. CAR   FIRST GOODWOOD MEETING

Not surprisingly the motoring press focused on the new Jaguar and showered it with informed praise. There was barely a publication that 9600 HP did not appear in at launch time or subsequently. Autosport carried John Bolster's eulogy based on his pre-launch acquaintance with 9600 HP and the magazine's editorial concluded that such a car could only have resulted from intensive development work and a racing history.

story, this must affect the shares". They were a good share anyway, so it didn't matter, but it really surprised me.'

Meanwhile, 9600 HP could not rest on its laurels as it had an active role to play during the show. Bob Berry was kept very busy demonstrating the Fixed Head, as he explains.

At that stage the Geneva Show had a test circuit. It was one of the great things about Geneva that it had a test circuit just outside Geneva on the south side of the lake. They closed the road and it was virtually a hill-climb and circuit. It was just a service road. There was a right turn, originally where the very wide road [which ran along the southern side of the lake] became a very much narrower single road. It went uphill to a right-hand hairpin, up to a left-hand bend and then it went up the hill and round a left-hander. It was very bumpy and steep and then you trundled through the rest of the little village and there was an approximately three-quarter mile narrow road, very heavily cambered, very bumpy, which ran down the middle of a field. At the far end, there was a little bridge or a bump, and then it petered out into the village as you did a left turn and dropped down to the main road again. It was a downhill first section, and it was absolutely straight, a straight blind, but it was very heavily cambered and very bumpy and when the authorities realized the speed that some of the quicker cars were reaching – there was a 250GT Ferrari and the two E-types – they put a chicane in it. One of the cars, might have been a Peugeot, actually went over the bump and went off the road. Nobody was hurt but it frightened the authorities to death. So they put a straw bale chicane in, just before the bump. But in an E-type you could do 130 down there without any difficulty. The speed built up very quickly because the first bit was downhill.

'Norman Dewis brought the roadster 77 RW out from England, I think on the first Saturday, and he and I spent all our time up there. The original concept was that people would go on to the stand, would get a ticket for a test drive, and would then be driven out in one of the cars. But there were so many people – there was literally hundreds of people – waiting to have a run.'

'Each day,' recalls Norman Dewis, 'we were setting up a new record and the Ferraris and Mercs were trying to beat it. We were supposed to be demonstrating to customers – the poor devils! There we were, trying to beat each other, and when they got out, these poor devils would walk away saying, "Thank you very much" and be shaking!'

So when Dewis arrived with the second car, [Berry continues], we had so many people waiting for drives that we decided to leave the cars permanently out on the hill-climb circuit because it went on all day. We ferried people out in other cars and we'd just circulate round and round. The cars took a tremendous battering because they were driven literally flat out.

There was a bit of a contest between Dewis and me to see who could get up fastest. It was pretty quick and used to make the customers sit up and take notice. What I did, and I think Norman did, was to give them the choice of going leisurely, quickly or as quickly as possible. They had the choice because it's too easy to frighten people. I was taken up the hill in the 250 Ferrari driven by their test driver and it was not something I would ever want to repeat. In actual fact [said Bob, rocking with laughter], it was slower than the E-type. That was the difference between sitting in the driving seat and the passenger's seat, I guess.

You never quite understood what the customer wanted. You could talk to them but you had to really keep an eye on them. Some of them wanted to go as quickly as possible with no concept of what that meant. Throwing it into an uphill corner, you can go into a corner very much more quickly than if it was level. Some of them really got a fright and we used to back off if they were showing signs of not being happy about it. The idea was to demonstrate the car, not to frighten them to bloody death.

I mentioned Norman's comment about the victims being rather white-faced. 'That's absolutely true,' said Berry. 'The vast majority, if not all of them, had never experienced that performance or being driven in that sort of way.'

So we just went round and round and round. I suppose a complete circuit was no more than ten minutes. It was very heavily policed and you didn't dare do anything silly on the road. So we used to trickle back very slowly, to indicate just how flexible the car was. Every run consisted of a full-blown standing start so we got through quite a fair amount of tyre.

There were thousands of people lining the course. It was rather like Shelsley or Prescott. What we found was that people were duplicating the tickets for a test drive and all sorts of people who had never been near the stand had got hold of them. There were queues of people with thirty or forty waiting. They'd stand there for ages just to have a ride. Neither of the cars gave us any trouble at all. It was quite extraordinary.

There's no doubt they took an awful hammering. As far as I remember, we didn't touch them. I don't think we put a spanner on either of them during the entire period. So it was amazing. It really was rough and there were quite a few occasions when the suspensions hit the bump stops, certainly on the high-speed run. Unless you kept it straight down the middle, it was sufficiently cambered to really pull you down. It was quite taxing really.

That was the great thing about Jaguar. Mechanically it was always 93–94 per cent right and the remainder was done by the customer, if indeed they were ever 100 per cent!

But it created quite a sensation. The hot car at that stage was the Ferrari. There were two models there and neither of them was anything like as quick round that circuit as the E-types were. It was quite interesting because I knew the guy who was the Ferrari test driver and we swapped cars. There was no doubt that the E-types were quicker, certainly on that circuit.

Also it was interesting that having driven both the E-types extensively, 9600 was undoubtedly the quicker of the two, despite the fact that it was slightly heavier. It was quicker on acceleration as well as top speed, but I think it was just a well-thrashed engine.'

The story goes that one potential customer walked into Jaguar's Piccadilly show-rooms in London and demanded a test drive, to be told that the only demonstrator was in Geneva. 'Book me a run,' he instructed, 'I'll fly out.'

There were quite a number of higher profile people, Bob Berry recalls. 'I remember the Chairman of SKF Ball Bearings flew in specially from Stockholm to drive it. The head of Swiss Railways lived just outside Geneva and I took it up there the second Sunday. I had to take it up to his mansion, a huge place just outside town. It was the first time I had ever had lunch in a private house where all the butlers and the footmen wore white gloves.'

Following its dramatic launch role, the car was pressed into service as the demonstrator for the dura-tion of the Geneva Show. Driven by Bob Berry, it spent hours each day pounding round the test course (generally flat out) and proved to be quicker than the current Ferraris and Mercedes-Benz, though the E-type cost a fraction of the price.

During the show, says Berry, 'there were a whole list of celebrities. We didn't necessarily know who all these people were, to be frank with you. Marcel Fleury and Emil Frey [Swiss French and Swiss German importers, respectively] brought down the VIPs themselves and therefore the Chairman of Swiss Railways came down with Emil Frey with a great deal of ceremony. It was quite possible that film stars got a ride and we didn't know who they were.'

One of those who drove 9600 HP at Geneva was Le Mans winner, Grand Prix driver and highly distinguished international motoring journalist Paul Frère. 'I was at Geneva and it was acclaimed as the car of the show. I remember taking the Fixed Head out with Bob Berry and it was quite an experience. We didn't do the course, we went out on the road. I think we drove from the Motor Show in the direction of Lyon. I did the driving. I was very impressed with the car, very impressed with the performance and with the accuracy of the steering. The performance/price ratio was exceptional.' As to the shape, 'It was absolutely gorgeous. It recalled the D-type very much of course. It was very striking.'

Frère and I also chatted in the pits at Le Mans in the late eighties. Some thirty years before he had raced D-types there for the factory during a long and very successful career. 'I thought it was a logical continuation from the D-type and I always felt that, after they had done the D-type Jaguars, they could do so much better than the XK150, and the E-type was the answer to that. It was really a fabulous car when it came out.

'It was an enormous step forward but it had, also, some terrible faults. I remember driving one of the early cars to Rome in summer and the heat was absolutely unbearable. You could hardly put your hand on the tunnel over the gearbox, but it was a magnificent car nevertheless.'

I suggested to Frère that the performance of 9600 HP was perhaps a little better than the production cars which could not quite manage the magic 150mph. He smiled knowingly and said, 'Exactly!'

On his return from the Show, Norman Dewis filed a 'Report on Geneva Motor Show Demonstration – E-type' to Heynes on 31 March, with copies to various people including Sir William. He noted that the two cars had covered a total of 3400 miles. His comments included, 'Bonnet: better locks required, the use of a metal tie key is not in keeping with the appearance of the car. Seats: driving non stop from Dunkirk to Geneva, I found that had more shoulder support been afforded I would have suffered less aching of the shoulder muscles. Ashtray is ornamental but has no practical use, it being far too small.'

'We both had to make a report,' says Berry. 'There wasn't much in it. One of the things we noticed was that the car was not completely watertight. There was quite a lot of water entry in through the footwells. They subsequently did quite a lot of work on that. Quite a lot of water got in around the rear door on the coupé – enough to fill the wheel well. But these were trivialities. As far as the cars were concerned, there were lots of bumps and squeaks and rattles when we got them back, but considering what they had gone through, it was remarkable. They were tough old cars, they really were.'

Dewis concluded, 'The handling and general comfort of the car throughout the journey was very good and I feel if urgent attention as to modifications and possible redesign is applied to the above report then we will be able to produce a first-class sports car'.

CHAPTER EIGHT

Press Hack

That British institution *Pathé News* dubbed 1961 'A Year to Remember' and it seems like a fair title. The year's news and events included the inauguration of Kennedy, the building of the Berlin Wall and the first American in space. France was said to be on the brink of civil war, with troubles in Algeria and de Gaulle being defied by his armed forces. A Channel Tunnel was being advocated and estimated to cost £130m with completion in about five years. Mini-cabs hit London, an early version of the hovercraft was being put through its trials, Elizabeth Taylor won an Oscar, Christine Trueman and Angela Mortimer contested an all-British ladies final at Wimbledon, and Cliff Richard was 21.

Prior to launch 9600 HP was given the title 'Press Car', and this was the role that the car was to play for the next year or so. Barely able to regain her breath after returning from the triumph of Geneva and the hard work being thrashed around the test circuit for the duration of the Show, the old girl was now lent to a never-ending succession of publications from around the globe.

Bob Berry, who had driven the car back from Geneva on about 27 March, recalls the pressure his department was under from the national and international press. 'The clamour to borrow the car was enormous. Absolutely. Once we had taken it to Geneva, the roof fell in in terms of people wanting to borrow the car to test it and that sort of thing. We were anxious to give it as wide a publicity as possible and therefore we lent it to *Quattroruote* in Italy and *Auto Motor und Sport* in Germany, and *Auto Journal* in France, and all the major influences throughout Europe.'

Meanwhile, in the UK the first monthly motoring magazines were appearing. Bill Boddy, Editor of *Motor Sport* was one of those to whom 9600 HP had been entrusted before launch. Clearly he was pretty peeved that others had had the car for more than a few hours and he had some harsh things to say about road works on the M1 (has anything changed?) and the then-Minister of Transport, Ernest Marples, but was lavish with his praise for the car. He even stated that he and Michael Tee had *cruised* at 155mph!

What Sir William Lyons has done is to use all that was best in the race-bred and inspired C and D-type Jaguars, learn some useful lessons from the 3-litre Cunningham Jaguar built for the last Le Mans race, evolve stylish new bodywork and combine all these ingredients in a new British Grand Touring Jaguar that is about as fast as they come, immensely accelerative, endowed with extremely good roadholding, handling and braking characteristics, able to be driven by grandma at 15mph or less in top gear, of returning some 20mpg of fuel under fast-travel conditions and which sells in GT coupé form, even after the Chancellor has had his levy of well over £618, for a mere £2,196 19s 2d. Sir William Lyons has bred another winner!

Just over a week before the announcement date of the new Jaguar I was allowed to sample it for a few hours on the roads near Coventry. I was aware that other motoring journalists had been permitted to venture as far afield as Italy in E-types but after many years' experience of the motor industry I have learnt to be thankful for small miracles, and thus I gratefully headed a coupé towards M1 – a road, Mr Marples, that was reduced to single-line traffic in several places while men toiled to plough up and re-lay its so-called hard shoulders!

What followed was quite fantastic – remembering that an honoured British name and not one hailing from Modena, Maranello or Stuttgart graced our motor car. Getting the feel of the E-type and then encountering those aforementioned single-lane sections of the great Marples Motor Road, we nevertheless found ourselves as far away as St Albans within an hour of accelerating out of the gates of the Jaguar factory. Put the E-type in top gear and it just goes faster and faster, until it is cruising along M1 at 6,100rpm, which we calculated to be a pretty genuine 155mph. At this speed it is possible for driver to converse with passenger in normal tones, wind-noise being low and little noise coming from transmission or final-drive – a fantastic experience! The E-type felt as if it would have been happy to go the length of M1 at this speed – equal to a sustained 6,100rpm – had not vehicles crawling along the outside lane at 90/100mph occasionally impeded its progress! After dropping to 4,000rpm or approximately 102mph, it was possible to accelerate to 5,000rpm (127mph) in a mere eight seconds.

In my brief two-hour run in this remarkable car (it used three-quarters of a tank of fuel and covered something like 155 miles, by no means all of them on M1, including several stops for photography and others in rush-hour Coventry traffic!) I was not able to assess it fully but I learnt enough to know that Jaguar have produced a GT car which fully deserves the honoured Gran Turismo designation. The E-type is a staggering motor car on all counts; safety, acceleration, speed, equipment, appearance - all are there, for a basic price of only £1,480. Staggering! I extend to Sir William Lyons, his design team, technicians and workers my humble congratulations. WB

Bob Berry explains Jaguar's thinking about the leading motor magazines and the order in which they were allowed to test new cars:

I think we regarded *Motor Sport* as being a motor sport magazine with a peripheral interest in the motor industry and motor cars. Whereas we saw *Motor* and *Autocar* as being general papers with a very wide and very diffuse circulation, and therefore they always had the first call on any new car for road test purposes and we used to alternate, by agreement, who got the first test. We operated this process rigidly so there was no favour between the two of them.

Our integrity was always accepted by the press. If we said, ' This is a 150mph motor car,' they were happy to accept it as such. That was why the *Motor* and *Autocar*, which were truly independent, were so important to us. It was the same with the two main European papers. *Quattroruote* and *Auto Motor und Sport* had a policy of almost testing a car to destruction. There was a destructive element to their testing which we found not acceptable but nevertheless we did lend cars. They'd take cars apart. We knew for certain that *Auto Motor und Sport* certainly took the E-type road test car engine out and bench-tested it because we learnt subsequently that Mercedes-Benz were interested in the figures. We know that *Quattroruote* had a hotline into Alfa Romeo and, to a lesser extent, into Ferrari, and we know the engine came out of the car that we lent them for bench-testing.

As mentioned, French journalist Bernard Cahier wrote up his pre-launch sampling in no less than ten magazines, including the April issue of *Motor Racing* and the June issue of the US magazine *Sports Car Graphic*. The former quoted Keats in its editorial under a photo of 9600 HP. 'A thing of beauty is a joy for ever. The phrase could well have been coined for the unveiling of the Jaguar 'E' type range.' In his article Cahier wrote: 'It would be exceptional to find a car with no points of criticism, and there were a number of these. The gearbox was hard to operate, and – most surprisingly – the brakes gave an impression of sponginess and did not seem to be responding quickly at first. The bucket seats on the test car were not too comfortable, failing to give sufficient support, but the Jaguar people explained that this was being corrected in the production models.'

Having taken some acceleration times, he commented: ' These are remarkable figures, comparing extremely favourably with most rivals at double the price. The acceleration figures are better than those of the normal GT Ferrari and the 300SL Mercedes.' He stated that maximum speed was 149mph.

'Jaguar have succeeded in developing an exciting, very fast GT at an unbelievable price,' Cahier concluded.

In the US magazine for which he was European Editor, he asked, 'What is the new E-type Jaguar? How does it look? What does it do?' This was his answer: 'Thanks to Bob Berry of Jaguar and Harry Mundy of the well-known English weekly *Autocar*, *Sports Car Graphic* was fortunate in being the first American magazine to

Post-Geneva, the car continued to be used as the Press vehicle for another year. Having proved its 150mph capability, 9600 HP did a lot of posing during a varied year.

try out this exciting new automobile. With automobiles, as with women, that first contact is very important, and in our opinion Jaguar has succeeded in making this first rendezvous a striking one.

'Yes, the E-type Jaguar GT is very striking indeed because it is very different from all its direct competitors and because it looks so fast just standing still. Its style is not Italian nor German nor, in a way, even English. It has its own Jaguar style, a style which caused quite a sensation in 1949 [sic] when the then-new, very slim and low XK120 was presented.

'When we tried out the E-type, we were very fortunate in having one of those rare beautiful sunny English days, and it was February, truly incredible. The traffic on the narrow English roads is always quite heavy but we still managed to find some good straights to do the acceleration figures, while the maximum speed was on a freeway another day. We were most enthusiastic about driving the Jaguar and particularly impressed by the superb handling of this car, combined with the outstanding acceleration.' He went on to make many other flattering comments and enjoyed having fun with over-steer.

'Long awaited, but now here, the E-type is assured of a fine career, especially if the Jaguar people are willing always to look into the future and to make the changes necessary to cope with the fast moving competitors. I say this because in the past too many manufacturers have come out with something good and then left it unchanged for too long.' How true.

Road testing was done to suit Jaguar [states Berry]. Therefore we had a group of people who we thought were people of influence. That was the whole object of the road test programme. Of the nationals, there was Harold Nockolds of *The Times*; Dudley Noble of the *Financial Times* had an early crack on a one-day loan basis. They would come up to the factory, we'd introduce them to the car and they would go away and drive it for the day. They'd come back in the evening and we'd talk about it, answer their questions. If they wanted to see it being made, we weren't too keen on that as there wasn't much happening! All the national dailies were done that way and all the Sundays.

We ran it through what we considered to be our road test list and therefore people like Basil Cardew had it, and Courtenay Edwards, and John Langley of the *Telegraph*, Robert Glenton on the *Sunday Express*. Max Boyd on the *Sunday Times*. We got to know some of these guys quite well although we always kept a distance. None of them became personal friends, because Sir William's view of that was that it could distort the relationship.

They all had to collect the car from the factory. I don't think that for the first twelve months we delivered cars. They had to come to the factory and we'd actually take them through it and stress the importance of the tyre pressures, and all that sort of thing. They would stand running at 150mph on standard pressure but not for too great a distance. Very few people actually tried in my experience.

After the newspaper men had had the car for a day, it seems that various magazines had it for a little longer as Berry recounts. First, he explains why 9600 HP was retained for this work.

'As far as I was concerned, I was always using something that was a known quantity. We would turn the car round in five days. Dewis would take it to MIRA and do a set of times and if the times were OK, and they invariably were, then it was just a case of making sure the paintwork wasn't damaged, that the trim was OK, that there were no rattles and squeaks, and the thing was up to standard. We used to have a three days test period – they would borrow it on a Friday through to Monday or Tuesday, and the rest of the week, we'd actually refurbish ready for the next one. So these cars [9600 HP and 77 RW] did a very, very substantial mileage and all the tests were done at high speed so we were always careful about the brakes and made sure the tyres were OK.'

Ironically, in spite of the overwhelming publicity which 9600 HP and 77 RW were garnering, production was desperately slow to get going. Of course, the lack of cars only served to make them even more desirable. A trickle of Roadsters began to leave the factory in May (11) and June (84) but, unbelievably, no Fixed Heads passed out of the factory gates until August (3) and September (34). It seems, hard though it is to believe, that Jaguar were not even certain they were going to produce the FHC. About 15 years ago, Harry Rogers, with whom Lyons worked closely, told me this story.

I worked a lot with Lyons. He had a telephone switchboard on his desk with ten switches and I was one of those, so I was all right!

He'd ring me up about six [in the evening] and you could always tell it was him because it wasn't an ordinary ring. It was one long blast, and never stopped. He'd say, 'You're not keen on getting away tonight, are you Rogers?'

Not particularly, no.' I mean, what could you say?

When I've signed these letters, I'll come and have a word with you.' Then he used to come down when the shop was cleared and discuss all the jobs. We would talk for blinking hours! I thought he was never going to go!

On one occasion, I had to attend a meeting with all his directors to discuss the E-type Fixed Head and decide whether it should go into production. Heynes got up and said the car was too noisy. Teddy Orr said, 'It's got 10-thou-itis.' He felt it was too finicky – too many parts in it. And so it went on, about half a dozen stood up. Of course, Lyons was running the meeting. 'Right-ho, chaps,' he said, 'we've heard enough of the complaints. Now, Rogers, what do you say?'

'I got up and I said, 'I've done no end of miles in it and I've found it no different to any of the other cars. It is a sports car and you expect a little bit of noise. As regards there's too many bits in it,' which was Mr Orr's feelings – they were all my gaffers, remember – I said, 'It's only got one more panel in than the open one, and that's the roof.' And then regarding the 10-thou-it is, I said, 'I can't see it. As a matter of fact, it will hold body and soul together. It hasn't got a big gap in the middle so that it can whip.'

'He stopped me then because I was pulling all his gaffers to bits. 'All right, Rogers, you've made your point. I think what I'll do is, I'll take it home with me tonight and see what I think about it.'

'Next morning the long blast went. 'Rogers, I tried that car and it's all you said it is. It's a lovely car. So we're going into production.'

For 8 May, 1961 Norman Dewis's log reads: 'MIRA. J. Barker Autocar, photographs. E 9600 HP.' Quite what these photographs were for is now lost in the mists of time.

On 14 June 'Britain's first automatic car wash and high density laundry' opened at St. George's Garage, Brompton Road in London. The opening was filmed by *Pathé News* and showed Stirling Moss driving through in his 'new car'. The car was 9600 HP, though sadly it was never actually owned by the great man. It is, however, good to know it was driven by him, albeit briefly. This sequence is also included on a video compilation of 1961 *Pathé News* items.

'Yes, I remember that occasion,' comments Moss. 'That's interesting,' he muttered looking, at a recording. ' I didn't realize the significance of that car at the time, I am sure. The car was beautiful, as all Jags are. That was the great thing about Jags.'

When the owners of Britain's first automatic car wash wanted to gain the maximum publicity for its opening, they hired the country's most famous racing driver, Stirling Moss. As his supposed own car, they needed the most dramatic and newsworthy machine of the moment.

'Bill Rankin probably organized it. The shortest drive I ever had!'

Looking at his 1961 diary, Stirling read, "Wednesday. Open Five Minute car wash. More work. Lunch with Frank Faulkner. Work. Re-opened car wash." I must have done it twice. Isn't that interesting. I don't know why. Maybe they had a double opening, or something.'

In his log for 5–11 July 1961 Dewis wrote: 'Testing 9600 HP on Continent. Southern France (Bayonne). Standard production dampers & oil separation dampers tested. RS5 Special Dunlop tyres fitted. 2,800 miles completed.'

'The continental test had two objectives,' wrote Dewis in his report to Heynes, with copies to Lyons, England and Knight. They were 'firstly to compare the … dampers, and secondly to reconnoitre various territories for mileage testing of the Zenith.' Zenith was the code-name for the large Mark X saloon which would be launched at the London show that October. Early examples proved troublesome and in the States they preferred the word 'Lemon'!

Norman visited a variety of areas in France and a limited area of Belgium, giving his conclusions as to where the test should be carried out. As to the dampers, he had this to report'. 'The car left England fitted with a standard production set of damper units and impressions formed over about 1000 miles of varied road surfaces. The "ride" was found to fall "off" after 120 miles and when negotiating undulating surfaces the damping had little control. This led to the suspension hitting the bump stops very forcefully, which became more aggravated when the car was driven non-stop for six hours.'

Early E-types were not exactly trouble-free, as Pat Smart, who originally registered 9600 HP, recalls. He was doing his apprenticeship and had been seconded to the Service Department. 'Not long after the car was introduced, it was announced that Mr So-and-So had arrived with his E-type, would I go and meet him and take his details. I went outside and the door of this Roadster opened, and a chap got out. He was wearing a frog suit, complete with flippers and mask. He pushed the mask up and said, with a straight face, "I have one or two water leak problems!"

Richard Hassan had been working with George Buck on petrol injection development and was particularly enjoying the work. When he was told that he was to be transferred, he mentioned his disappointment to Buck, who said he would see what he could do. The transfer was dropped and George explained to Richard that he had applied the '13 inch rule' – he had had a word with Bill Heynes!

Later Hassan went on a Sales and Service week in the South West with a fellow called Jim Stirland.

They told me that they had this very difficult customer, who had got an E-type and was prepared to settle at nothing. He wanted the world and as far as he was concerned this was a terrible motor car. He was, apparently, talking in terms of suing the company.

At these Sales and Service weeks, you had all the manufacturers' representatives – from Lucas, from Borg-Warner, SU, Laycocks, etc. They were all very experienced and this was my first such week, whereas they did about 12 a year. They were all there to offer advice to the owners.

Everyone was very worried about this guy and he had been told that he would be introduced to the chap from the factory. Jim had said to me, 'You ought to see him. You're more *au fait* with E-types, that's why you're here – it'll be good experience for you.'

The appointment was for two o'clock and he arrived in a white roadster. He started laying into me about what's wrong with the car and so on. I'm apologizing, trying to struggle out excuses, but before I could get a chance to answer one complaint, he'd be on to the next one. We were talking our way from the front of the car to the back. He pointed out the water leaks, for example, and showed me that the carpets were soaking wet.

Then he put his hand inside the door and pulled the bootlid release. He lifted the boot floor and the spare wheel was semi-immersed. He said, 'Look. There's a bloody fish in there.'

There was a goldfish swimming in and out of the spokes!

I looked round and the Lucas rep was bent double trying to contain himself, and I realized that I was being had. I stared round the place and there were people behind pillars, behind cars, all killing themselves. I realized this was the life for me, and three weeks later transferred to the Service Department!'

There were no problems when Graham Hill, in Tommy Sopwith's *Equipe Endeavour* Roadster, and Roy Salvadori in Coombs's example began the E-type's racing career with a fine victory at Oulton Park. At Snetterton on 23 July Mike Parkes scored another win in the Scott-Brown Memorial Trophy race in Sopwith's Roadster. ' Lofty' England had lent Parkes his Roadster, 1600 RW, and Mike was returning it to Coventry on the Sunday evening. He was, however, pretty exhausted as he had collected a Ferrari from Italy a day or so before. At Fillongley, near Coventry, he fell asleep and stuffed Lofty's car through a hedge. Next day ' Lofty' and a young John Pearson jumped in 9600 HP and went off to 'fetch it out of the ditch,' as John puts it. 'He had made a great hole in the hedge and Mr England was not best pleased.'

The cars were so scarce that even Grand Prix driver Bruce McLaren had to wait a while. Pop star Adam Faith telephoned Lyons and pleaded with him. This rarity, plus the extraordinary amount of publicity, combined with the dramatic appearance, led even the normally staid British to lose their cool whenever a car was spotted.

Mike MacDowel, the unfortunate employee who got into hot water for showing a customer the top-secret E-type prototype, still worked under 'Lofty' in the Service Department, and also had responsibility for various competition exploits such as the Tour de France. 'I used to be very honoured to drive an E-type around at times. If you pulled up anywhere it was quite incredible. There would be a spontaneous reaction. If you pulled up outside a pub, for example, people would flock round it. I can't remember another motor car, in my 36 years man and boy in the motor business that created such public interest. People would say. "Ooh look at that! Fantastic! Unbelievable!" It was a very exciting time. I've never seen it since. It has all become such big time, huge launches and expensive parties, and God knows what else. But nothing has created the excitement that the E-type did. Aura is the word.'

Not everyone was impressed, though. Denis Jenkinson, Continental Correspondent of *Motor Sport*, led an extraordinary life during the summer months following the Grand Prix circus around Europe and virtually living in his car. DSJ was not one to mince his words and would later become an E-type owner.

> The concept when it appeared was terrific. I thought at last the British motor industry had made a proper GT car. Astons had been trying for years and failed by my standards. My standards, during the fifties, started with the Lancia Aurelia, Alfa 1900C and small Porsches. As to the big cars, I grew up on the 300SL – a monster, but a super monster. Aston Martins never did anything for me.
>
> I thought the E-type was somewhere on the right lines – until I drove one. Then I thought it was awful, a dreadful thing.
>
> My requirements of a GT car were to average 1,000 miles a week, which would be just Tuesday, Wednesday and Thursday. It had to cruise effortlessly on any sort of roads. It had to be fun going up the mountains, totally reliable and a pleasure to look at.
>
> When I saw the first one, I thought that's got to fulfil all the requirements. But I was not prepared to live with that awful gearbox, the dreadful seats and the fact that you couldn't see at night. The thing you couldn't argue about was the performance. That is still a landmark.

'The performance did feel good,' states Jackie Stewart. 'You could do 100mph in an E-type just like eating bread off the table. There was no speed limit, so one did it all the time. Some of the horrific drives – I can't think how I survived!' Stewart vividly recalls the first one he drove, as do most people:

> I remember the ' E' before its launch. I was deeply involved with my family's garage in Dunbarton. It was called R.P. Stewart and Sons, and my father, who had started the business way back, built it up really, brick by brick. We were Austin agents to begin with, then we became Jaguar dealers and then main dealers for Dunbartonshire. So when I used to go up and down the road collecting new cars from Coventry, and because my brother was very involved with Jaguar and had driven for the factory team, we had the benefit, if you like, of knowing many of the people within Jaguar from Sir William to 'Lofty' England, to Bob Berry. So I saw photographs long before it came out, both in the drophead form and the coupé form.
>
> We got our demonstrator very early on. It was one of the first in Scotland and really was so far ahead of its time. I think it was easily the most spectacular car that had ever come out of the British motor industry.'

The car was photographed extensively by Jaguar for brochures and advertising, including a session at Hickstead horse trials. Even though the E-type was destined to become an inseparable part of the 'Swinging Sixties', the fashions famously associated with the decade were still a couple of years away.

Bob Berry sums up the impact. 'It put Jaguar back to where it was when the XK120 was launched. The impact was quite profound. It was impossible to drive the car anywhere. You literally did get stopped.

'People would pull in front of you and try to get you to stop so that they could talk to you about it. The number of times one got stopped by the police just so they could talk about it was quite extraordinary. It was an embarrassment to drive the car. No matter where you parked it, people would swarm around. It went on for many months and, as they were very slow coming through, they had a rarity value for a year or more.

'Even at the October Motor Show, they were greeted as though they were new cars.'

One of the many thousands of visitors to the Jaguar stand at Earls Court in 1961 was Innes Ireland, fresh from his Grand Prix win, which was also Lotus's first, in the United States GP. at Watkins Glen. 'I had already ordered a car in white with black leather. When I went to the Motor Show, there was a white one with black interior on the stand. So I quickly got a hold of 'Lofty' England and said; "Hey 'Lofty', that must be my car up there!"'

'So, by "beating him round the head", he finally agreed that I could have it after the Show.'

One of the apprentices on duty at the Motor Show was Richard Hassan. 'You couldn't get on and off the stand. I was only 20, and the excitement and the feeling you had when you had to fight your way on to the stand, was quite something for us – it was quite a thrill. Jim Clark came to the stand, with his pal Ian Scott Watson, and started looking at the E-type and said, "What's the delivery?"

'We were telling everybody it was impossible and I told him he hadn't a hope in Hell! So he said, "Well, what about this one?"

"Funnily enough," I said, "that one's just gone." When I mentioned that Innes Ireland had been along, his face was a picture. But Innes was the one who had just won the Grand Prix and "Lofty" had obviously decided that he was the one who should have the car to show round Europe.'

Another apprentice and great pal of Richard's was the late Roger Woodley. 'I had the good fortune to be at that October Motor Show. We were besieged. In our little stall where we handed out the leaflets and so on, we were trapped. The crowds surged around the thing and would stay. It wasn't a matter of people coming and going. The throng got bigger. It was a great sensation.'

Meanwhile 9600 HP was continuing to earn its keep through 1961 and into 1962. In January 1962 a chart of Comparative Performance Figures were produced at Jaguar for the latest tests on petrol injection and compared with those figures recorded for 9600 HP nearly a year previously. The old girl was still the quickest to complete the standing ¼ mile, apart from the old blue prototype Roadster fitted with a fabricated inlet manifold.

The same month *Autosport* carried an article which presumably was not a spoof!

During its combination year of posing and more serious driving work, Norman Dewis had taken 9600 HP to southern France and, with the ex-Le Mans driver at the wheel, this was no picnic.

It consisted of what purported to be a reprint of a piece published in Russia reviewing that country's previous year's racing. In their introduction to the piece *Autosport*, whilst expressing concern for any race commentator who had to mention competitor U. Bugrov, stated: 'The appearance of the E-type Jaguar reported to have been delivered to the Soviet Embassy in London in the Formula Libre class next season might make a few faces redder than red." Make what you will of that!

In February, 1962 *The Motor* published an article under the title, 'GRAND TOURING – Expedition by E-type' penned by Tommy Wisdom. The car he drove was 9600 HP.

'The Wisdom Winter Expedition to the Swiss Lakes,' wrote Wisdom, 'provided a chance to discover how that superb example of the car maker's art – the Jaguar E-type coupé – performed under Grand Touring conditions.'

In the course of a long and fascinating career, Tommy Wisdom drove the works SS100 at Brooklands, competed in numerous Alpine Rallies, owned and competed with one of the semi-works XK120s which he also lent to young Stirling Moss for the 1950 TT, his first big win, and co-owned a C-type. By profession, he was a motoring journalist and his wife Elsie (known as 'Bill') was also a regular competitor and navigator. Later, their daughter Ann became a well-known rally competitor and enjoyed great success with Pat Moss, sister of Stirling. Together with her boyfriend and fellow works rally driver Peter Riley, Ann accompanied Tommy and 'Bill' on their winter challenge. Each sampled 9600 HP. This is Wisdom's account of the winter expedition:

'Mrs W., despite fond memories of stark Rileys and MG Magnettes at Brooklands, is nowadays only interested in high performance cars so long as their speed is achieved in comfort and silence. Ann is more used to tough rally cars that resemble to a certain degree the old-type sports models on which I cut my competition teeth.

On our winter run to Switzerland the journey south-east through France was naturally over main roads - my favourite short cuts are inadvisable in the winter and, in any case, traffic is relatively light. Including stops for petrol and the frontier crossing, the Jaguar averaged 49½ mph to Montreux. And this was dawdling, for we were changing drivers (we had Peter Riley's Volvo as tender car) to give everyone the opportunity of sampling the E-type under winter conditions.

The journey back was made under more pressure. The same route was followed –

When *The Motor* had originally road-tested the E-type, they had borrowed the Press Roadster, 77 RW. But 9600 HP appeared in the magazine when Tommy and 'Bill' (seen here) Wisdom, in company with daughter Ann and rally driver/boyfriend Peter Riley, took the car to the Swiss Alps in December, 1961. Note, the factory had now converted the car to right-hand drive.

from Montreux round the lake to Lausanne, over intermittent ice to Vallorbe, where the sun shone on the skiers on the nursery slopes of Mont d'Or, then rain through the Jura, and by way of Pontarlier, Chaumont, Chalon-sur-Saône, Rheims and Arras to Dunkirk, the last 100 miles being in that wet mist so typical of northern France. Our best hour was just after St Dizier to Rheims – 71 miles. The overall average was 60.3. This involved frequent cruising at 100mph and three times the speedometer needle exceeded 120mph. This statement should shock no one, for the car was under complete control at all times; genuinely I took no risks. But I could not rid myself of the recurring thought – the racing Jaguar 3½-litre SS100 at Brooklands before the war was not as fast as this. (Then we managed a lap at 118mph).

Pleasant surprise – the round trip of 1,378 miles was covered at an average petrol consumption of 21.2 mpg.

All four of us were impressed by the easy pace of the Jaguar, its quietness and comfort; in the favourite phrase of the motor testers, it fairly eats up the miles.

On the open roads of France, despite rain and snow, fog and ice in turn, it put 60 miles into the hour with almost contemptuous ease. The car was as steady as a rock at three-figure speeds; the pronounced camber of some of the northern *routes nationales* had no effect on the steering wheel. It is at these touring speeds that the driver must keep alert; there is no physical effort required. On the open road, with its 20mph to maximum in top gear, there is no need to change gear in the Jaguar - and therefore the mind must be attuned to the possible emergency.

Maximum speed? I don't know. But I can say from experience that this E-type will do exactly 100mph in third gear at 5,500rpm. What I do like is the ability to trickle quietly and smoothly through traffic at less than 20mph and then accelerate away into the three-figure regions.

Luggage accommodation? It is ample on the coupé, not so on the open model. But it is only older folk who raise this question; the modern motorist travels light. The cabin trunk and the Gladstone bag went out with the aspidistra. Air transport has brought this about. Today the younger people set off to the South of France with a couple of hold-alls, but it is difficult for the middle-aged to appreciate the change. A wine merchant friend in my age-group who complained about the lack of space on the E-type needed to be reminded that 30 years ago he set off blithely on 3,000 miles of Alpine Trial in an open MG with his grip lashed to the spare wheel.

Un-witchlike (or should it be Un-Which?-like?) the female side of the expedition was quite uncritical; they *were* persuaded to say the apparatus to provide audible means of approach was not really up to the standard of the rest of the machine; the E-type really deserves a *Fulgor* to awaken the more somnolent of the camion pilots. My own slight criticism is that the lights are adequate: no more. *Cockpit Comments* – Bill Wisdom: 'Surprisingly comfortable car.' Ann Wisdom: 'It's smooth and it steers like a dream.' Peter Riley: 'A genuine grand tourer – I can think of nothing more desirable for Continental touring.' My own: ' Here is a car which, like a pedigree gun or a green-heart trout rod, is so worth learning to use properly.'

Peter and Ann remember it well. His parents had retired to Switzerland in 1958 and lived above Montreux overlooking the lake. Mr. Riley Snr had a 250GT Ferrari at the time.

Ann Riley: 'It was Christmas 1961 and we had got engaged that October. Peter's parents had invited all four of us – my parents, Peter and I – to go and stay for Christmas and my father said, "I'll find a nice car, something interesting." And it turned out to be the E-type and he allowed us to drive it.

Peter Riley: 'It was very new and very exciting. We had lunch somewhere [*en route*] and he said, "I expect you'd like to drive the E-type". I said, "Yep," and he said, "Right, you take it this afternoon." I just had a Volvo Amazon and he and Bill set off behind us and I think we drove all the way to Switzerland.'

Ann confirms that they did. 'Thoroughly enjoyed it,' says Peter. 'Decided we had to have an E-type. There must be an E-type in our future. So we bought a large china pig and wrote E-type in lipstick on the side of it. We kept putting half-crowns rather hopefully in it,' recalls Riley with great amusement. 'But we never got our E-type.'

'The children came along and that was the end of that,' chips in Ann.

Peter is probably best remembered for rallying the big Healeys and continued until 1964. 'I finished in 1962,' states Mrs Riley. 'I was pregnant when we won the Tulip. We got our legs pulled about three people in the car and hoping it was a girl so it was an all-woman team!'

Peter Riley: 'I'd known Tommy since the early fifties when we were next-door numbers in the Alpine [Rally] – 1951 I think. He didn't know then that he was going to be my father-in-law. He knew my father was a keen motoring man so he thought he'd look for something really new and exciting, and he got the E-type off Bill Lyons who was a great mate of his. All the Jaguar people were friends. He dated back to the SS100 days. He could really have the pick of what he wanted. So he got this and we enjoyed it terribly.

'Then he went off somewhere during the holiday, down to Lausanne or Geneva or somewhere to see a friend. On the way back – in the middle of the Vevey – there is a very slight kink in one of the streets which is a bridge and under which flows an icy stream. It was cold winter and in the middle of town was sheet ice, on which he spun it hard against the bridge. Anybody could have done it. He bent the front all-right, I reckon he bent a wishbone. We were all very sympathetic. I think it probably went down to the Geneva dealer and a new wishbone, or whatever, was flown out and it was fixed.'

Trying to recall the route, Peter states, 'The logical thing to do would be to drive from the Midlands to Reims and stay just after Reims at Sept Saulx for the night, and then go on to Geneva. There were no motorways, plenty of traffic and the boats were slower. We doubt whether the old folk would have consented to do it in one hop, especially if they wanted to stop for lunch, which Tom always did!'

'He was welcomed with open arms by all the lovely hostesses across Europe, "Ahhh, Tommee"!' chuckles Ann.

Peter Riley sums up his memories. 'It was slightly daunting because it was very fast. E-types in their early days were very fast. There were those of us who were quite happy with 125mph. You could touch 120mph in a Works Healey, more or less on demand, but not much more. But you knew this thing would go on to 150 odd. And that was a rather different ballpark. And motorways were new in the late fifties/early sixties and one didn't quite trust a motor car to use its performance. Before motorways, you got to the end of the straight in four minutes, however long it was and however fast you were going. So the idea of doing over 100 for 15 minutes at a time was a different thing altogether. So one was cautious about the top end of its performance until you began to realize it was a new generation of cars and it operated within its performance envelope quite happily.

'The ride! I couldn't believe how good the ride was. I was used to my father's Ferraris!'

The publicity continued for a long time to come and the orders flooded in. But Tony Cochran, who was the Southern Region Sales Manager, remembers that there was a slight catch in the long delivery times that were building up. 'People were so

Such was the impact, rarity and subsequent fame of 9600 HP, that people such as Tony Alden, even recall photographing the car in 1961. Seen at Silverstone, this shot confirms the recollections of those who talk about the amazing crowd-drawing capabilities of the E-type.

desperate to get an E-type that they would order one from ten different dealers. Then, when theirs came through, they would cancel the other nine!'

At some stage Jaguar Cars organized a reprint of the original *Autocar* road test for dealers to hand out. The curious thing is that they changed all the photographs of 9600 HP for ones of an anonymous, unregistered car. This reprint was clearly created some time after late 1961, for the ' E' shown is not an external bonnet lock car. 9600 HP was now unrepresentative in that respect and also the D-type breather arrangement on the cam covers was not exactly standard!

Jaguar also had the *Autosport* road test from the 17 March issue reprinted as a four-page handout. This one retained the 9600 HP photos (though when tested by them the car did not have the cam breathers) including the dramatic head-on shot without overriders and bonnet badge bar.

Autosport also published their own 80-page booklet of reprinted road tests and articles under the title of *High Performance Cars 1961–1962*. It had a superb Michael Turner painting of Graham Hill in Tommy Sopwith's E-type ECD 400 and

During a busy year, the car appeared at many events and was believed to have been used as the Course Car at such places as Shelsley Walsh, Britain's premier hillclimb and the oldest venue of motorsport in the world still being run on its original course today. We believe this shot was taken at Brands Hatch.

This concertina-style colour brochure was produced by Jaguar to illustrate the entire range, with a shot of 9600 HP to represent the E-type. From the fact that the S-type saloon is included, we can date this as 1963–4 – at least a year after 9600 HP had been sold by Jaguar.

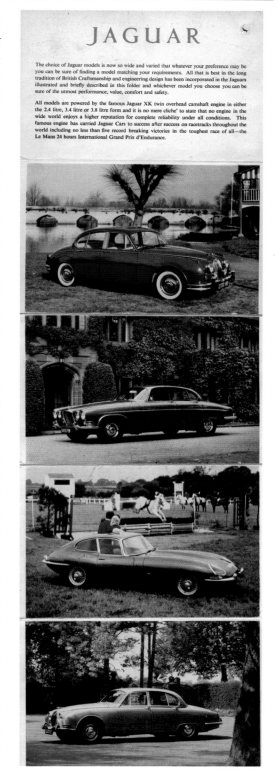

Roy Salvadori in BUY 1 at Oulton Park on the front cover, and the report featuring 9600 HP was the first test inside.

On 19 February, Norman Dewis and Barrie Wood, an apprentice who worked on 9600 HP and would later occupy a senior position at AC Delco, carried out performance tests on a new press Fixed Head (860010) which was registered 6162 RW. The figures were all slower than 9600 HP by just a few tenths of a second and the 90–110mph time was nearly a second slower. The standing quarter mile took .75 sec longer, all of which indicates that 9600 HP was not representative of standard performance. The average of five runs through the timing lights worked out at 133.3mph. Though not a genuine maximum due to the position of the lights, Dewis was regularly reaching around 143 in 9600 HP at this point which may be very telling.

The report concluded with the cryptic comment, 'Head has been removed and re-fitted by engine section.' Perhaps a little work was done on this head, because on 15 March the figures were a little better with 139.1 being clocked.

As to what else 9600 HP was doing during this period, it is now rather difficult to tell, though odd snippets are gradually coming to light. Paul Skilleter acquired some photos of the car which were believed taken at Brands Hatch. Tony Alden made contact to say that he had photographed the car at the Daily Express International Trophy meeting at Silverstone in 1961. Understandably Bob Berry's memory of this period in the car's life is now a little hazy. 'I am not sure if it didn't appear as a course car at Shelsley and/or Prescott.'

Even though the E-type was entering its second year, the sight of an example was still something noteworthy, as Pat Smart recalls. 'I saw an E-type parked outside the pub I'd had lunch in. At that time, it was the same as it had been when the XK120s had first come out. Everybody said, "Ooh! Look at that car".

'There were two people sitting in it with white linen, or buckskin, helmets on. Looking at the passenger, I thought, "I have never seen such an incredibly ugly woman". I thought it was his wife, or his girlfriend. Anyway, I was going the same way as them, so I followed. They went to the Service Department [at the factory] and the bloke got out and said, "Wait there". This other person just sat there.

'I walked nearer and nearer. It was a boxer dog!'

'Clearly the XK120,' states Jackie Stewart, 'was a fantastic car when it was first introduced but I think the E-type was so ahead of its time, and has remained a classic of its kind. It brought Ferraris and Maseratis down to people who could not afford them. It had not only elegance but it had sophistication, it was smooth, well-appointed – it really was a beautifully thought-out motor car. It's at times like this, thinking back, that you see how advanced British design and aesthetic values have been an influence within the world of the motor industry.

'One thinks of so many countries, particularly Italy, as being trend-setters, but really that Jaguar E-type, and the XK120, were the real trend-setters. They marked everybody's card for the rest of time.'

On 4 May 1962, after about 18 months and some four lives at Jaguar, the company sold 9600 HP to the famous Jaguar garage, Coombs of Guildford.

'Jaguar has always been like this,' states Bob Berry. 'Once a car had finished its usefulness, it was just disposed of. The concept that we might keep 9600 as the first one never entered our minds. Coombs probably wanted to buy it because he had some customer wanting it. He was always on the *qv* for something. So the car just went and that was the end of it.'

Actually, it was not quite the end of it. Apart from having another five lives to come, this cat clung on to its fourth life posthumously. Jaguar produced a small, concertina'd brochure covering the range – Mark 2 saloon, Mark 10 saloon, E-type and S-type saloon. Each model was photographed and the E-type shot was one of the early publicity photos taken at Hickstead of 9600 HP. The date? From the fact that the S-type was included, it had to be late '63 or '64.

CHAPTER NINE

The Next Custodians

John Coombs had a close relationship with Jaguar and is particularly remembered for running the smaller Jaguar saloons in racing, piloted by the likes of Roy Salvadori and Graham Hill. He also had the sixth E-type Roadster, which he registered BUY 1, and which would be raced extensively and gradually metamorphose into the prototype Lightweight E-type, a model that Jaguar half-heartedly developed for international racing. John Coombs told me that Jaguar disposed of most of their former press cars through his garage.

Coombs of Guildford was one of the best-known Jaguar dealerships but was lost to the opposition during the dreadful British Leyland debacle, when BL followed a suicidal policy of sacking existing dealers and merging the Jaguar marque in with every other ratbag model in their diverse and sprawling range. Ever since Coombs has been a most successful BMW dealership.

Roger Putnam has been Sales & Marketing Director of Jaguar since 1986, when he had the job of picking up the pieces. Before the tide was reversed Jaguar was represented by 300 multi-franchise dealers 'giving away' 17 Jaguars a year each. Putnam and colleagues reorganized so that Jaguar had just over a hundred dedicated dealers selling 70 cars a year. Back in 1987, he told me, 'Jaguar had lost worldwide a good number of its solus [single make] outlets including the excellent garages like John Coombs at Guildford and Mike Hughes at Beaconsfield – people who really knew the specialist and luxury car business.'

By chance I found myself sitting next to Michael Hughes at a dinner at about this time. After mentioning that the press had been trying to photograph and eavesdrop on Prince Andrew and Miss Sarah Ferguson in his garden, we talked of Jaguar. His company had been a Jaguar dealership for 22 years, but he had not been happy about handling the rest of the British Leyland products following the merging of the companies. Having arranged a meeting with the Leyland people, he merely mentioned this and a young BL chap who looked no more than about 19, said to him,

'Right, terminated. Thirty days notice!' That was the end of the conversation.

Within a few hours Hughes had become a Mercedes-Benz dealer and would build up another highly successful dealership.

I wonder if arrogance is a common trait among junior and middle management in the motor industry. Even today, it seems to be so. Roger Putnam is jetting round the world all the time, yet replies to letters immediately, sometimes within hours. He treats one with great courtesy and respect. However, at lower levels there is so much arrogance and you are treated with contempt. When will they learn?

Returning to the story of 9600 HP and 1962, Coombs sold the car to a gentleman by the name of John Paddy Carstairs. Best known during this period as a leading film director, he found that the glamour of the E-type suited his lifestyle and the stars who surrounded him. John Coombs had good connections with the film industry. 'I made a film in 1956,' says Coombs, 'called Checkpoint with DB3S Astons and that is how I got to know a lot of people in the film world.'

Carstairs led a fascinating life and packed an enormous amount into his 60 short years, including having three successful careers concurrently. Born in London, he was one of four sons of the celebrated comedian Nelson 'Bunch' Keys, who was described as 'the man with a hundred faces'. Carstairs was educated at Repton, where he formed a cinema club and produced what is believed to be the first ever full-length feature film made at a British public school. It was entitled *The Hero of St Jim's*. His headmaster, Lord Fisher of Lambeth, demanded to see the film and then, rather unusually to say the least, did his best to publicize and encourage the boy. As a result Carstairs was invited into the film industry by Herbert Wilcox and began working, in 1928, as an assistant cameraman. This film starred Dame Sybil Thorndyke. Herbert Wilcox is best remembered as the husband of Dame Anna Neagle. They were introduced to each other by Carstairs.

He changed his name because everyone expected the son of Nelson Keys to be humorous. Following experience as a general factotum, continuity clerk, film editor, camera operator and assistant director, he went to Hollywood at the age of 19. His first job was in a drugstore and his second was as a gate man at Paramount Studios. He was not a great success in this role and was fired when he refused admission to B.P. Shulberg, who just happened to be the head of the studios!

He joined the Christie Studios and worked as a dialogue writer on a production of *Charlie's Aunt*. In the next few years he alternated between working as an assistant director and scenario writer for Basil Dean at RKO films in England and trips to Hollywood, including working for MGM as a contract scriptwriter in Culver City.

With my interest in Holmesian matters, I was intrigued to find during my researches that in 1932 Carstairs co-wrote the script for *The Sign of Four*, one of the Sherlock Holmes long stories, produced by Associated Radio Pictures and starring Arthur Wontner, a highly regarded Holmes. Indeed Tony Howlett, President of the Sherlock Holmes Society of London and doyen of Holmesians, rated Wontner very highly. 'For years he was my favourite. Of all the actors who played Holmes, I think he was the closest in appearance to the Sidney Paget illustrations that originally accompanied the stories in the *Strand Magazine*. His interpretation was very thirties but he was pre-eminent until Basil Rathbone came along.'

Carstairs began directing at the newly opened Pinewood Studios and his first big assignment was *Incident in Shanghai* in 1937, starring George Sanders and Sally Gray. Later he was staying at a hotel in the South of France where he was kept awake by the sound of mule trains taking the French army to the Italian border. A fellow guest was R.A. Butler.

'Does it mean war, sir?' he asked the famous politician.

'Well, if I leave the hotel for London in the morning – do the same thing,' was the reply.

Next morning at breakfast, Carstairs addressed a member of staff. 'Bonjour, M. Maître d'hôtel. Has Mr Butler come down to breakfast yet?'

'Mr Butlerrr, 'ee left very earlee ziss morning, monsieur.'

In 1940 Carstairs made one of the best George Formby films, *Spare a Copper*. The same year he volunteered for the Royal Navy and served with the Fleet Air Arm. Perhaps not surprisingly, he was seconded to the film section. From 1944 he was with Naval Intelligence and, that same year, married his delightful wife, Molly.

'I was a driver in the WAAF,' states Molly, 'and I knew him even before that. We were all Westcliff people and my young brother went to school with his younger brother. I was 16 when I met Paddy.'

After the war he studied at the Slade School of Art. Apart from painting, he was keen to try his hand at sculpture. One day he entered a life class and, watching the other students, observed that they were measuring the less public parts of the female model's anatomy with calipers. Not feeling quite able to do this himself, he concentrated instead on the Chinaman who was also modelling. Carstairs applied his calipers to this gentleman's head but, much to the surprise and considerable anger of the Oriental gent, they stuck in his ears!

From now on Carstairs alternated between painting and film making. In 1946 he made one of his favourite films, *Dancing with Crime*, with a young Richard Attenborough. *Sleeping Car to Trieste* followed in 1948 and *The Chiltern Hundreds* starring A.E. Matthews, appeared a year later. During the fifties he directed a host of films, taking his total to over fifty. He made Sir Norman Wisdom's first six films, including *Trouble in Store* in 1953, plus *Tommy the Toreador* with Tommy Steele in 1959 and *Weekend with Lulu* with Bob Monkhouse in 1961.

'Paddy was a dear man,' says Monkhouse, 'and I loved him but we only ever worked together once – in 1960 or '61 on a seemingly 'lost' film called *Weekend With Lulu*. He lusted after my enormous Cadillac convertible in those days before the E-type effervesced in his blood. Everyone fell for Molly, an irresistible lady.'

He clearly had an interest in cars for he owned an Allard K3 in the fifties, which suggests he was quite an enthusiast. In his book on Allards, David Kinsella states

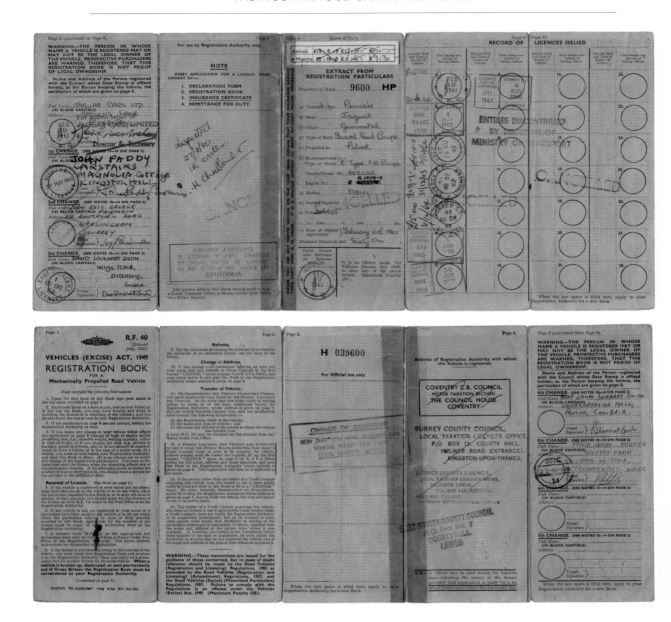

The birth certificate - 9600 HP's original log book. To paraphrase Sherlock Holmes, who was referring to Bradshaw (the Victorian publication that listed train times), the language is terse and the style
limited. However, the facts are incontrovertible. A potted history.

that the K3 was launched at the Motor Show in 1952. 'One K3,' wrote Kinsella,
'Chassis 3286, was finished in ming blue with grey trim and sold to John Paddy
Carstairs.' Kinsella states that the car would have cost around £250 then and have
been worth about £50,000 by the end of the century.

'We went to Italy with our Allard,' recalls Molly, 'but mostly we used to fly and leave the car. Paddy was always so exhausted at the end of a film. He packed so much into his life. When he wasn't filming, he was writing. When he wasn't writing, he was painting for another exhibition – he had a lot of exhibitions in Bond Street and the Royal Academy, and the Paris Salon. He was a very busy man and he couldn't sit still for a minute. He wasn't a typical man at all.

'He discovered Norman Wisdom. He did a lot of the Frankie Howerds and films with Charlie Drake. They always hired him [JPC] for comedy because he was particularly quick on comedy.' But this most energetic of men did not stick merely to films and art.

'He wrote about 29 books. They were what I would call pot-boilers. He wrote a couple of biographies, he wrote a children's book, a book on painting. He was very prolific in every direction.' Interspersed with his novels were short stories, a biography of his father, the autobiographical *Honest Injun* and a number of thrillers.

'I thought thrillers would be easy,' he told one journalist. 'It all started easily enough, then round about page something-or-other, I thought, "It's time the heroine was abducted". So I arranged to have her abducted. Easy enough, so far. But then – I couldn't find her! Where had she gone? I spent days walking up and down trying to find where she'd been abducted to!'

He did not restrict himself to the cinema but worked on productions for the small screen as well. In the early sixties he made a series of *The Saint* short stories for ATV and produced and directed the *Meet The Wife* series for the BBC, starring Thora Hird and Freddie Frinton.

However, amid this frenetic life Carstairs found the time, in 1962, to purchase 9600 HP from John Coombs and registered it on 31 May 1962.

'He bought it more or less for me,' says Molly. 'I said I wanted one. It was *the* thing at the time. I came back from a holiday in the South of France and there it was. I really drove it more than he did, because very often when he was working on a picture, he'd have a chauffeur car. He'd find at the end of a day's directing, he was tired and he didn't want to drive. So I had it more than he did.

'I used to go down to Devon a lot where I had a friend at that time. I didn't do any foreign driving with it.' Molly thinks the car did still cause great interest from the public but, because she and Paddy lived such a jet-set lifestyle surrounded by famous film stars, they did not notice whether crowds were gathering around the car or a famous companion. Certainly, the car was the perfect complement to this glamorous lifestyle.

'My whole life then was so exciting. We were always doing something that was particular. We went to America when we had a film on Broadway and it was all TV appearances. I was very young at the time and I couldn't absorb it all. Now, when I try and think back it's all connected to that time running up to when he was not too well. I suppose your mind blocks things out. It still hurts now when I think about it all these years later.'

The fame and glamour brought its disadvantages, though. 'We were living at

Kingston in a big house there and we were always being burgled, being in the film business. I was burgled 14 times at Kingston. Every time we went away on a plane, there'd be a photographer – 'Paddy Carstairs and his latest book' – you know, and it was good publicity for him. He didn't mind too much being burgled – men don't, do they? – but for me it was an awful shock.'

Apart from his life as a leading and prolific film director and his life as novelist, John Paddy Carstairs was a highly regarded artist with a distinctive style of his own. His paintings were often full of movement which seems entirely appropriate for this most energetic of men.

Then, in 1970, poor Molly had an even worse and desperately traumatic shock. 'He died sitting next to me – of a heart attack. Boomph, like that. For a year I was really quite ill. When Paddy died, I went right off the map.' Her recall of the sixties and their time with 9600 HP is something she subconsciously blanked out of her memory as a way of dealing with the sudden, shocking loss. Somehow, you feel that that loss was made even greater because not one person, but two, three or four people died when John Paddy Carstairs passed away. He was a man of such disparate talents and had, unusually, the energy to pursue each of his fields with single-minded purpose.

'He was extremely tiring. I don't know whether I could live with him if he were alive today, but I still miss his vitality because most people seem lukewarm when I think about him. He had such terrific energy.

'He would be scribbling in the middle of the night. He would get an idea. He didn't sleep, he'd have a few hours' cat-nap and then he would think again and start writing.'

'I never thought I would live alone but once you have lived with somebody like that, it's very difficult to live with somebody else. I have dabbled in this and that but it hasn't for one minute made me think I must settle down with someone else. That's how strong his impression is still, thirty years later.'

Molly recalls that her husband's father and three of the four sons all suffered from heart trouble. 'The father, Nelson Keys, had a stroke.' All the sons were in the film industry, occupying a variety of roles.

His surviving brother, who wishes to remain anonymous, thinks Paddy died of a broken heart. The Rank Organization changed direction in 1970 and pulled out of light comedy. Suddenly Carstairs had no work in what was his first love. 'Couldn't paint when he was not working. When he didn't work it ruined his life. When he died, the family was amazed by the number of letters which they received from people whom he had helped. He was most friendly and everybody was very fond of him.'

One of those was Norman Wisdom, of whom Carstairs had said, 'He will do anything – if you dare him!'

'This is a great appalling loss,' Wisdom said at the time, 'to show business and to me personally. I shall always be grateful that he was the man who introduced me to filmland. There was this great feeling between us. We gelled nicely and he had the same sort of sense of humour as I did.'

Recently octogenarian Sir Norman, as he now is, recalled Paddy Carstairs with great fondness. 'He was a smashing bloke and a marvellous director. He was responsible for my early successes and I have a silver spoon which he gave me for every film we made together. He was a very down to earth person and we were good friends.'

On one occasion Wisdom suggested a different way of doing a sequence in one of the films. 'Paddy said, "We'll do it both ways and then decide." So we did and then he came over to me and said, "I do apologize Norman, you're absolutely right. We'll do it your way."' They had an excellent rapport and his approach made Carstairs a pleasure to work with. I mentioned the theory that he died of a broken heart. 'It's quite possible. The film industry went out of sight around that time.'

We then talked of cars. 'I was mad on cars. I had a Two-Door Mulliner Continental Bentley.'

I asked if he remembered 9600 HP. 'I do. It was a lovely sports car. I went in it several times aound the lanes near Pinewood. There were a lot of good country roads round there. I certainly do remember the car, but my memory is not so good now as

I am getting on a bit. There are three problems with getting old. You lose your memory.' Pause. 'Oh dear, I can't remember what the other two are.'

What a delightful man. It might sound corny on the page, but the great old pro made it very funny. 'You haven't changed!' I responded.

'Only my under-clothes.'

'I have a feeling you may have used that one before.'

'I can't remember! I do remember his E-type though. It was a beautiful sports car with very good acceleration.'

Derek Malcolm, writing in the *Guardian* of John Paddy Carstairs at the time of his death, stated, '... his best work, either as director or script-writer, has an honourable place in the history of the British cinema.'

Molly Carstairs has lived as a virtual recluse ever since but is a most delightful and vivacious lady. Though she has blanked out the sixties, she still has fond memories of 9600 HP.

'It always looked beautiful. It was such a pretty car. I don't think there's ever been a prettier car than the E-type.'

The Carstairs kept 9600 HP for three years, and the next registered keeper, who acquired the car in June 1965, was Jack Fairman. Jack enjoyed a long and distinguished motor racing career in international sports car racing and, to a lesser extent, in Grand Prix cars. On his mother's side, he was descended from a Quaker family, his great-great-great grandmother being Elizabeth Fry, the prison reformer. Jack's father started up one of the first steam laundries. Born in 1920 Jack learnt to drive at the age of eleven on his father's 1913 10hp GWK. During holidays from Reigate Grammar School he accompanied the laundry van drivers, unofficially driving out in the country. The fact that he was taught to hoist a heavy hamper full of sheets on to his back and then cart this load up several flights of stairs, thereby developing unusually powerful back and shoulder muscles, may not sound of great importance. However, some years hence it would play a vital role in Aston Martin annexing the World Sports Car Championship!

Fairman's father had also developed a garage business and young Jack worked there at weekends. Leaving school at 17, he went to the College of Aeronautical and Automobile Engineering at Chelsea for two years, gaining his diploma. He then joined the august firm of Daimler in Coventry and after another two years moved to Armstrong Siddeley. His competitive motoring began with an Alvis 12/50 which he drove in trials, hill-climbs and at Brooklands. He served with the Tank Regiment during the war, was involved in the Normandy operations and finished up as Town Major of Kiel.

Returning to the family company, he became a director of the garage business and then Managing Director of Fairman Precision Tools, which he built up to a level where it was employing a staff of over 100 by 1960. His post-war competition career commenced at Shelsley Walsh hill-climb, which was and still is one of the premier motoring events of the year, driving an elderly Bugatti. To his surprise he was asked to drive an HRG at Le Mans in 1949. He asked why he had been chosen. 'Answer was that my Bugatti efforts had been observed and if I could cope with that ancient monument, I could cope with anything!' On another occasion he crashed a Riley and ended up on the roof of a trackside building!

Paired at Le Mans with Eric Thompson, he finished eighth, and first in class, at his virgin attempt and would race at Le Mans every year for the next twelve years, bar 1957. For 1951 he was paired with a young chap called Moss in the number one C-type as the car and the works team made their debuts. The drivers had tried the cars a couple of times at Silverstone and MIRA, but there was nowhere within the UK that had a sufficiently long straight to replicate the Mulsanne Straight at Le Mans and allow the new Jaguars to test at maximum speed.

'So it was not until we arrived there for the first practice session that we knew for certain that the C-types would attain their designed speed of 150mph. This was my first experience, and Stirling's also, of that kind of speed. It takes some time to get used to it after dark.

'At 4pm on the Saturday, in the incredible electric atmosphere which permeates Le Mans before the start, Stirling took first spell and within four laps was in the lead. During the next three hours or so he remained there, breaking the lap record in the process.'

Thanks to Malcolm Sayer's superb aerodynamic work, Moss found he could still reach 150mph on half throttle. However, he was taking the two right-hand bends between Mulsanne and Arnage completely flat out and saving the brakes by not using them at White House and the Dunlop Curve. Or so it appeared: 'As you come up to a corner, you want everybody to think you're taking it flat, so I was rolling back on the throttle for the Dunlop Curve way before the pits, then going through the pits with it hard on the floor. I appeared to be going flat out but the point was that I had dropped 2–3mph!'

'I took over the car,' continues Jack, 'at about 7.30, and by 8.30 it had started to rain, apart from getting dark. This was my first experience of 150mph in the dark *and* the wet. I was kept pretty busy, dealing with incipient slides and making horrible decisions, such as wondering whether to overtake a cloud of spray before the next bend, or wait and thus lose time.

'In the middle of it all I had one of those sudden flashes of awareness. Here was I achieving an ambition by driving in a works team at Le Mans, I had just equalled Stirling's lap record despite the rain and also had overtaken the legendary Juan Manuel Fangio, who was driving a Lago-Talbot. As a result, I braked just a little too late at the end of the fast straight, forgetting the road was wet. I had to take the escape road and stopped at what seemed to be halfway to Tours!'

Autosport noted there was great cheering from the crowd as 'the British driver passes the Argentinian crack. Fangio must have been astonished. A 'GP' Talbot being passed by a British sports car – well, well!'

Fairman handed back to Moss with their lead intact, but sadly the C-type retired soon after with a lack of oil pressure. However, Stirling and Jack had done their job. 'By bashing on regardless,' as Jack puts it, 'most of the opposition, including Fangio, had run into trouble in their attempt to keep up with us.' Team-mates Walker and Whitehead cruised to an easy, but famous, victory. 'William Lyons had tears in his eyes,' says Fairman.

In 1952 Jack drove an Allard J2 X with Sydney Allard but retired during the 14th hour with a ruptured fuel tank. The year after he began a very successful association with Bristols and Tommy Wisdom, resulting in eighth place in '54 and ninth in '55. For 1956 he was back in the Jaguar works team, so he had the unique distinction of being in the team for its first and last years. But it was not a happy race for the factory team. Paul Frère, who would drive 9600 HP at Geneva, had the misfortune to spin his D-type in the Esses on the second lap as it began to rain. His team-mate Fairman spun his 'D' to avoid Frère and escaped unscathed – until he was hit by the spinning Ferrari of the Marquis de Portago.

Phil Hill (14), Jimmy Reece (24), Jack Fairman (4), Maurice Trintignant (15) impegnati sulla sopraelevata durante la 500 Miglia del '58.

Jack Fairman earned his nickname 'Fearless' at the 500 mile races at Monza. Here we see him in the 1958 event in the Ecurie Ecosse D-type in close company with future World Champion Phil Hill in a Formula 1 Ferrari, plus Jimmy Reece (Hoyt Machine) and Maurice Trintignant (Sclavi and Amos) in Indianapolis cars.

Jack had been doing a lot of testing and racing for Connaught in Grand Prix events and finished fourth at the British GP. When Jaguar retired from racing and Connaughts lost their sponsorship, he found himself high and dry for 1957. He joined Ecurie Ecosse, who were running a team of D-types. As a result he took part in the curious Monzanapolis Race of Two Worlds in Italy. This was supposed to be a 500-mile contest on a banked oval between US Indianapolis cars and European racing cars. However, the European GP teams refused to play. Ecurie Ecosse, though, fancied a slice of the £30,000 prize money.

Before the event the Americans, whose cars were designed specifically for this type of event, had been winding up the Scottish team. However, the US cars were only fitted with two gears and they were slow off the start. To his surprise, 'Jolly Jack', as 'Lofty' called him, found himself well in the lead by the end of the first lap. He was laughing so much he nearly went off the track!

During practice he had lived up to his other nickname of 'Fearless Fairman'. 'Just as I was approaching the banking at about 165mph, the entire right-hand back tread came off with a noise like a six-inch shell.' As a result the Jaguar D-types were restricted to 160mph, but the American cars gradually fell apart until only three of the 20 were left. Jack led the D-types home and claimed to be the first European driver ever to cover 500 miles at over 150mph.

For 1959 Fairman joined the Aston Martin works team and was paired on occasions once again with the maestro Moss. At the Nürburgring, the lone DBR-1 was up against the might of Ferrari, Maserati and Porsche. Jack had the misfortune to slip off the road and Moss, back in the pits, was packing up to go home. But, with his exceptionally strong back muscles, Fairman was able to lift the car back on to the road. After a demon drive by Stirling, the duo took a remarkable win. At Le Mans Moss and Fairman retired, but Salvadori and Shelby won and clocked up more points for Aston Martin. After his own car, which he was sharing with Salvadori, caught fire in the pits at the Tourist Trophy, Moss took over Fairman's car and put in another epic drive to clinch for the British team the World Sports Car Championship.

As team owner David Brown commented, 'Aston Martin win World Championship as a direct result of one driver trained by laundry!'

After Aston Martin retired from racing, Fairman was retained by Ferguson to carry out testing on various four-wheel-drive vehicles including their prototype P99 Grand Prix car. He raced this twice – at the British GP and the British Empire Trophy. At the GP he was in 13th place out of 30 starters by the 15th lap, but had to pit when the car ran over some debris and was damaged. The push-start infringed the rules, but Fairman continued under appeal. Meanwhile Moss had to retire his Lotus while lying second. Jack was called in and Stirling took over, only to be disqualified within a few laps. Jack claimed to have received a letter from Fergusons to say that had he been allowed to carry on, a study of the lap times suggested he would have finished as winner.

In 1963 he spent six months in Italy working with Dunlop and BP on the new ATS GP car designed by Carlo Chiti, of Ferrari and later Alfa Romeo fame. In 1965 Jack was testing at Indianapolis for two months developing the Thompson Special, the first rear-engined Indy car to be built in the US.

The same year, in June, Jack Fairman purchased 9600 HP. A few years ago I asked him how he acquired the car.

Some dealer in London had got hold of it. I saw it standing outside and stopped and looked. I thought, 'That looks like the car that broke the records'. So I went inside but didn't say anything about what I thought the car was.

'Is that car for sale?' I asked.

'Yes, it is,' was the reply.

The dealer who had it for sale had no clue whatsoever that that was the actual car. So I bought it for less than a thousand quid, and ran it for several years. I drove it a lot and it was a nice car to drive. When the motorways opened, it was nice to have a car you really could cruise at 80 or 90 and not turn a hair.

The police did chase me one day. They followed me for 30 miles and I never dropped below 100mph. Something had happened ahead and there was a traffic jam. So I stopped and the police car came up behind. A chap got out and said, 'I admire the speed your car goes at, sir, but we think you should ease off a bit because you might have run into this little lot, mightn't you sir?' I think they were only

In his BEN residential home, Jack Fairman – now in his eighties – is surrounded by many reminders of his illustrious motoring life, including a print of 9600 HP in one of my barns.

joking. They were jealous because their police car couldn't keep up!

The cop said, 'I wish our car could keep up with yours. We could use one of these in the police!'

I ran it on the road for a couple of years, used to take the kids to school in the morning in it. Created some interest, especially amongst the schoolboys. Jack Playford did a few things to it at my suggestion, made it steer better. I had better linings for the brakes.

I was rather conscious that there was I driving around the roads of Great Britain in the fastest road car in the world. There was nothing else as quick as that, no Yanks. There might have been a few Italian Ferraris, but that's not a normal sort of car. The

Ferrari's not the sort of car you put the kids in to take to school, but I could do that with the Jag. I only sold it because the kids were growing up and there was not room for them. There were no back seats but when they were little they could climb in the back. When they started getting bigger, they couldn't climb in the back and it got dangerous. So, reluctantly, I had to sell it.

Having bought the car in June 1965, Jack advertised it for sale car in *Autosport* in December 1966. The 9600 HP advert makes interesting and amusing reading now, and also tells us a little more about the history of the car.

9600 HP – The first FHC E-type as tested by *Autosport*, 17th March, 1961, and exhibited by Jaguar at Geneva, after which it stood around for ages. (Mileage today is only 30,000). Recently resprayed by Rowe's of Chichester and rechromed. Maintained and modified entirely by Playford's of Croydon. Konis, comp. Roll bar, new discs. Will be collectors' piece in few years. £950. Full details to serious enquirers from Jack Fairman, Betchworh (Surrey) 3252.

Unfortunately Rowe's no longer exists in its original form, but Playfords were a well-known Jaguar specialist until quite recently. The company was run by Jack and his two sons, John and Brian. 'We used to fit,' states Brian, 'competition torsion bars and springs, but we never used factory shockers. We always used Konis and often fitted a larger diameter roll bar. The Jaguar shock absorbers used to leak and were pretty unreliable. Anybody who was anybody had Konis. Engine-wise, I would very much doubt if we had done anything for him. Normal servicing would have been Jaguar servicing. I vaguely remember the car.'

It seems that Fairman failed to sell the car for what was probably a rather ambitious price at the time. Even though Jack had the foresight to suggest that it would become a collector's item, the classic car craze was still a few years off. The same magazine, for example, had a 1962 25,000-mile, one lady owner Roadster for £825. It appears that Fairman kept the car for another year or so. Then, needing to sell the car, Jack approached Richardsons, the well-known sports car, and particularly MG, specialists. Based in Pease Pottage, Sussex, the company was about ten miles from Jack's place at Betchworth. This business had been started by Stanley Richardson, who had three sons in the business – Michael, Ian and Clive, though Clive was later killed on the Reigate Road. The garage closed down when the land was acquired to make room for the M23. They also had a depot in Moor Lane, Staines.

Their Manager was Geoff Linssen and he clearly remembers 9600 HP passing through his hands. 'I bought 9600 HP from Mr Fairman. The price paid was £650 and he assured me of its unique history.

'Fairman just rolled up. "Do you sell Jags? My name is Jack Fairman. I used to drive for Jaguar."' The deal was done and Geoff 'paid him on the spot' .

'I took it home a few times. I was keen to see how it went in comparison with ordinary 3.8s. It stood in the showroom in the right-hand front window.'

Keen to know more about the car, Linssen telephoned no less a person than Engineering Director Bill Heynes, who was 'very friendly. He said, "Hang on a minute, give me the chassis number to make sure it isn't a fake." He told me it had had three engines and that it was registered two months before the world had heard of it. He said, "I personally drove it down the M1." I also remember sending for the 1961 back-issues of *Autosport*, which contained pictures and road tests.

'I sold it for £800 or £850 in view of its history. I was very pleased to get that for it. In fact, I damn nearly owned the car myself. I had a very nice dark blue XK150 3.8 'S' Fixed Head Coupé. I thought about buying it but I'd paid more for 9600 HP [on behalf of the company] because of its history and couldn't afford it. My 150 was worth about £400/450.'

Following my discussions with Linssen, I decided to study the original logbook with renewed interest in the hope that I could glean, or deduce, a little more from this ageing brown document. Jaguar taxed it for a year from 10/2/61 until 31/1/62. Curiously, it appears that it was not taxed again until 4/5/62, the date it was sold to Coombs. This suggests that either the car was not used in early 1962 (Fairman's ad did say it 'stood around for ages') or that it was used on Trade Plates, or most likely it was an oversight. The tax then expired on 31/8/62, which is a four-month period. In those days, you could tax a vehicle for four or twelve months.

Carstairs registered the car on 31/5/62 and renewed the tax on 24/8/62 – again for a four-month period. We then have periods of twelve months from 18/12/62 to 31/12/63 and 18/12/63 to 31/12/64. It was renewed on 5/1/65 and lapsed in April of that year – another four-month period. It appears to have been untaxed for May and June, was acquired by Fairman on 28/6/65 and taxed two days later until June the following year.

It would seem that Jack forgot to tax it, or was not using it, for a couple of months because it was next taxed on 9/8/66 until July 1967. Meanwhile he had advertised it at the end of December, '66. Confused? I am not surprised! Incidentally, the annual rate was £15 in 1961, which increased to £17 10s (£17.50) and again to £25. Unfortunately, the information on taxing runs out there because there is a stamp saying 'ENTRIES DISCONTINUED BY DIRECTION OF MINISTRY OF TRANSPORT'.

Meanwhile, a photograph of 9600 HP going through the car wash in 1961 appeared in the 29 February issue of Country Life in 1968 accompanying, and totally irrelevant to, an article on mergers in the motor industry.

At this stage in the game, our next fixed point is a Richardsons advert in the 21 June 1968 issue of *Autosport*.

E-type Fixed Head, an historic car, being the first one made, registered 10th Feb, 1961. Shown at Geneva and Road Tested by *Autosport*, etc, Feb/Mar 1961. Three famous owners including Jaguar Cars Ltd. Mileage 45,000. Full history and maintenance, in superb condition and perfectly original. A collector's item that will never depreciate. Taxed. £975!

With Fairman selling it to Richardsons, no other owner appearing in the log book and the above advert being dated June 1968, it appears that Fairman must have kept it for around another year before parting with the car. Also the mileage had

This remarkable house – Wings Place in Sussex – was home to 9600 HP for a period in the late sixties when both were owned by David Lockhart Smith.

increased between December 1966 and June 1968 from 30,000 to 45,000.

Peter Lockhart Smith, who was then just 20, had a great interest in cars and motor racing. 'I saw the ad in *Autosport*.' He immediately showed it to his father, David. 'We went straight away to look at the car. I think we had looked at a couple before seeing 9600 advertised. My parents had known Antony Hopkins, the broadcaster and musician, for many years and he owned a Lightweight E-type, so the idea of buying 9600 did not seem so eccentric. We were nervous of buying a problem car requiring a lot of work, but the history of 9600 persuaded my father to take the plunge.' At that time, the Lockhart Smiths lived at Wings Place (also known as Ann of Cleves House), Ditchling – about six miles north of Brighton.

David Lockhart Smith was born in Hong Kong where his father was Colonial Secretary. He was educated at Cambridge and, during the war, became a Captain in the Royal Marines. He was attached to the Fleet Air Arm and flew Swordfishes, Barracudas and Albacores on operational service and as an instructor in torpedo dropping. He then qualified and practised as an architect in the City of London, his projects including Sir John Lyon House, Broken Wharf House on the waterfront and the restoration of a Wren church after war damage. He died in 1984.

There was some delay before the car was usable. 'It was rather embarrassing for me when we discovered how much work the car needed before we were able to renew the MOT,' recalls Peter.

Though the car was not registered in David Lockhart Smith's name until October 1969, it seems that he had purchased the car some months earlier, for I have bills made out to him dated May '69. A new battery was fitted and an assessment made of the work required to pass the MOT test. During July a new clutch was installed, together with various new oil seals, brake parts and a flywheel. The car duly passed the MOT test on 9 October 1969, and the mileage on the certificate was given as 46,750 which tallies with Richardsons's last advert.

In 1969 we used the car, [states Peter Lockhart Smith] for a couple of trips up to Cumberland to look at Stonegarthside Hall. This was before the completion of the M6 through the Lake Hills and I remember driving past Penrith in the snow on the old A6.

In 1970 we decided, at the last moment, to go to Monte Carlo for the Grand Prix. We set off, I think, via Newhaven at night and stopped off for early morning coffee with a cousin who lived just south of Paris. After the race, which was memorably exciting, I flew off to Italy for a day or so. When I met my father at Nice Airport, the car had acquired a dent in the rear caused by an enthusiastic local driver following too closely.

We returned via the Cévennes and my father was kind enough to let me do most of the driving. We visited Sonia Holmes, the artist, and her then-husband Peter who had just sold their house in Ditchling and had bought for restoration Château Montvaillant near Anduze. I recall that we had to hurry back to the coast to catch the ferry. It was an interesting experience using the amazing acceleration to overtake slower cars.

In June we moved from Sussex up to Cumberland, where my parents had acquired

Stonegarthside Hall, which is north-east of Carlisle, right on the border with Scotland. The house needed complete restoration and the Jaguar was put away in a barn. [The late C17th hall is described in a book on historic buildings as 'arguably the most remote country house in England'.]

Again I was allowed to drive it up north on my own via the M1 and Scotch Corner, which was the quickest way before the completion of the M6 through Birmingham. The highest speed I recall doing was 135mph in a brief burst.

I recall that when we started the car again after a year or so, we discovered that the engine wouldn't hold water and overheated. In any event, the car was hardly used from 1971 to 1975 and this is borne out by the small increase in mileage on the MOTs.

When the Lockhart Smith family moved up to Stonegarthside Hall in Cumbria, the car resided in this rather fine barn, the first of several barns it was to be imprisoned in over the next thirty-odd years.

In March 1972 Lockhart Smith had written to Jaguar about the car. From the reply, we can deduce that he was contemplating some renovation work and had also enquired whether Jaguar would be interested in the car. Geoff Pindar, the Service Director, replied and it makes rather amusing reading now.

Thank you for your letter of 7th March, from which I note you own the above car bearing the registration No. 9600 HP which was, indeed, a very early car in the ' E' type series.

It is difficult to be precise and unfortunately we cannot arrange to send an engineer to visit you to assess the condition of the car at the present time. You will appreciate also that a great deal will depend upon what is found on dismantling as to the requirements for replacements and having regard to our present commitments and the possibility of the Service Department being moved a little later in the year, I must confess I hesitate to undertake this work at the present time.

As far as the possibility of the car being on display is concerned, I do not think there is any possibility of this company being interested in purchase of the car, but I am not sure whether Lord Montague [sic] has a similar car in his collection at Beaulieu. I personally believe that he has an example of the 3.8 litre ' E' type but I will check when the individual concerned returns to the factory.

'I do not recall,' states Peter, 'offering to sell them the car outright. I think I had an arrangement in mind where they might buy a share in the car, put it in good order and put it on display.

'In late 1975 my father became ill and I decided that, as it was obvious the car needed total restoration, it should be sold as this was not something we could contemplate at that time. Cumberland is rather a damp place and I was worried that the rot in the car's body might become irreversible. I think the car was sold in early 1976.'

Peter Lockhart Smith, whose name also appears in the logbook though it was never stamped, thinks the car was advertised in *Autosport* yet again. He is absolutely correct, for the following appeared in the 15 and 22 January issues.

HISTORIC 3.8 'E' TYPE, pre-production prototype, chassis no. 002, reg. 9600 h.p. First FHC in world, Geneva Show model. Tested Autosport 1961 at over 150 m.p.h., 5,500 miles. Full history, some work needed, £1,350 o.n.o. – 054-121 xxx (Cumbria).'

With the exception of the phone number, this is exactly as the advert appeared, complete with its amusing misprints. It appears that the power was even greater than we thought and the mileage even less! Almost certainly the mileage should have read 50,500.

At this point matters become a little vague, though I am confident that we shall tie up the loose ends with a little more time and research. It seems that Lockhart Smith sold it to someone in the Manchester area by name of Evans. He may have been a dealer, for the next owner, who resided in South London, saw the car advertised in *The Sunday Times* and recalls going up to Manchester to complete the purchase. Research proved that their memories were not at fault. The following advertisement appeared, a shade under two months later, in the 7 March, 1976 edition of *The Sunday Times*.

First FHC E-Type Jaguar. Geneva Motor Show model and tested by Autosport 1961. Good running order. Genuine 50,000 miles. Full history. £1600. Tel. 061 865 xxx or 061 969 xxx.

We are working on tracing Mr Evans but have not had any luck as yet. We do know, however, exactly who bought the car, and this was a gentleman by the name of Derek Brant, and when I use the word *gentleman* I do so intentionally. Like so many people who have come into contact with 9600 HP, he is a remarkable chap.

Keen on items of a mechanical nature, Derek bought, at the age of 16, a motorbike and sold it at a profit though still a schoolboy. While attending Epsom Grammar School, he had spotted the bike in someone's back yard one day. Then a friend gave him a KTT Velocette, which was not working. Derek got it going and advertised it in the local paper for something like £30 and an older gentleman came to see it. He said it was a racing bike and far too cheap. He paid Derek double the asking price and considered he still had a bargain! Being an entirely honourable chap, Brant told his friend who insisted he keep all the money.

Brant then bought his first car, which was a TR2, and in 1962 he purchased a brand new TR3A. This lacked appeal for him because, being new, there was nothing to do to it. So he sold it and subsequently bought others on which he did a little work. A succession of friends spotted the cars and gave him a small profit each time. It was nothing more than a hobby but he was keen to graduate to E-types, which he had always loved.

In similar vein he bought a 16,000-mile XK120 from a customer who was Chairman of British Airports Authority, to whom he paid the price asked. Later he sold it for a profit of £1000 and, even more amazing, this was to a well-known dealer. In this way Derek managed to buy and sell several E-types.

One day in 1976, he opened a copy of *The Sunday Times* to see a classified advert which immediately caught his eye.

I knew it was number two. I knew it was the Geneva Show car because I think it was in the advert. The irony was that I knew where number one was as well. In Beaconsfield a man had a factory full of probably 200 cars of which number one was one of them. I went the first time to look at a TR3A and saw the Jaguar there among MG TFs and MGAs and that sort of thing. The car that took my fancy was a ten-year old 3.4 S-type saloon which had done about 2000 miles. So I bought that off him.

Having had a satisfactory deal, from the seller's viewpoint, an important relationship had been formed. Derek never gave any hint of his serious interest in the first production right-hand-drive car and this gent never volunteered a price. Indeed it is unlikely he had plans to sell it, but he was a builder and, as builders do, he needed cash from time to time. Brant decided to bide his time.

Meanwhile he saw the advert for 9600 HP and immediately telephoned the vendor. Brant merely enquired as to whether the condition was such that he had a fair chance of making it back to London if he went up by train.

> We agreed on the 'phone that I was a buyer of this car and money was not an issue. I was not going to haggle about it.
>
> The guy hadn't had it very long so I should think he probably was a trader. I explained to him that I couldn't get to a bank until ten, I think it was in those days. "I will draw the money out in cash and get the train." I phoned him back half an hour later and said, "The train leaves at xyz." I wasn't with the guy more than ten minutes at the station. He was in the car park there. We did drive it round the block, literally, less than a mile. This was more from the point of view of getting back to London than anything else. I paid him the money and that's exactly what happened.
>
> The thing drove back down perfectly satisfactorily. On the way home, I passed by Beaconsfield and parked round the corner and went in to see the builder who had number one and bought it. So I bought one and two within a day, which then made me run out of money a bit. I think I bought 848 CRY a few months later. I think there was an Aston advertised in *Motor Sport* and then, as a little afterthought, it said, 'Also 12th E-type Roadster'.

Number one is actually a much later car than number two. This apparent paradox is explained by the fact that, as we have seen, 9600 HP was originally a left-hand-drive car and was the second one made. Because Jaguar were so slow getting the E-type, and particularly the Fixed Head Coupé model, into production, right-hand-drive number one was not built until August 1961, around a year after number two!

Superficially, number one appeared to be in very presentable condition, whereas 9600 HP was starting to look rather tatty. From photographs which Derek took, one can see a few dents. Of course photos usually flatter cars and it seems the car was quite a bit rougher than it looked. As a result, Derek gave thought to having some work done. First, he visited the famous leather suppliers, Connollys, to see if they could match the distinctive, heavy grain.

I phoned up and explained I had this early E-type,' continues Brant. 'So they suggested I come up and had a look. They took me up into their warehouse with massive great roles of leather. I had with me a cutting, or maybe the cushion, and it was quite a bumpy sort of hide.' This was easy for the long-established company and they showed Derek a hide of a similar texture.

From an MOT certificate, we know that Brant had the car tested on 12 December, 1976 and the mileage was 50,988, just some 4238 miles greater than when Lockhart Smith had first had the car MOT'd. The test was carried out by Palace Service Station. 'That's a mile up the road,' Derek commented when I visited him 24 years later.

'I had a number of lock-up garages around the Surbiton area where my little business is. I really wanted to get it rebuilt. Somehow I got to know Punters over at

Hillingdon. They had a Polish guy who was a welder, but I was bothered that he wasn't doing the job well enough.'

At this point Paul Skilleter enters the scene. To anyone in the Jaguar world, Skilleter's name will be very well known. He joined the staff of *The Motor* in 1966 as a young photographer and his passion then was XKs. In 1975 he wrote

During Derek Brant's brief ownership, he took the car to a small garage with the evocative name of Punters! Here Paul Skilleter photographed 9600 HP in late 1976 or early 1977. The bonnet had been temporarily removed and it can be seen that the old girl was now showing her age.

Jaguar Sports Cars, the first of several Jaguar books, and included a photo of 9600 HP with Lyons at Geneva. He was an early member of the original team which was responsible for producing *Classic Car*, the first magazine devoted to the subject. Interestingly this small team included, as Editorial Director, Maurice Smith who had conducted the original *Autocar* road test and Jonathan Wood who will appear in this story shortly. Paul edited the *Jaguar Drivers' Club* magazine during the 1970s and in the June 1976 issue of the *Jaguar Driver* wrote the following in his editorial under the heading 'WANTED, E-TYPE FOR T & CC': 'Those who take *Thoroughbred & Classic Cars* magazine [as the magazine had been renamed] should be pleased to know that there should soon be an increase in its Jaguar bias because an E-type is to be added to its fleet of staff cars.'

After stating that it would be run by himself, he continued, 'we're looking for the most rust-free example of a 3.8 fixed-head coupé which we can find. If anyone knows of such a beast which may be for sale, perhaps they could let me know...'

As a result, on 14 June, 1976 Derek Brant wrote, as follows, to Paul Skilleter.

I currently have four E-types. The first fixed head is chassis no. 860001. I also have the second fixed head, the Geneva Show car 9600 HP (shown beautifully in your book), and also the twelfth, and two hundred and thirty-second drop heads. Now, as you can imagine it is going to take me some time to get these cars up to excellent condition; I have nearly completed the '232' drop-head and have no particular preference as to the next one to start ... so, you could either 'borrow' for an arranged time, or be 'partners in' either the first or second fixed heads. The photograph [enclosed] of the 'first' is rather flattering but is really quite solid. The second, is of course, quite 'famous' since the early road tests were of this car, and much publicity. Unfortunately it does need a lot doing to the body, and again, the interior.

The above gist 'states the case', but perhaps they may interest you. Come and see, or write, phone, whatever, it will be interesting for both of us, I would think.

Paul replied to the effect that he had found and acquired a suitable E-type but expressed interest in the early cars. On 30 July Derek wrote again and, after congratulating Paul on finding a sound car, continued, 'Funds make my rebuilding project a long-term situation because, having done the 232 chassis drop-head, I am very reluctant to sell it, just to finance the remaining three. I can save, and do them in time, with the experience gained from this one. I would still like to meet you...'

Clearly they did meet, for Paul photographed 9600 HP at the small workshop in Hillingdon. Thankfully, they had done very little to the car other than remove the bonnet, boot floor and rear quarters. They had tacked in place a new factory rear panel and that seems to be as far as they got.

'I had bought these cars with a long-term view of selling them and paying off my mortgage, and for the family as an investment. However, I saw that the people doing the restoration weren't really skilled enough and neither were my contacts, and maybe Paul Skilleter could have helped me.

'The Jaguar factory, maybe through Paul Skilleter, wrote to me and I went up there and they took me round the factory. They had a few cars in a little museum there and they were very keen for me to put one or two in their place.'

A couple of years before, Derek Brant had holidayed in southern Spain, where he had visited an American who ran a church with a mission for drug addicts, alcoholics and other young folk from all over the world. Derek discovered religion for the first time and became a devout Christian, an experience that would change the course of his life.

In the latter part of January, we nearly always used to go abroad to Spain because we fostered children – two little black girls and their brother – and we had two children of our own. The only time we ever had without the foster children was when we would scoot over, after the busy time in my shop, and have a little family time for two weeks at the same hotel in southern Spain.

It was also a bit of a pilgrimage to go back to the church I got 'saved' in. I was sitting about three rows back, just praying, and I really felt God speak to me about selling these cars. 'They are a millstone around your neck.' I hadn't seen that. There was almost a debate going on, as happens when you are praying, trying to hear what God is saying.

I said, 'No, these are for my family.'

He said, 'It's not my plan for you. I have other plans for you.'

Derek returned from Spain with this on his mind. But how could he go about selling them? He recalls that Paul was planning to write about at least one of them and phoned to suggest taking some more photographs.

'"Sure," I replied. "I'll meet you up there." Then, and it seemed like an afterthought, Paul said, "Have you ever thought about selling them?"

'"It's funny you say that," I replied. I think I told him what had happened and that I might have to sell them because someone bigger than me had said so. He actually said, "I have an American client who would be very happy to buy them, or an English guy who could restore them. He is into rebuilding XKs and so on and so forth." I decided to pray about this and that's why I wanted them all to go as a package. That's why I insisted on this.'

Derek told Paul that he would give him a price based on what he had spent on the cars. 'I have no idea what I paid for them but I made no profit on them. Paul then phoned you, Philip, and you said, "Yes".'

Derek recalls that he and I had a verbal agreement that I would keep the historic cars for a minimum of three years. 'I felt they were a worthwhile collection,' he continues, 'and that they should go to the right home. I just saw that I had got hold of something that was a bit beyond me. So when this came up, especially in the light of what had happened in Spain, I just felt this was a excellent opportunity. I really

wanted them to go to someone who knew what they were doing. I have told probably a hundred people all over the world in the last few years how thrilled I am that
you've kept them, thereby keeping your part of the deal in the extreme.'

Derek went on to do good works in many parts of the world. He has been a mis-
sionary in Papua New Guinea, Australia, the Philippines, Hong Kong (living with
drug addicts), Singapore, Spain, Jamaica, Newfoundland, Canada, Uruguay, Uganda
and others. Derek, and his wife Jackie, are currently, and have been for some years,
on the lay leadership team of Holy Trinity Brompton, a large Anglican church in
London.

'The ownership of these historic cars was a delight and to be involved again today
has brought things full circle.' For Derek, however, the pursuit of God's plans for his
life remains the challenge. Tongue in cheek, he quips, ' Matthew 6–19 "put not your
trust where moth and rust destroys and where thieves break in and steal". God must
know all about E-types!'

The bill! Some explanation is needed. XVE 1 was the first production RHD car which had been re-registered with this number. Derek's thinking was that, with the addition of a well placed and appropriately coloured attachment stud on the number plate, this would almost read XKE 1. Brant was in the process of re-registering the twelfth Roadster DJB 61, but I later short-circuited this, retained 848 CRY and would be very pleased later that I had. It was sheer luck, though, like so much of this story.

CHAPTER TEN

Rusting in Peace

My personal passion for motor cars started at a ridiculously early age. I am told that, at the age of about three, I would sit in the front of my father's car as he drove and name all the cars that went the other way – couldn't do it today! My particular love of Jaguars was no doubt inspired by my father owning several examples in the fifties and sixties.

He formed and ran several precision engineering companies that principally did work for most of the major aircraft and motor manufacturers, and so I was brought up in an atmosphere of knowing and revering these great names. Also the company purchased *The Motor* magazine to be put in the reception at the factory, and these were passed on to me. They were a fundamental part of my education and so names like Charles Bulmer, Paul Frère, Maurice Rowe and others, who are quoted in this book and have been so helpful, were well-known to me in my formative years. My mother and father spoilt me with every new Dinky model, as it appeared, and I lived in my pedal car. Friends used to push me down a track we had formed in my parents' garden as we tried harder and harder to break our previous course record. I learnt a lot about understeer!

Later my father's colleagues fitted a small petrol engine in my pedal car. It was a splendid idea and thrilled me but did tend to be a bit on the temperamental side. I suppose I was then aged about 12. Friends used to call in on the way home from school to have a demonstration. After much pushing, it would, if we were lucky, finally go and I would rocket off up the long back garden. Trouble was, once it was going it was reluctant to stop, or even slow down. Progress was generally terminated by something solid or rolling it. There would be much shaking of heads by the mother in attendance with her offspring as she hauled her little darling away with indecenthaste, never to be seen again. Clearly, I was dangerous company!

On one occasion I let a friend drive it – Christopher Guy was his name – around my parents' front drive. He was supposed to go round in circles but panicked and

149

drove straight into the front door of the house. Unfortunately, or perhaps fortunately, it was shut at the time.

In between other makes, my father had examples of XK120, 3.4 Mark 1 (he swore had been rescued from the factory fire!), Mark VIIM (for about three weeks), 3.4 Mark 2, Mark X and XJ6.

My hobby in my mid-teens was model car racing, otherwise known as slot racing or Scalextric. I used to build my own cars, constructing chassis, etc., and race them against grown-ups at clubs all over the country with some success. One particular event I recall was the National Junior Championships. With some tips from an experienced adult called 'Mac' Pinches, I found myself, to my amazement, in the final. I would become a very competitive person but, at this stage of my life, I was very content with fourth. To my even greater astonishment, I found myself in second place after three of the four races. The leading driver then changed the tyres on his car which was not allowed. However, his father had sought permission from the National Steward and he, without thinking, had given the OK. It was then suggested they should be refitted, but the father, who was no fool, said he had cut them off. The Steward took some awful stick because he was actually the Chairman of our club. However, I was more than pleased with second overall.

My first car was an Austin Healey Sprite Mark III. Friends thought I was crazy to take my test, a few weeks after my 17th birthday, in a sports car. However, I knew I had a reasonable chance of success when the examiner put his clipboard to one side, adjusted his sunglasses and began smiling at any young ladies in the vicinity.

When I left school, I went into accountancy but could not stand the pace. It was so slow and I was in a hurry. This was also the period when John Cleese was making merciless jokes about accountants. For example, a fellow stopped by an interviewer in the street, stated, 'I am a chartered accountant and consequently too boring to be of interest.' I owe him a great debt of gratitude. Though it had never been known before in this firm, I escaped from accountancy and, after studying business including accountancy, began working for my father's engineering company. I worked on every section on the shop floor before being sent out on the road, which I hated. Not happy to be simply the boss's son, I also started my own business concurrently.

After about a year an MG Midget had replaced the Sprite. Keen to get into competitions, I took this to Ralph Broad of Broadspeed, who was making a big name for himself preparing cars for saloon car racing. He did a superb job tuning it to half-race spec and I did some sprints and hill-climbs. I then went the whole hog and built up a full-race Sprite, with help from a young company called Aldon Automotive. With this I won about 12 events in 1970 and, when a new championship was planned for 1300cc sports racers, the brilliant Don Loughlin started to design a car for this. The plan was to use my engine and I would drive it for them. However, they moved premises and Alan and Don's small business was a bit stretched for a while. The project slowed down and I was not sure if it would ever happen. With the impetuosity of youth, I pulled out my small contribution. Some time later the car was completed and easily won the Championship.

How different life might have been! However, I sank my modest funds into a growing passion of mine and bought a couple of Jaguars XKs. I had fond, even if vague, memories of my father's 120. Like the gardening personality Prof Stefan Buczacki, I treasured my Dinky model of an XK120 and I was still reading *The Motor*, in which a young staff photographer would write from time to time about his aluminium-bodied XK120. His name was Paul Skilleter.

I bought an XK140 FHC, which was scruffy but on the road, for about £280 and an XK120 Roadster in need of total restoration for £400. I remember thinking that I had to have the 120 as it was probably the last example left that needed restoring and that I would ever be able to afford. This was 1972 and prices had already started to creep up.

There was no looking back. I was now hooked. The disease had taken a hold. The next year, 1973, was a particularly bad one for me. I acquired an XK140 Drop Head

In 1973 I acquired this rare right-hand drive XK140 Roadster from John Pearson. For many years it was the only one of my growing collection of rusty relics that was on the road and it gave me immense pleasure. Here I am going through the famous Esses at Shelsley Walsh hillclimb in the seventies.

Coupé for £340, an XK150 'S' FHC, a part-restored 120 Roadster for £800, a rare
RHD XK120 FHC for £150, a very rare RHD XK140 Roadster for £800 and the
21st RHD E-type Roadster for £350. I hasten to add that, with the exception of the
140 R, they were all in need of total restoration, though the 140 DHC and E-type
were just about on the road.

The 150 was being sold by a gentleman called Owen Wyn Owen, who is particularly known for digging up *Babs*, the World's Land Speed Record car, from Pendine
Sands where it had been buried after a drive chain beheaded its unfortunate driver
Parry Thomas. Owen Wyn Owen completed the restoration some years ago, but it
was in his workshop in 'as found' state when I visited in '73. He had advertised the
XK150 for £225. I drove up to North Wales and viewed it. A few days later I telephoned him and I well remember the conversation.

'I am very interested,' I said, 'but I wondered if you would take an offer?'

'Ooh, I don't know about that,' he replied in his broad Welsh accent.

'What had you in mind?'

'I was thinking of the round two hundred,' I ventured.

'Ooooh no, I couldn't possibly accept that. I might knock the five pounds off as
you had a long way to come.'

I later discovered that the car had been owned by Jack Fairman.

Furthermore, many years later, when I was preparing to interview Jack who was
coming up to stay for the weekend, I looked up in *Autosport* a famous article entitled 'The Sound and The Fury' by Chris Nixon, recounting his experience of being
driven around on the road for a weekend in the works Aston Martin DBR1 sports
racer by Fairman. During the article, they mention going to collect Jack's XK150.
But can you guess what car was on the front cover, the subject of the preceding article and featured extensively? Answer – 9600 HP!

A few years later Jack Fairman would replace the XK150 with the E-type. With
my owning both cars, at a much later date, it was a coincidence upon coincidence
upon coincidence!

The XK140 Roadster I bought from John Pearson, who has become a great friend.
As recounted earlier, he used to skive off school and walk up to Silverstone to watch
his Jaguar heroes testing. Some years later he would ride in 9600 HP with Jack.
Another coincidence.

The 120 FHC, I discovered, was the third RHD example and the earliest one sold
by Jaguar. It was rallied by Jack Hallay. By this stage I had joined the Jaguar Drivers'
Club (JDC) and had seen it advertised in the *XK Bulletin*, which had first been edited by Paul Skilleter and was then being edited by Jeremy Broad. I was the first of 17
people to phone up about it that night. I said I would have it, but the kindly gentleman insisted I must view it before deciding. At that time, I had a small flat in
Birmingham but was keen to move to the country. I could not afford Warwickshire,
a county in which I knew most of the country pubs intimately. The exceedingly grot-
ty XK was in a delightful part of west Worcestershire in a shed behind a defunct tiny

filling station. I confirmed that I would like to become the owner of this sad relic and asked if the vendor happened to know of any cottages for sale locally. He did and I bought a derelict cottage at auction a few days later. As it was not too far from Shelsley Walsh Hill-climb, another passion from childhood, and was on an incline, I named it Hill Climb Cottage! I was to learn a lot about building in the next five years.

Incidentally, I had seen my first E-type at Shelsley, back in 1961. It was a red Roadster driven by the Leicestershire Jaguar distributor Robin Sturgess.

I had gone beserk buying everything I could possibly afford because I could see that, with rising values, they were all going to be out of reach soon. I was aware that I had ahead of me a lifetime's worth of restoration but, although expensive and lengthy, full restoration is the only sure way of knowing the true condition of the car. Irrespective of that, I had no choice as I could not afford anything else. My one regret is that I was not a little older, as then I might have been able to afford a C-type or a D-type! Older cars were already becoming eagerly sought after and one had to move fast. My *modus operandi* was to get up on Thursdays at 5.30am, when the local newsagent was just opening his shop, purchase a copy of *Exchange & Mart*, in which such treasures lurked, and immediately phone up people.

They were not always too pleased to be woken by some nutter in the early hours of a Thursday morning and, in their sleepy state, were not even sure if they owned an XK. With some gentle prompting, they recalled that perhaps they did have such a car and, after a few salient questions, which they struggled through, I announced that I was on my way. In this manner, I beat everyone else to it and acquired some bargains.

My parents, though, were not amused by these strange antics. Why couldn't I be normal, like everyone else? My mother had been steadfastly against my racing, and my father didn't approve of me wasting my money on these funny old heaps of rusty junk. I was particularly hurt when I very proudly drove up to their house in the newly acquired 140 R and offered him a run round the block. A very jolly lady, who lived next door at that time, was enthusing about the car, which did not please my father. He declined.

The XK Register used to have monthly meetings at pubs around the country. The Midland Area, which had been organised by Jeremy Broad at one of my favourite pubs, The Winged Spur at Ullenhall, had fizzled out a few years previously. I revived the meetings at an establishment near Warwick and made a number of lasting friendships. One of those whom I had recently got to know, and who would become one of my closest friends, was a chap called Steve Gilhooly but always simply known as 'Gil'.

Also in 1973, another great friendship began. Nick Baldwin would later have a considerable influence on the direction my life took and has much to be blamed for. Nick was then working for *Autocar*.

A chap by the name of Peter Spackman had floated the idea of an E-type Register, a section of the JDC to be devoted specifically to this model. Being busy with business, he had not had time to get it off the ground. Paul Skilleter was then editing the

Jaguar Driver magazine and had asked for volunteers to take over the embryonic E-type Register and get things going. I was young, foolish and keen. I wrote to him. I formed one of those ghastly things called a committee, roped in Gil and several others, and we organized the first International E-type Day at the newly opened museum at Donington Park in 1974. I had put a particular effort into persuading as many owners as possible of historic Jaguars to attend. Nigel Dawes responded with his C-type and D-type, Sir Anthony Bamford provided a Lightweight E and an XKSS and, among the line-up, was the first RHD production Fixed Head E-type.

I had another bad year in '74 and acquired a very rare Austin Seven van, a Seven Opal, a Chevron B8, the Chevron B16 Spyder (which I swapped for a Hewland gearbox), a Mirage GT40 bodyshell, sold my first 120 R and met Jeremy Wade. Destined to become another great pal, he had been offered my 140 R when he spotted it at a filling station while on a bicycle ride from school in the late 1960s. The price was £150 and he has been kicking himself ever since. When, some time later, a photo of the car was featured in an article on XKs by Bill Boddy in *Mayfair* magazine, I went into a newsagents and proudly bought four copies. I received some very strange looks!

Around this time, Nick Baldwin left *Autocar* and became Editor of a splendid magazine called *Old Motor* which was published by Prince Marshall. Though they tended to specialize in pre-war subjects, they decided they would like an article on Jaguar XKs. Nick contacted me and asked me to write it. As a result, I went and interviewed Wally Hassan in April 1975. A charming gentleman, he put me at my ease and we had a delightful evening. During this period, still young and naïve, I decided to form a small restoration company and one of the first jobs was making some wings for Nick's 1912 Caledon lorry which he was restoring. The subsequent London to Brighton Commercial Run was a splendid adventure. A month later, in June, Gil and I were returning from Shelsley Walsh in his 4.2 E-type when Gil ran out of opposite lock, the long nose glanced the verge and it just flipped over. Luckily it was a Fixed Head and we were fine but the car was not. However, we did manage to *just* miss the sign marking the first motoring fatality in Britain. The cruel irony is that poor Gil had purchased an ancient 2CV van for regular transport and was going to take the E-type off the road, for a while, the very next day.

Eleven days later Paul Skilleter came up to photograph the XK140 R and the Austin Seven Opal, which I had brush-painted a bright red the night before at his request, for the front cover of *Classic Cars* magazine. He brought with him his then-colleague Jonathan Wood. A month later I was in the paddock at Shelsley where the MAC Secretary, Steve Perry, introduced me to the local policeman. He rejoiced in the wonderful nickname of 'Phil the Fuzz'. As I was to find, he was no conventional policeman, but he was universally liked and respected, a proper and very effective village 'bobby', sadly now retired.

'Welcome to the area,' he said. 'Anything you want to know, just ask me.'

'Could you please tell me where the late-drinking pubs are,' I said, trying to be funny.

'Dear, oh dear,' he replied, 'I couldn't answer a question like that. I go to The Lion. See you in there.'

Over the next few years we had some tremendous fun and escapades, most of which are totally unprintable. On one occasion there were three of us left in The Lion at around one in the morning. Phil walked in in uniform and said, in his sternest voice, 'Right, nobody moves.' Dramatic pause. 'I'm buying a round.' Another time we were in there in the early hours and there was a meeting at Shelsley that coming weekend. The night before a refreshment caravan had been broken into and Phil needed to go and check it. He asked me to drive him. I had my 140 R with me, in which I happened to be competing at the event. We drove down to the hill-climb and Phil told me to stop on the startline. He took hold of his stopwatch and shouted, 'Go!'

I shot up the hill and, as we approached the caravan at the first of the Esses, enquired as to whether he would wish me to stop. 'No, you b———, keep going.' We completed the course, checked the caravan and retired to another hostelry to check all was well. We left at four.

The next night, we did a precise re-run, except that we left at five!

One bank holiday that year saw Nick Baldwin, John Smith and myself at the Transport Extravaganza at Crich Tramway Museum in Derbyshire. Behind one of the flea market stalls was a large ancient chassis on wooden spoke wheels and solid tyres. Nobody could identify it, except Nick. It was a 1912 lorry called a Yorkshire. The three of us purchased it and Baldwin published a photo in the next edition of *Old Motor* with a caption stating it had been 'bought by a syndicate of Warwickshire collectors'. We paid £25 for it! Some years later, John announced that he felt, on balance, he could probably pass the rest of his life without his one-third share in these remains and, if we bought him another pint, we could have his share.

The collection of disparate motor vehicles was growing, but suddenly things took a dramatic turn. On Monday 28 February 1977, Paul Skilleter telephoned to say that someone he knew of was thinking of selling his collection of four E-types, which included the first 'E', but he wanted to sell them as a job-lot rather than individually. More than fascinated, I was instantly hooked. But there was a problem. I could not afford the total, which amounted to £8250. My only hope was my father. I had always been very ambitious and my father was fed up with me forever going to him with business ideas and bargain cars. He was not amused by my collecting habit, even though he had been quite keen on cars himself.

I could not see him that Monday because I had a very full day planned. My new, high-powered and very attractive secretary started that day. At 12.00 we had a meeting with the late Graig Hinton at the Bradford Arms on the A5 to discuss a forthcoming auction we were jointly organizing. On the way back down the M6 motorway I was in a hurry. We were in my ageing DBS-V8 Aston which, as we were in the middle of the first of the world's fuel crises, I had acquired for a ridiculously modest sum. We touched 130mph a couple of times. That evening, I gently turned right off

By 1976 the twelfth roadster, though complete, was in pretty poor condition. When I purchased it from Brant in 1977, I was aware that it was an early car and was delighted to later learn that it had been successfully raced by Robin Sturgess in 1961. I did not discover two further facts of great interest until much later.

the main Hagley Road in Birmingham on to a side road and thought for a nano-second I had hit an enormous pothole. The steering had fallen apart on the nearside and, at 20mph, I mounted the pavement, smote and came to rest upon a tall steel pole. I had demolished and parked on top of a 'No Waiting' sign!

On the Tuesday I saw my father at his office and, to my amazement, he did not dismiss out-of-hand the subject of the E-types.

Paul did his bit to try and help. My father was likely to be far more impressed if someone else argued the case rather than his impetuous son. I used to often tell him that old cars were going to be worth a lot of money in the future and were, therefore, a first-class investment. That was not my motivation in collecting, but I thought it would appeal to the businessman in him and please him that I wasn't wasting my money. He was never impressed. But one day he came back from lunch with one of his garage-owning friends and said, 'Graham says those old XKs are going to be worth a lot more in the future.' Ahhhhhh!

Vintage Bentleys led the way in those days and were already showing a hefty appreciation. I remember trying to persuade my father to buy one for £250! So Paul wrote a short report stating that, in his opinion, these E-types were the vintage Bentleys of tomorrow. For my benefit, because I wasn't a complete fool, he also wrote the following report on 9600 HP.

Notes on 885002, 9600 HP

- Body number V1002 (i.e. second fhc body built). Original engine number 1009–9 (might be 1019) but factory note which says car was sold with engine number E5020–9. Present engine is R1019-9, which given that I took the first engine no. mentioned down wrongly from AJAW [the late Andrew Whyte, then heading up the Press Office, having succeeded Bob Berry, and later a highly distinguished Jaguar author], indicates that the car still has its original engine. Or that a coincidentally close engine was later fitted (log book is altered to read R1019 but no Local Authority stamp which may mean engine change was made before the car was actually licensed.
- First registered 10th Feb 1961 (month before car was officially announced).
- Colour: opalescent gunmetal with black trim.
- Period with Experimental Dept. under Heynes, where given appellation 'Car No. 7'.
- Almost certainly driven out to Geneva by Bob Berry, where it was used as the demonstrator. Used as road test car by 'Autocar', 'Autosport' etc., and in many publicity photographs in dailies etc.
- Sold to John Coombs first week in May 1962.
- Fitted with modified engine for 153mph road test maximum – see D-type breathing arrangement on cam covers!!
- Three owners subsequent to Coombs, whose name did not appear in the logbook.
- When car was converted to rhd is unknown, but very likely Coombs did it before retailing the car in 1962. Certainly road tested while in factory ownership in lhd form.
- Car as owned by Derek Brandt [sic] is genuine I believe because of the following points:
  - It has the original logbook
  - It has an engine with numbers that appear to tie in with the documentation (logbook & factory records)
  - It has the unusual black, heavily-engrained trim as shown in pictures of 9600 HP on test in 1961
  - It has Perspex luggage door and rear quarterlight windows; this is not mentioned in contemporary literature (neither was the 'D'? engine!), but merely points strongly to the fact that the car was in Experimental for some time. Plus the luggage lid itself is made in aluminium – a unique feature.
- The car is not, however, the vehicle actually displayed inside the exhibition hall at Geneva – this is believed to have been 885005, later sold via a Geneva dealer. Proof of this is that pictures of the show stand car indicate it had light coloured upholstery, not the black of 9600 HP.
- Also, when photographed at Geneva during the show, 9600 HP lacked front over-riders and bonnet mouth medallion strip; show stand car had both.
- Whilst I do not think it invalidates any of the above points, I could not locate a chassis number stamp on the front subframe of 9600 HP, and as the boot well area which includes the number plate face is missing, having been replaced by a new unit, I couldn't check the body number tag. The chassis date plate is still fixed to the offside sill, however, and looks suitably decayed.

I was at an Association of Engineering Distributors seminar, which sounds truly thrilling, on the Wednesday but saw my father again on the Thursday. To my considerable surprise, but total joy, he was receptive. To his great credit, he had the imagination to see what important cars these were and what an opportunity it was. Perhaps there was a slight chink in his armour. Perhaps for once he allowed his heart to rule his head. I shall always be immensely grateful to him, for without him none of this would have been possible and I would certainly not be writing this book.

To remind you, the four cars consisted of the first RHD Fixed Head which initially, I seem to recall, appealed to me most as I thought it must be the most important of the quartet; 9600 HP, about which we knew little in those days; the twelfth Roadster, about which we knew nothing other than that it was an early car, and a later white 3.8 Roadster. I think the FHC was in theory on the road, but 9600 HP was definitely not. The later Roadster had been restored by Derek and the twelfth open car was very rough and in need of total renovation. My father agreed to help me on the strict understanding that the running Roadster be sold. Though it would have been nice to have kept it, this was not an historic car and so I was more than happy to agree with his terms.

That Friday evening, I left Birmingham at 8.45pm and arrived at Paul and June Skilleter's house in Enfield at 10.30. Next morning I drove with Paul and June in their Mark 2 Jaguar to Farnham, where Paul was to photograph a couple of cars outside a pleasant house in the town for the cover of Jonathan Wood's first book. After lunch and drinks at The Donkey, we called on Paul's uncle and aunt. We did not stay long for we had an important appointment. 'Derek Brant – 3.00,' reads my diary. 'Tried 3.8 Roadster (White) – viewed 1st FHC & 12th Roadster. Pd him cheque for £5200. Paul picked up baby Fiat, I drove Mark 2 back to Enfield.' The ultimate irony is that I think I must have bought 9600 HP without even seeing it!

None of us remembers much about this eventful day! Obviously we had agreed that I would pay the balance outstanding at a future date. Next day Paul and I worked on his early aluminium-bodied XK120 R, LXK 48, which had helped to fire my enthusiasm when I had read about it in *Motor*. It had not been on the road for ages, but we tow-started it and went for a run.

Having raced it on occasions in the past, Paul decided he wouldn't be using it in 1977 and very generously lent it to me for a season. I had some fantastic journeys in this very quick, highly modified car and did a few hill-climbs, winning at Castle Howard.

Back to work with a vengeance, I had a very full day of meetings, including lunch with Jeremy Broad. I was then running our engineering supplies business, but the economy was in recession and so my job mainly consisted of ruthlessly operating credit control to ensure we got paid before firms went bust, the trauma of making nice people redundant and fighting industrial tribunals. It was not a pleasant time. Two years previously, when I was Financial Director, one of our reps had come to me and told me the Managing Director and Sales Director were planning to set up in opposition. In the second half of that year, we turned the company round from a loss-making situation into a profit by the year end. But it was not an easy business and my heart was not really in it.

On the Wednesday I phoned Derek Brant and the same day I insured the white Roadster. Next day I attended an auction at Alexandra Palace and the diary says 'Collect E-types' but it is not specific. The white Roadster, ANB 800B must have been one of them because my girlfriend and I took it to Silverstone for a JDC meeting that Saturday. We met up with Paul and June, who were staying with us for the weekend, but it was not a very happy journey back for Paul in LXK – 'slow puncture, exhaust dropped, total brake failure on way back,' according to my diary.

On Monday I arose at 6.30am, departed at 6.45 and arrived at Derek Brant's in Surrey at 8.15 to collect Number One. I didn't dally for I had, as usual, a long day ahead of me at the office in Birmingham. That Saturday I went up to The Lion in the white Roadster and bumped into a friend called John Thomas. I casually mentioned I was selling the car and he said he had always wanted one. To my astonishment, he said he would buy it off me. The following Monday I telephoned Andrew Whyte and asked him to look up number 12 in the chassis records. A couple of weeks later I was delighted to receive a note from him saying it had been raced by Robin Sturgess in 1961. This was, therefore, the very first E-type I ever saw. Another coincidence.

Three days later I did a 20-hour day and some 600 miles. Needing to eat, and interested in the concept from a business standpoint, I sampled one of the first UK McDonald's, which was adjacent to Charing Cross Station. My diary records my thoughts in one, succinct word. 'Rotten'. In late April, I sent Derek another cheque and in early May a young man from Ford Credit called at our company. Our accountants had advised it would be tax efficient to purchase our company cars on HP. His name was Steve Barratt and he would later start a parts business specializing in E-type spares and would supply most of the parts for 9600 HP.

On 21 July Derek Brant wrote to me about various matters and closed by gently reminding me I still had one car to collect. Accordingly, on August 17th I made another foray down to London and met him between 2.00 and 3.30.

My diary notes, 'Key – down alley – rear entrance to garage under flowerpot. Key through letterbox – 73 V———.'

Meanwhile in July Paul had joined our small restoration company to look after marketing and help run it, as I was very stretched. Together with an E-type spares specialist in Yorkshire, we also formed another company to concentrate on E-types. I had what, to me, was an hilarious experience that month when I went down to London to collect a customer's XK140 R for restoration. He had a steep drive in front of his house in a suburban part of London and I parked my tow vehicle and trailer across the road so that we could push the car straight on to it. There was some urgency as I was totally blocking the road. The car was in a sad state but he assured me the handbrake worked. I was on the driver's side, he on the passenger's side, as we eased it out of the garage to the top of his very steep drive and the point of no return. I was steering. As it inevitably gained momentum, I leant over and applied

When photographer Tim Andrew visited my place in the early eighties in connection with a book we were working on together, he took this stunning shot for his own interest and had ideas of producing a poster. The shot shows, from the foreground rearwards, 9600 HP, XK120 Roadster, XK120 Fixed Head Coupé and XK150 'S' FHC.

the handbrake. As you will have guessed, it made not a jot of difference to our progress, which was becoming alarming. I was faced with the prospect of mounting the trailer, going clean over the front end and ramming my car. Decisive action was needed. I turned left into his garden wall. It stopped the car, but at some cost to the wall, which fell into the pavement.

At this stage it became even more embarrassing because I found the whole episode agonizingly funny and was bent double. To my surprise he was also suffering convulsions but I noticed he was trying, with great difficulty, to speak. Finally, amid gales of laughter, he managed to gradually stutter out, 'Thank – you – I – I – never – did – like – that – wall – thank – you!'

Towards the end of the year I was invited to join the XK Register committee and took over the editing of the *XK Bulletin*, which was fun and good experience. At that time the *Old Motor* team of Prince Marshall, my great pal Nick Baldwin and designer Brian Harris were publishing books on rather rarefied subjects and, deciding to try something more mainstream, commissioned me to write a history of Jaguar.

During this period I had to store the cars in various rented barns and workshops, which was far from ideal. It became something of a joke amongst my friends that all I ever did with the cars was move them from barn to barn. Not content with the problems I already owned, I had continued to add to what I used to refer to as 'the world's largest collection of rust'! Meanwhile I had been restoring Hill Climb Cottage and learning the hard way about various building techniques, unreliable so-called professionals, architects, building inspectors (one was called Crippin) and planning officers. Of the five years I owned the place, it was habitable, after many hours of hard toil, for the last 18 months of that period.

On 14 January 1978, I viewed an old Tudor farmhouse with lots of barns. I looked at the barns first and, literally, said to my then girlfriend, 'The barns are OK, now what's the house like?' It was very run down but I thought the whole place was potentially terrific. After many tortuous delays obtaining a mortgage which was not easy on such a property in those days, I finally completed the purchase in April. Everyone thought I was mad.

Once again, I happened to be ahead of what would become a trend. I used to meet people locally who said, 'My God, you've bought that. We looked at it but we weren't that brave.' They meant insane. But I always say that, with such projects, you should go into them with your eyes well and truly – shut!

At last I could have all the cars, including 9600 HP, in one place, although the big Dutch barn was then completely open-fronted. One just did not think about security. Anyone driving or walking past could just look in at everything. Actually, it looked like the local scrapyard. Also the weather could get in, which was not good, but everything had to be a long-term plan and could only progress as I could afford it. The irony was that I fell in love with the house to such an extent that, for the next 12 years, I devoted all my time, energy and meagre funds to restoring the house and two cottages, and made no progress with the cars. No one believed I would ever do anything to the poor old cars, including 9600 HP, which looked sadder and sadder as the grime built up.

Around this time, Paul went back into writing and photography full-time. He had learnt a lot from the experience and would later start a very successful magazine called *Practical Classics* and still later enlisted one of our employees to edit it for him. The E-type company had moved up to Yorkshire and around that time my co-director was approached by some rather unsavoury characters who offered him some E-type parts of questionable background. I think we nicknamed them 'The Krays'. We contacted the security people at Unipart, the Jaguar parts distributors, and, allegedly, there was something naughty happening at quite a senior level. In true cloak and dagger fashion, we set up a 'sting' at my offices and later received a letter of thanks from the Unipart Chief Executive.

In March 1980 a Mrs Challoner called at the farm to view 9600 HP. She was from the motor taxation office and I think this was the time when we all had to re-register our old cars. Presumably she was satisfied, as new registration documents duly came through. Around this period I had vague, and ambitious, ideas of trying to complete No. 1 and 9600 HP in time for Geneva the following year, which would have been the 20th anniversary. I spoke to Jaguar about working together on this but nothing came of it.

I had always wanted to meet Jack Fairman, for obvious reasons, but no one seemed to know his whereabouts. Then he surfaced and I met him at Silverstone in June 1980. He was amazed to hear I had two of his former cars.

Unfortunately every motoring club seems to suffer politics and petty jealousies and suchlike. The JDC was no exception and was about to enter a decade or so of utter turmoil. Alternately, I was either vilified or lauded, depending on who had grabbed the reins of power during this period. In May 1981 I was voted Chairman of the XK Register and the Board of the JDC immediately brought in a rule banning any person with a connection with the trade from holding any office. It virtually wiped out the XK committee and a few others! I remember writing to the then Chairman and saying that it reminded me of Voltaire's satirical comment when Admiral Byng was shot for disobeying suicidal orders: 'In this country it is done to shoot an admiral from time to time to encourage the others.'

In 1981 I sold the engineering business, retaining the property, and decided to concentrate on writing and other pursuits. We opened a small dinner party restaurant in an old hop kiln at home and continued to work on the house. Following the sad and very premature death of Prince Marshall, the little publishing business was taken over by Frederick Warne, who were famous for publishing Beatrix Potter. They were

My first book had been published in 1984 and I was particularly proud to have had a foreword by the man who made Jaguar, Sir William Lyons. His was a remarkable career, combining pre-eminent styling ability with a shrewd head for business. From humble beginnings, he grew an empire which would eventually encompass such august names as Daimler, Coventry Climax, Guy and Meadows.

not sure if they wanted a Jaguar book, but finally decided they did. I progressed again and after a while they sold out to Penguin, who bought Warnes for Potter but got Porter thrown in, which must have reduced the price a bit. Now Penguin were not sure if they wanted a Jaguar book or not. Finally, they decided they did, I completed it, *Jaguar – The Complete Illustrated History* was eventually published in 1984, and Penguin immediately sold their motoring titles to Haynes. I had now written just one book but could boast of four publishers! After several new editions and many reprints, I am pleased to say it is still in print today.

I had closed down the one restoration business some time before and we would eventually close the E-type one down as well. In about eight years, we had worked on around 100 E-types, of which most were full restorations. My co-director developed other interests and it was not easy for me to have any influence being 100 miles away.

Meanwhile in 1983 the JDC AGM had witnessed much excitement. Jaguar were most unhappy with several persons in positions of power. They asked about five people, including myself, to attend. We had been armed with questions and it had been discovered that the constitution allowed Sir William Lyons, as President, to chair the meeting. He appointed 'Lofty' England, who came over from his retirement home in Austria, to deputize for him. 'Lofty' was magnificent and made mincemeat of the minnows. It ran something like, 'Mr Porter? You had a question you wished to ask?'

'But he can't ask anything without giving 21 days' notice.'

'Oh yes, I think he can. Go ahead Mr Porter.' Following the question,

'Good point, Mr Porter. Is there anything else you wish to add?'

'Bbbut...'

'Will you be quiet, please, or I will have you removed.' 'Lofty' involved not just me but each of the Gang of Five, as I nicknamed us. He was brilliant and it descended, at times, into pure farce. Unless I am much mistaken, the entire Board was suspended.

When Jaguar was privatized in 1984, the rush for shares was covered on the BBC *Nine O'Clock News*. Some archive footage was shown of Jaguar's past, including film of 9600 HP. Unfortunately, I have never been able to trace that footage.

During 1985 I briefly edited the *Jaguar Driver* magazine for the JDC, until I was sacked. I think I was one of five Editors that year. It was an extraordinary situation. Though Editor I was not allowed to see the proofs and control the content. After my fall from grace, I was a non-person. If anyone mentioned my name in the magazine, it was taken out before going to press. Tony Dudmesh, who contributed the E-type pages, found a novel way of getting around this. He called me Paul Philter! There was a great deal of unpleasantness around that time and even 'Lofty' could not defeat great blocks of proxies. It upset him greatly. Paul Skilleter and I were asking too many awkward questions and we were both expelled from the Club. Some time later, the police became involved and many years later very large sums of money had to be repaid to the Club by a former official.

In 1986 I was commissioned by Haynes to write a book on the forthcoming XJ40. I discussed with the Jaguar PR department the matter of a Foreword. Sir William had done me the honour of writing one for my first book and John Egan had written an Afterword. Jaguar offered to help and suggested a variety of people, including Prince Charles. My publishers thought he would be ideal and I communicated this to Jaguar. As with all these things, we had a deadline. After a few weeks, it was becoming urgent and Haynes were chasing me. Of course, as usual, Jaguar failed to reply to my letters and did not return calls. Finally, when we were desperate, I phoned five times one day and finally got through to the guy in charge. 'Ah yes,' he said. 'We decided it wouldn't be appropriate after all.'

'Right,' I said, 'I am going to try the Prime Minister, Mrs Thatcher.'

'Oh,' said a worried voice. 'Well, we can't help you there.' He was obviously uncomfortable. 'Please don't tell anyone if she says "No".'

I immediately sought the advice of Sir Pat Whitehouse, a Vice-Chairman of the Conservative Party, and my old friend Sir Sydney Chapman, who was a Government Whip. Sydney dropped her a note and within days we had a superb foreword from one of my great heroes.

I was enjoying the writing, but it was not a good way of creating the necessary funds to restore a certain collection of cars and it was extremely time-consuming. In 1988 I wrote the pilot for a new series of books and this was entitled Original Jaguar XK. Admittedly the publisher decided to double my royalty and so I did end up getting 20p per copy. Ever the glutton for more punishment, I foolishly suggested to Haynes that they might like a definitive history of the E-type. They would. 'How many words will it be?' I had no idea and hesitated.

'Well, a definitive history will have to be 100,000 to 150,000 words,' I was told.

'How on earth,' I thought to myself, 'could I possibly write that many about one car?' I started my research and began interviewing people all over the country and spent a frenetic two weeks dashing round the USA. Some nine months later I began to commit digit to keyboard and spent a similar length of time writing, on average 14 hours a day, seven days a week, and finally completed my magnum opus. The total number of words? A mere 300,000! But there was a benefit that I had not bargained for. In doing my research I learnt a great deal more about the early life of 9600 HP. I learnt that it was a prototype and the fate of the others which made it the oldest surviving example. Just in time, I interviewed people like Maurice Smith, who did the famous road test, and so on.

Meanwhile I had become involved in flying hot air balloons. I could not have had two better mentors, because Ian Bridge, for whom I had navigated in the World Championships in the USA in '85 as we finished eighth out of 100, and David Bareford, who taught me to fly, were the two top British balloon pilots. I was very lucky to find a first-class sponsor, Vax, and we had a superb relationship for ten years. In 1990 I persuaded Vax that we should aquire a hot air airship to supplement the balloon and did a deal whereby we were the factory team entry for competitions, representing the manufacturers, Thunder & Colt, a company then run by Per Lindstrand.

I learnt to fly hot air airships while acting as co-pilot to the designer, Mats Backlin, during the first European Hot Air Airship Championships which we, or more fairly, he won. I had many adventures in the airship and was retained as their Test Pilot by Thunder & Colt. I was the first person ever to fly an airship in South Africa and loved the cut and thrust of the competitions, which were pretty hairy. Vax put me on a very good retainer and we gave each other 110 per cent. By pursuing my ongoing motoring journalism for magazines like *Classic & Sports Car* and by continuing to work myself into the ground, I could now afford to make some progress with the cars. Also, with a unique touch of sanity, I had sold a few, which helped to fund the restoration of others.

We decided to begin with the twelfth Roadster. A few years before, I had telephoned the original owner, Robin Sturgess, and he said that he had been watching the film *The Italian Job* on TV a few days before. Did I realize that it was my car in the film? I did not.

He had raced the car with his registration 2 BBC, but changed that to 848 CRY when he sold it. At the next opportunity, I watched the film and he was absolutely correct.

In 1990 I visited a company called Vicarage, who had become famous for restoring and enhancing Mark 2 saloons, to write a piece about their new high-performance E-type for *Classic & Sports Car*. I met, and was very impressed by, their chief engineer, Andrew Tart. Meanwhile the Roadster bodyshell had gone off to E-type specialist Martin Robey to be rebuilt. At home, I was employing somebody on a casual, temporary basis before he went off to work in the States. Andrew was disenchanted with Vicarage and asked me if I would employ him as well. I couldn't possibly afford to do so and he suggested we start a small restoration company in one of my barns. 'No way,' was my immediate response, knowing what dreadfully difficult businesses they are to run.

Over the next few months we talked and I was persuaded. Andrew is a very clever guy and we got on extremely well. We spent a year creating a super workshop and, with our first customer lined up, we opened Feline Motor Works for business. The idea was to keep it very small, which I think is very important, and to specialize, which is vital. I sent out a press release to the effect that a certain Jaguar author and a pre-eminent Jaguar engineer had joined forces and *Classic Car* magazine ran a snippet. A very successful businessman by the name of Peter Neumark read it and contacted us. He wanted to buy an XK150 and have it restored. He found a car and gave us the job. This was to be a most significant meeting for us all.

Let down by an XK bodyshop, which much more recently has gone bankrupt, we decided we needed a panel beater and employed Peter Stant. To provide help on the management side, as I was still involved in many other things, Nick Goldthorp, the founder of Vicarage, joined us part-time. For 18 months all went very well. Every customer was satisfied, bar none, which is unique for this sort of business, but we had a fantastic team. However, unfortunately Andrew was not happy. He wanted to expand and I did not. So Peter Neumark set up Andrew and Nick as Classic Motor Cars and, with his backing, they have gone from strength to strength. Peter Stant remained with me and completed the oldest known Austin Seven Swallow Two-Seater for Jaguar Cars, who owned it. Stant was not an average panel beater, and used to spend his lunch hour reading Stephen Hawking. But sadly the work dried up. We advertised but it was money down the drain. I felt it was so ironic that so many rogues had plenty of business and here was a totally honest, very capable little set-up with none. Before the bank balance became too depleted, I had to let Peter go, which really upset me, but he found a good job and we are still friends.

Before he left, Andrew had completed the restoration of the *Italian Job* E-type and Nick Baldwin and I had joined 100 Minis for a trek to Italy a day after it was finished. The car went superbly and continues to be a great delight. Later, it was filmed extensively by *Top Gear* and presenter Quentin Willson, who has owned rather more than his fair share of E-types, described it as the best he had ever driven. The car was later featured in *The Car's the Star* but was not improved when one of the crew had the misfortune to drive into the back of it and did £12,000 worth of damage. The behaviour of the BBC was quite extraordinary and would make a brilliant edition of one of their own consumers' rights programmes.

In 1991 Jaguar Cars issued a press pack to celebrate the 30th anniversary of the E-type. They included a reprint of the original *Autocar* test, but this time it was complete with its original shots of 9600 HP.

In July, the same year, a well-known, larger restoration company telephoned me and said they would restore the car at an attractive price for the publicity. The chap stated that they normally charged £16,100 to rebuild the body and £4000/4600 for painting the shell, both plus VAT. They would do this work at cost, which was £15,000. I was not overly keen on this company but asked them, as a matter of course, to kindly put it in writing. Of course, I never heard another word. Subsequently, they have been slated by several of their customers and I saw an example of their appalling workmanship, so that was a narrow escape.

At some stage I was also contacted by a firm of trimmers who said that, as and when the car was restored, they would be pleased to trim it free of charge. Again, I asked them to kindly put it in writing and, again, I heard nothing more.

Also in 1991 9600 HP appeared in the *Daily Mail*'s colour supplement called *You* magazine. It was a profile of some fellow and the journalist painted a picture of a very strange eccentric. This was the price of achieving publicity for my sponsors, who were ecstatic, as the airship, emblazoned with their name, adorned a complete colour spread. On another page was a photograph of 9600 HP. Inevitably I had been asked what it was worth and, while saying I had no idea, mentioned that at the height of the silly prices of the late eighties I had been offered £100,000. I was quoted as saying the car was 'worth hundreds of thousands'. Ugh! The feature was appropriately entitled, 'An Open and Shut Basket Case'. I am not sure whether that was a reference to the car or its owner, but fear it was the latter!

On 27 October 1992 Channel 4 showed an arts programme devoted to the E-type. It was one in a series entitled *Without Walls*, and this edition was called *The Story of E*. The director Matthew Whiteman, who drives an E-type, was besotted with 9600 HP and featured the car extensively. He visited us in Worcestershire and brought with him a spider in a matchbox to film it walking across the dusty bonnet – very arty! Jonathan Glancey talked of the car and said, '9600 HP is probably the most famous E-type of all. The reason for that is this was the car that Jaguar used to get its maximum speed test runs. It took the car out to a Belgium motorway and shot it along at a genuine 150mph, and it was that speed that captured the public imagination, and that of the motoring press. But something that nobody knew at the time – well, the press knew but they weren't letting on – was the fact that 9600 HP had been specially doctored and lightened to get to that top speed. The production cars wouldn't quite do it. But Jaguar was learning more than a few things about publicity at the time. In fact, it would use the car for almost any purposes to get a publicity shot.'

The programme then cut into the *Pathé News* sequence with Stirling Moss and

The things one does for publicity for one's sponsors! Flying hot air airships led on from piloting balloons and apparently I was the first person ever to fly an airship of any sort in South Africa. The various World and European Airship Championships in which I competed were tremendously challenging and, at times, pretty hairy. One of the delights of the Sherlock Holmes Society is that it is a complete contrast from cars. Eccentric? Not in the least.

London's first automatic 'car laundry', and the programme closed with a static shot of the car and the inscription, '9600 HP is scheduled for restoration in Autumn 1993'!

Subsequently, Bob Berry would tell me that the car wash appearance would not have been organized by Jaguar. 'Sir William hated stunts. We never did anything like that.'

The Daily Telegraph chose *Without Walls* as one of the programmes to highlight on the day it was broadcast and even mentioned that 9600 HP would be appearing.

Since 1993 I have been writing on a professional basis for the JDC, as many of the unpleasant element have gone and Tony Dudmesh, he of the Paul Philter, is now the Editor. I just write my column and keep my head down.

In 1994 I spotted a very beautiful lady at a Jerome K. Jerome Society gathering. She was laughing a great deal and I thought, 'That's the lady for me.' Fate was on my side for she was single and, what was really remarkable when we subsequently met, she seemed to like me. Almost as remarkable, Julie had always taken an interest in cars and had owned an MG Midget. Variously an actress, theatre director and globe-trotting management consultant, she spotted the potential to have a tiny theatre in the old barn, which really explains her interest in me. We married in 1995.

There have been several articles in *Autocar* about 9600 HP, written either by Maurice Smith or myself, to commemorate various anniversaries. The old girl has also appeared on a number of occasions in *The Daily Telegraph*. In the *Weekend Telegraph* of 2 March 1991 under the headline 'E-type Deserved the Hype', the scene was set with the following introduction: 'In a remote barn in Worcestershire, John Langley reunites with an old friend in retirement'.

'Slumbering peacefully under its dust sheet in the barn of a Tudor farmhouse deep in the English countryside,' wrote Langley, 'rests a lithe gunmetal grey car that shook the motoring world at the Geneva Motor Show 30 years ago.' He went on to say that that year's show would have plenty of outstanding new models. 'But none of them can hope to match the impact created in 1961 by 9600 HP, the original E-type Jaguar. It was, in the words of Bob Berry, who drove it through the night to Geneva, "probably the most charismatic car that has ever been produced. I think possibly it will go down in history as a unique car."

'Some of us E-type enthusiasts fear that Berry is wrong to use such words. Caution and understatement are all very well, but one doesn't use words like 'probably' and 'possibly' when talking about the first production E-type. It was, simply, amazing.'

Langley went on to describe his pre-launch run and achieving high speeds on the M1. 'Somewhere I have a photograph of the needle nudging 150mph to prove it, taken by the photographer with me.

'It became, for better or worse, a symbol of the sixties, like the Mini Cooper and Stirling Moss. Subsequently I drove many other E-types, including the last and most powerful V12 models, but none made quite the same impression as that original car. So it was quite an emotional moment when quite by chance I met 9600 HP again...'

In October 1996 John Langley and colleagues sampled the new Jaguar XK8. Under the heading, 'The E-type is still my type,' John wrote lovingly of his old friend and was shown standing with her outside the Browns Lane main entrance. In the 17 January 1998 issue, Tony Dron wrote a guide to buying a classic Jaguar. A photo of 9600 HP appeared with Bob Berry and myself with the caption, 'Golden oldie: the oldest E-type in existence awaiting restoration'. In December the same year, John Langley was writing about early motorways and described his run in 9600 HP on the M1 as 'my most memorable motorway drive'.

We have now completed the XK120 Roadster, which is white with red upholstery just like my father's example in the fifties. Desperately sadly, he died in 1996 at the age of 68 before the car was completed. We then tackled the XK120 FHC which was progressing superbly until the paintshop had a small fire which caused a gas cylinder, standing by my bodyshell, to explode. It literally looked as though a bomb had

From left to right, in front of the old farmhouse, we see my faithful XK140 Roadster (still going strong in 1991), the XK120 Roadster nearing completion, Moriarty the hound, some very strange person and the E-type Roadster (which turned out to have been the very first E-type I ever saw) just painted.

gone off beside it. The painter's insurance had lapsed, but luckily I was covered and, with various fantastic help, we still had it finished in time for a tour we organized for the XK 50th anniversary in 1998. The previous year we had started the international XK Club, a very different club with no committees and no politics. Julie and I run it as a business, as a means of controlling it rather than as a way of making money, and have members in 33 countries.

In 1998 we did a rally in the XK120 Roadster and bumped into Andrew Tart. To be honest, relations had been a bit strained because I was not too happy about the way things had turned out. However, we immediately hit it off again and the old rapport was instantly re-ignited. It was to prove a most fortuitous meeting.

CHAPTER ELEVEN

Resurrection Begins

Though even my friends may have doubted it, my intention was always to restore 9600 HP. However, I was aware of the awesome responsibility upon my shoulders. Sadly, I do not have the experience, ability or time to have tackled it myself. Clearly, it was going to need highly skilled attention in many areas. But that was not all. Something more was needed as well. It was crucial that those involved had the right *attitude*, an understanding of the importance of the car and a sympathy for the job. It had to be rather more than just another E-type restoration.

Over the years, through naïvety and gullibility, I have allowed people to make a start on several of my cars. Often they have proved incompetent or unreliable, or even gone out of business, for restoration is not an easy business. Consequently, for 22 years I clung on to two guiding principles regarding 9600 HP.

Firstly, it was essential that whoever started the restoration finished it. That should be a requirement of any restoration project, but it was especially important, nay vital, with 9600 HP because I believed that we would discover so many unusual features. The careful stripping down and recording of details was as important as the rebuilding. A ham-fisted, uncaring approach would have destroyed the unique nature of the beast.

Secondly, it was crucial that the restorers were specialists with years of E-type experience. Without that background, they would simply not recognize the many differences. They needed to know the cars inside out.

The high level of skill that I required of the restorers in their various fields of work was necessary, not just to do a competent job, but also because, with this car, it was important to conserve and repair every single component wherever humanly possible. For reasons of cost, it is normal E-type restoration practice to replace most of the bodyshell with new panels. In this way, by the end, there is very little of the original remaining. The same is true of many of the components, from the mechanical parts to the exterior chromework. It is more economical to throw away most things and fit new, usually reproduction, items.

In a phrase the 9600 HP approach had to be 'restoration by repair rather than by replacement'.

Mention of costs reminds me that that was no small consideration. Proper, reputable restoration by real experts is extremely costly.

The old car world is freely littered with incompetents, rogues and outright crooks. Optimistic customers, often new to their hobby and fired by emotional enthusiasm, are prime targets. The firms are not always crooked but often naïve themselves and think restoration is an easy and quick way to make a buck. 'Don't you listen to any of those inflated prices, I can do it for half that cost. You're being ripped off, mate.' The figure they quote would barely cover the cost of the parts. The customer is taken in. He shows good faith and cheerfully pays a good proportion up-front, especially as early progress looks positive. Then it all goes wrong.

The firm has had his money but the work is taking longer and the parts bill is adding up. They ask for more, and more. The customer is trapped. The car he arrived with had some value, even though it needed restoring. Now it is a pile of parts with some work done to the body. It is worth a fraction of what it was. Does he go on and pour more money into a bottomless pit, not knowing whether the work when completed will be satisfactory? Or does he say 'enough' and lose virtually all the money he has spent so far? It is a nightmare scenario, but you would be amazed how often it happens.

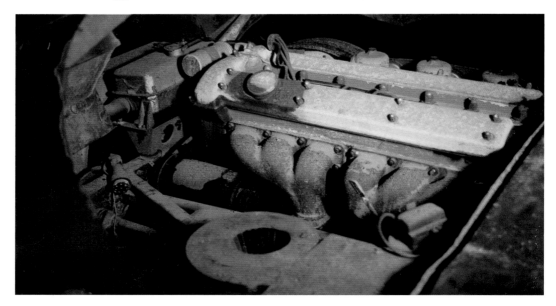

After 9600 HP had been mouldering in successive barns for over twenty years, the old girl looked pretty sad. Was she too far gone? What would we find? Was there any hope? Could she be revived and, if so, how much of the original could be saved? Would we, at best, end up with a replica that was simply a reminder of more glorious days?

Alternatively, it can all end with the company finishing the car by taking disastrous short-cuts. Thus the poor customer ends up with a car that needs restoring again. Often the company simply goes bankrupt half-way through.

You enter these shark-infested waters at your peril. I knew that one wrong move with 9600 HP could prove fatal. For this reason, and because of the staggering cost of doing this car justice, I sat on 9600 HP for over 20 years.

When Andrew Tart had been based at our little workshop, we occasionally touched on the subject of 9600 HP and it was clear that this was a challenge he relished. Peter Neumark, as a customer who became a friend, was aware of the car and its significance. We then went our separate ways. *Classic Motor Cars* (CMC) was formed in 1994 by Peter, Andrew and Nick Goldthorp, who all contributed considerable experience in their respective fields.

Andrew is a highly gifted engineer with a background working on a wide variety of sports, racing, vintage and classic cars. Former Chief Engineer of Vicarage, the world-renowned Jaguar Mark II specialists, he developed most of the upgrading technical modifications that they were famous for. He does not suffer fools gladly and demands very high standards from himself and those working under him. Above all, though, he loves his work. Nick founded Vicarage, in 1982 and with others helped to build up the business, gaining much vital experience of restoration company day-to-day management. Today Nick carries out the same role for CMC and looks after car sales.

The company occupies smart modern, 10,000 sq ft premises on the Stanmore Industrial Estate just outside Bridgnorth in Shropshire (to the West of Birmingham) and the team consists of eight craftsmen covering skills in panel beating, mechanical work, engine rebuilding and electrics. They specialize in E-types, XKs and Mark II saloons.

Peter, as CMC's Chairman, brings his wide business experience to bear in guiding the company and has the resources to have established CMC on a sound financial footing, which is so vital. A great enthusiast, he has a burning ambition to make CMC the best restoration company in the world and *the* E-type specialists.

'I grew up with cars,' says Peter, who comes from the northern town of Blackburn. 'My earliest recollection of a car was my father's cream 1955 Vauxhall Velox. I was about six years old. My father was a commercial traveller, as they were called, a manufacturer's agent. Of course, to do that job you needed a car but most people didn't have cars in those days. My dad always had cars and he changed them every two years. My grandfather and uncle were in the same business and I think my grandfather's greatest claim to fame would be that he introduced plastic flowers into this country,' chuckles Peter.

'A near relative I called Uncle Jack used to race Jaguar saloons and I remember going to Aintree with him in the sixties, and another relative, Auntie Lotta, had an XK150, and this is probably how my love of Jaguars started. In my teens I got my first job which was in a car wash. I used to wash the car with a sponge by hand and they had a gantry, which spurted water out, and you pushed it back and forth over the car. I got half-a-crown an hour, plus tips!' Around this time, Neumark had his first ride in an E-type. 'I can remember to this day the surge of acceleration was like nothing I had ever experienced before.'

He was actually 23 before he had a car, and that was a company car. 'As a penniless student, I just couldn't afford one.' After university, he decided it was 'about time I did something with my life. I had always had a hankering to be a salesman, I'd grown up with selling and it was in my blood. But I could not get a job – I was too heavily qualified. In those days you just didn't go into sales with a degree. So I went on the "knocker" selling brushes for Betterware, to keep body and soul together. I knew that if I was going to get a good training, I needed to be in food, computers, energy or medicine.' Eventually, he became a medical rep and after 18 months he instituted some research, with the results published in *The Lancet*. 'So I can lay claim to being the first medical rep to get his name in *The Lancet*! That did my stock in the company no harm and suddenly I was a regional sales manager at 24.' He then joined a transport company as their sales manager, followed by a successful period at International Paper and then, in his early thirties, he joined a company that became TNT, the international carriers, and ended up as National Sales Manager.

'In 1982 three other guys and I started Target Express. Over the next 15 years we expanded it to become the largest privately owned and most profitable transport company in the UK. We started with two vans out of a shed – and it *was* a shed – in Preston. The office was a 20-year-old caravan with gas lights. For six months we had no money but believed we had the skill, knowledge and talent to grow a reasonable business but had no idea we would end up with two thousand people and a turnover of £100m. As the company grew, that allowed me to indulge my passion in cars again and that's how I met you!

'I remember you showing me 9600 HP one day and I recall thinking it was something incredibly special. Then I got to know you better and I just thought, "One day we're going to have to restore that car". I felt then, as I do now, that it is one of the most important cars that has ever been built – not just the most important Jaguar. In the annals of motoring history, it will go down as a landmark car and I wanted to see it on the road. It was not right that it was in that barn. It was so important that it had to be enjoyed by others as well.'

Over the years I had toyed with the idea of selling the first RHD production car. It was obviously a very historic car but nothing like as significant or important as 9600 HP. Trying hard to be objective, rather than emotional, I felt it was a bit greedy to have *two* Fixed Head E-types. Gradually, over the years, I had made some progress with restoring number one. The body had been repaired, though restoration standards were not then what they are today. The rear suspension and engine had been rebuilt. Then, in 1986, I took it to a specialist in Birmingham who was going to have it painted and assemble the car in four-and-a-half months in time for the 25th anniversary celebrations in Switzerland that year. I regained possession of it four-an-a-half *years* later, after going to arbitration. I won against the painters (the paint was micro-blistering) and, in what I believe to be a total travesty of justice (with no right of appeal) I lost against the Jaguar specialist and had to pay four times what they originally quoted me. Furthermore, the car was not even completed. It was just this sort of experience that made me so very wary about making any move with 9600 HP.

Some time later I sought a value for the first RHD Fixed Head and phoned a specialist auction house. To my amazement, they said it was just another FHC that happened to be the first production one. They did not have the imagination to realize the importance of the car and thought it might fetch about £25,000 when restored. To complete the work was going to cost something like that, so I put such thoughts to the back of my mind.

Intriguingly, during 1995 Peter Neumark asked one of his advisors, Roy Hurdley, to request someone that Roy knew, who apparently knew me, to enquire if I would ever consider selling 9600 HP. I cannot recall anyone raising the subject and as Hurdley died in 1998, we cannot now find out who the go-between was.

During 1998, after our chance meeting had brought us back in contact, I bumped into Andrew in the paddock at the Coys Silverstone event where Peter had just done his first race in his Monza Alfa. Andrew took me over to Peter's motorhome, where we had a chat over a glass of wine. It was good to see Peter again. He is a very charismatic character and we get on well. 'We realized,' recalls Peter of that fortuitous meeting, 'that, really, we had a lot in common. I remember saying to you, "Life's too short and we really should do something about 9600 HP."'

I knew it was an ambition of Andrew's to restore the car and he knew I had toyed with the idea of selling number one. Peter had the imagination to realize how important number one was and so was seriously interested in acquiring the car. He knew that he would be selling Target and would then have the time to devote to CMC. 'I wanted to do something that would distance CMC from the mass of restorers. We decided we would try and restore a very important car and the first thought was 9600 HP.'

To restore 9600 HP, CMC then quoted for parts at cost and estimated 1500 to 1700 hours, to be charged at a special rate. The total was £68,577. Peter's offer for number one did not match that figure and also this was an estimate and thus open-ended. I loved the idea, and was grateful for the constructive suggestions, but could not take it any further.

With perfect timing, an ex-pat Englishman with a restoration company in the USA made contact to say he was desperate to restore the car and made various tempting offers.

Peter then discussed matters further with Andrew and Nick, and another proposition was put to me. This suggestion entailed me selling number one for the princely sum of £1. However, in return CMC would totally restore the car to a standard that we would all be proud of. I did not hesitate for long, because although I was a little sad to think of losing number one, it was a patently fair deal from my point of view and, perhaps, most important of all, I totally trusted Peter and his colleagues. I knew that CMC were one of the very few firms in the entire world, perhaps the only company, that matched up to my very demanding criteria. With Peter behind them, they had not only the technical expertise, but the financial strength to see it through.

CMC brought in E-type parts specialists, SNG Barratt. This company was formed by the husband and wife team of Steve, whom I had first met in 1977, and Hazel Barratt. Working initially from home, with Hazel on the 'phone and Steve out collecting parts, the business grew rapidly. They moved first to the Old Workhouse, a rather different address, and then in 1995 to their present modern premises in Bridgnorth. The warehousing was supplemented in 1997 when they took on an adjacent building for the production department, and they were proud to achieve the ISO 9002 international quality standard in 1997.

However, in spite of all our combined experience, we were still stepping into the unknown. Until CMC made a start, no one could know the true condition of the car under the accumulated grime and fading paint. It was going to be a challenge, and that challenge was going to be all the more demanding for the spotlight was going to be on each guy all the way through. The media interest was extraordinary.

As a result of this, and the grapevine, enthusiasts all around the world came to hear of the project and we received a barrage of questions and advice. We thought we were taking the project pretty seriously, but we had enthusiasts telling us we must retain and preserve every minute sliver of varnish that parted company with the wood-rim steering wheel. 'I am really pleased,' wrote another enthusiast, 'she still has a dent in the nose, which is now part of her personality. A good wash, a new glass eye and a careful engine job is about as far as I would go. Please don't remanufacture her'…' Today we live in an age when the art of conservation has, quite rightly, assumed a new level of importance, and this was forcefully emphasized by the many and varied communications. What a responsibility!

In parallel with the 9600 HP discussions, we had been going down the tortuous route of seeking various permissions to restore our old Elizabethan barn for discreet offices and a small museum for the XK Club, my archives and 9600 HP. We had many battles as we wanted to retain the authenticity. For reasons of weight and originality, we wanted to thatch the roof. The first young conservation officer told us she *could* make us keep the corrugated tin. After 18 months we were able to start and obtained the first grant from the newly-created Rural Development Agency. It was decided to have a joint launch party for the barn and 9600 HP on 1 April – really! To our surprise no less than four TV crews attended and many publications were represented.

We had tried to contact a number of people who had played a role in the car's life. Bob Berry was unfortunately abroad. Jack Fairman joined us, which was splendid. Peter Lockhart Smith regretably could not but it was a great pleasure to see Derek

Brant again, after some 22 years. Another who sadly could not be with us was John Langley, who had recently retired as Motoring Correspondent of *The Daily Telegraph*.

'I am so sorry,' he wrote, 'that I shall not be able to attend the start of the renaissance of my old friend 9600 HP... I have very fond memories of the car after my high speed burst on the M1 in 1961. Only one other new model stands out in my memory so vividly in some 45 years of testing new cars – the original Citroën DS, although in terms of sheer performance this was not, of course, in the same league. ...I shall certainly be thinking of you all.'

Christian Frost came over from Denmark. Christian is a motoring journalist and superb photographer (a number of his shots grace this book) with *Bil Magasinet* magazine, and we first met in 1995. His first brush with 9600 HP was, he told me, some years before when he asked Jaguar about it and they told him it had been scrapped!

On 6 April Nick Goldthorp and I loaded the car on to a trailer and the ensemble disappeared through the gate bound for Bridgnorth. It was quite an emotional moment and the first positive thing that had happened to the poor old car for many a long year. A couple of days later I had a two-page article in the Motoring Section of *The Daily Telegraph*. Consequently, a number of people contacted me which

The first positive thing that had happened to 9600 HP in over twenty years. On 6 April 1999, the barn (on left) restoration started and Nick Goldthorp, of restorers CMC, collected the car. It was bound for the workshops in Bridgnorth, Shropshire and eleven months of hard, highly skilled and very challenging work under pressure.

kick-started my 9600 HP research once again. I propose to tell the story of the restoration and the research in parallel, as CMC rebuilt the legend and I aimed to piece together the car's life.

The very first job for CMC was a humble one. The car was thoroughly cleaned! With the use of a high-pressure cold water jet wash, the accumulated years of grime and grease were chased off the bodyshell and all mechanical components.

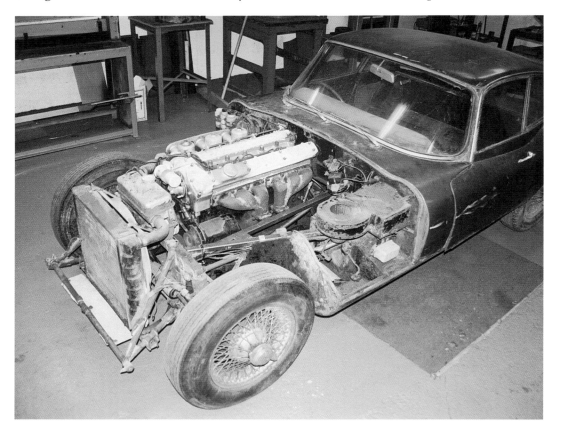

First job was to simply remove the semi-attached bonnet and thoroughly clean the car to be able to see and assess what was under all the accumulated grime. Immediately the car started to reveal the first of the many tiny discoveries that made the project even more fun. An example was parts of the old left-hand drive throttle linkage still attached to the bulkhead, adjacent to the heater box, and which the Jaguar engineers had not bothered to remove back in 1961.

Thankfully the car was very complete and was all in one piece, with the odd exception. The old boot floor was long gone, and some of the trim was simply lying strewn around the interior. The original engine was intact but had not run since 1976, when Brant drove it back from Manchester. Even something as simple as cleaning made the car look very different. Already the unique features were becoming apparent. The excitement was starting at long last.

Highlighting some of these differences might seem a tad fanatical, but it is all part of what makes the car special. The bulkhead was flat, with no indentation for the mounting of the servo, and here was an odd quirk – the old LHD throttle linkage was still attached to the bulkhead. The chassis plate would have been on the offside but was taken off and moved to the nearside when the car was changed from LHD to RHD. One could still see the rivet holes where it had been. The door shut faces were different, with a separate door striker panel let into the 'B' post, and the tailgate trims appeared much wider than normal. The guys also noticed the tailgate hinges were completely different from production cars. Of course Paul Skilleter had noticed the aluminium tailgate and Perspex rear window and rear quarterlights back in 1977.

Careful examination and cleaning of the all-important chassis plate, which carries the chassis, body, engine and gearbox numbers, revealed that the chassis number was stamped as 875002 D/N. On the XK140s and 150s, the D/N, standing for De Normanville, indicates that overdrive is fitted. How interesting! The E-type was never fitted with overdrive because there was simply no room. Can we deduce that it was intended to fit overdrive to 9600 HP, or did the man with the stamps make a mistake?

The target, incidentally, we had all set ourselves for the completion of the restoration was the exact anniversary of Berry's original mad dash to Geneva – 13 March 2000. It might seem strange to celebrate the 39th anniversary, but we could not wait another year and anyway it would be a dress rehearsal for 2001. With ordinary restoration often taking 18 months plus, this was to be an exacting challenge for all concerned. Eleven months to go!

The dismantling was carried out by Colin Howell, because he would be assembling 9600 HP again. Colin worked closely with Andrew as they very carefully took the car apart, making copious notes and photographing everything. CMC acquired a digital camera especially for this job and it proved ideal. Colleague Simon Prytherch took no less than 300 photos at this stage alone, as they painstakingly catalogued every minute part. Considering the car was seemingly so rusty, everything came apart relatively easily.

Unless unsafe to do so, or just plain impossible, CMC were going to move

The bodyshell was then completely stripped of every component. This simple statement glosses over the fact that this in itself was a carefully executed and painstaking exercise. Several hundred photographs were taken as every minute feature was recorded to ensure the car would be put back together in precisely the same way in every possible detail. Greater care could not have been taken had it been a Renoir.

heaven and earth to re-use every single component. Even if the parts could not be used, they were going to keep them both as patterns and for my museum. Even the nuts and bolts were part of history!

The *Telegraph* article included a plea for information about John Paddy Carstairs, about whom I knew little. Bob Jennings wrote to say that John Coombs, who sold the car to Carstairs, had a lot of connections with the film industry. 'At functions at the garage, which I attended, I met people from Elstree and Pinewood studios. It was the time of Hammer films and Dracula.' Jennings himself used to hill-climb one of the 12 Lightweight E-types and I have photographs of the combination which I took at Shelsley as a teenager. David Kinsella wrote to tell me that Carstairs had owned an Allard and enclosed a copy of a page from his book on Allards in which he mentioned JPC. Then, and this was a great piece of luck, a Mr and Mrs Phillips wrote to say that Mrs Carstairs was still very much alive.

The stripped 9600 HP body revealed more previously clothed secrets. For a start the bulkhead has a multitude of extra holes. Obviously, during its development life, things were fitted, removed, refitted elsewhere and that type of thing. This was a living testbed and the signs were still there for us to see and deduce from. Theories were flying around as various people examined the car. The inner face of the bulkhead (behind the dashboard) was, I thought, particularly fascinating. When I saw a series of scribe lines, it recalled days spent on the shopfloor of the engineering business. These lines had been made by the engineers when they were working out where to

position items. I suggested that this area should be preserved and not painted over. The guys agreed.

The shell was a curious mixture of beautiful craftsmanship and, seemingly, hurried bodging. Perhaps that is not too surprising when you reflect. As this was a prototype, the panels were made by hand, rather than being pressed. So the roof was made of sections butt-welded – edge to edge – rather than overlapped as

After removing the dashboard and facia panels, the metal bulkhead panels behind revealed more history. Rather like discovering prehistoric carvings in caves, we were excited to find the scribe lines the engineers had originally made when they built this car by hand in 1960. Rather than paint over this area and lose this little bit of history forever, the guys at CMC treated the small areas of rust and preserved this area as found.

was production practice. With the seams between sections cleaned up, there was little evidence of the joins. Thus the roof and rear wings looked like one large, beautiful piece of work. So the body was built to a high standard and then internally modified to meet ongoing development requirements. Time was short during this phase; finesse was now a luxury. Holes were hacked out.

Sometimes we could follow the logic; sometimes we could not. The transmission tunnel had several large apertures which were presumably for access, but to what? Nobody was quite sure. It is all part of the mystery. On the other hand the hacked-out rectangular apertures for the RHD pedal box were done when the car was converted from LHD. The inner wings were made up of about six different shaped patches welded together because the tooling had not yet been made. The anti-roll bar was found to be larger than standard, but that could have been a remnant of the uprating work by Playfords during Fairman's ownership.

As the stripping continued, the guys found a curious mixture of superb craftsmanship and crude work. Clearly the body had been beautifully made by hand and later had been hurriedly modified at various times to incorporate changes during its development and Press roles. An example of terrible workmanship was the cutting out of the apertures for the right-hand drive pedal components. The metal was removed by drilling a series of holes and the rough edges were not even filed smooth – real back street stuff!

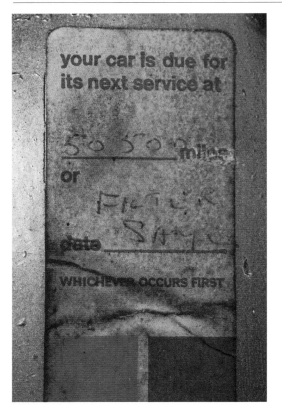

A delightful little period feature was the Castrol sticker that was visible with the driver's door open. It suggests that the next service is due at 50,500 miles and as the car did very little mileage in the seventies, it is almost certain this sticker was affixed to the car in the late sixties.

A delightful little feature was an old Castrol Motor Oil sticker on the 'B' post which stated, 'Your car is due for its next service at 50,500 miles....' With great care, Colin successfully removed it intact.

The next stage was shot-blasting. Now, this was positively worrying. Shot-blasting takes no prisoners. Corroded metal just disappears into dust under the scourge of the grit fired under pressure. Many a proud owner has had the trauma of an apparently quite sound shell returning from the shot-blasters like a string vest that has cohabited with a pack of under-nourished moths. As the E-type has no conventional chassis, the structural bodyshell is the item of both the greatest mass and most importance. Without that, we would have no continuous history. The car would lose its soul and become a clone rather than a true reincarnation. There could be no compromises; it had to be done.

It was a tense couple of days and then Andrew phoned. I held my breath but the news was good. What a relief. The shell had come through the process and was better than we all expected. Of course, it was not perfect. Some structural areas would need replacement and there would be myriad minor repairs, but overall it was not at all bad considering its age.

Meanwhile, I was attempting to research a variety of unrelated fields – Sayer, the original journalists, Carstairs, the other owners, the 'Geneva Conundrum' and every aspect of its life and this story! I am lucky enough to have a great friend in Geneva, who has been a Jaguar owner and enthusiast for many years. Eric Herbert Biass is a distinguished aviation journalist who takes a particular interest in 9600 HP. Naturally, I turned to him for help, reasoning that with all the photographers ringed around the car, there must be copies available somewhere. Surely there must be some local journalists who would remember the event.

In early May, Eric telephoned. He had had no luck. Then his wife, Paula, had the idea of trying the library. So he duly went there and, yes, they had some shots. Bravo! However, Eric could not find anybody still alive who could help us. Emile Frey, the original Swiss agent, is no longer with us, the guy who ran Marcel Fleury likewise. Every one a cul-de-sac.

From the start, Peter Neumark had tried to involve Jaguar. He felt, understandably, that it would be mutually beneficial to work together. The guys at CMC would appreciate any information that might be available in the archives that would assist their challenge. He was just asking for an indication of interest and (non-monetary) support. In the past he had had to listen to me moaning about Jaguar and the unprofessional and ill-mannered way certain departments behaved, ignoring letters, not returning calls, utter rudeness and regular failure to do what they had promised. He thought, he has since admitted, I was exaggerating. Having experienced the same treatment first-hand, he found I was not.

One day engine specialist Dave Butcher telephoned CMC. He had been chatting to a neighbour whose father had originally worked on 9600 HP, on development and testing, and had loads of photos. Eureka! Sadly, though, he had died a few weeks previously. Oh dear. And the whole lot had been thrown away – negs, prints, the lot! Pass the gin.

When the naked body returned from shot-blasting it looked like a beautiful piece of sculpture, as the stripped roof flowed seamlessly into the rounded haunches of the

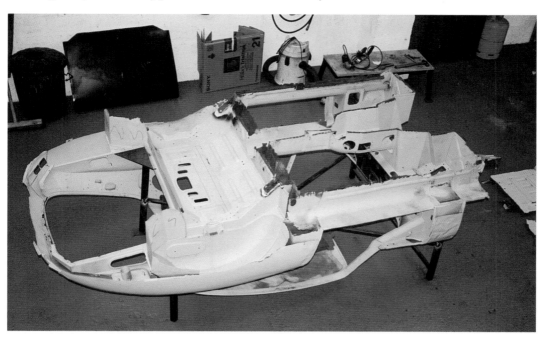

Following stripping, the bodyshell was sent for careful shot-blasting. This process can be totally vicious and completely uncompromising, yet it had to be done. The fear was that little of the original body would remain after blasting. To our immense relief, the shell was nothing like as bad as we feared and it had superficially appeared. On its return to CMC, the shell was turned upside-down for ease of working and the old floors were removed.

rear wings. At this stage Tim Griffin, a highly skilled panel beater with plenty of E-type experience, entered the stage. Tim was to live, breathe and sleep 9600 HP for the next six months as he grappled with the complex challenges. Though mechanical work is his main forte, Andrew worked closely alongside Tim. They turned the whole shell upside down and mounted it on a special cradle. First job was to remove the floors. They were rotten and furthermore showed evidence of dubious repairs.

The floors and sills are important structural members on an E-type, and there was no question these had to be replaced. However, the original floors had no drain holes but had an extra strengthening rib pressed in. New replacement floors were obtained and the drain holes welded up. Andrew had had some male and female tools made up and then modified the new floors by pressing in an extra rib. Extra stiffeners were added. In this way the new floors were exact, faithful reproductions of the originals. They were built up on a jig to ensure accuracy.

On one of my regular visits, Tim showed me the sub-frames which attach to the front bulkhead and carry the engine and front suspension. 'A lot of them have stress fractures by the engine mountings but there are no real stress fractures on these, but there is pitting which suggests they are the age of the car rather than later replacements.' Good news. We could keep the original sub-frames. Tim actually found differences between the construction of the car on one side of the shell to the other. He explained about making a new section for the 'B' post area. 'Normally when you are doing E-types, you make a pattern for one side and then reverse it for the other side. So I made the pattern, reversed it, made the other panel – didn't fit! Thought, "What's going on here?" Apart from both sides being totally different, the inner wheel arch is welded on the *outside* of the inner quarter, as opposed to the opposite the other side. They looked the same but wouldn't fit.' Such eccentricities were keeping him on his toes but he was thoroughly relishing the challenge. It was proving time-consuming though and the clock was ticking. Nine months to go!

'We're trying to recreate all the little faults,' added Tim. 'It's no good replacing something and making it perfect when Jaguar had a little fault in it and they originally bashed it to make it fit. This is what's taking the time.'

In June two gentleman closely involved in originally creating the E-type came over to Bridgnorth. Tom Jones had been Chief Engineer under Heynes, and Cyril Crouch was in charge of the body structure. Cyril ruefully recalled that there was so little money available for tooling that his task was not easy. He would, he stated, have done quite a number of things rather differently without the financial strictures and predicted low volume. He would, for example, have had a star shape pressed into the floors instead of a series of straight ribs.

Cyril Crouch: 'The first bodies were hand wheeled by Abbey Panels before Pressed Steel Fisher came on the scene. We were told we were only going to build five hundred so why do any proper tooling?'

Tom Jones: 'The panels were done on a stretcher press. The master panel was very thick and it was filled with concrete, and then a rubber section came down in the

In June we had a visit from two men who played a leading role in designing the E-type. Tom Jones (left) was Chief Engineer and Cyril Crouch was in charge of the body structure. By examining the body in its naked state, they were able to give the restorers some invaluable pointers as to how and why things were done the way they were originally.

press to pull the metal around the concrete block, and then you'd finish it off in the wheeling machine. They were then hand-trimmed.'

In mid-June Peter contacted a Coventry newspaper and asked them to print an appeal for information. Before the Goodwood Festival of Speed, I had dinner with Sir Jack Brabham and would kick myself when I later discovered that Sayer claimed to have done work on GP bodies for him. Next night I was having a drink with the Jaguar crowd in a hotel and got hauled into reception to do a telephone interview with a Coventry radio station who had spotted the newspaper piece.

Meanwhile Tim and Andrew were carrying out a number of localized repairs to the bottom edges of the front and rear bulkheads, the rear chassis legs, footwells, prop shaft tunnel, and the 'A' and 'B' post areas. Curiously, Tim found that quite a few panels were more closely related to Roadster panels than production FHC

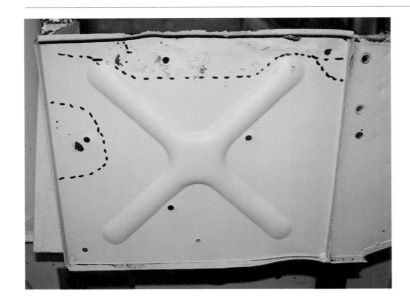

It was imperative with this car to retain every fraction of the original body wherever humanely possible and that is what made this E-type restoration unique. Whereas it would be normal practice, and far quicker and cheaper, to replace entire panels, the conservation approach dictated minimal new metal. The areas that absolutely had to be replaced were thus marked up before cutting out.

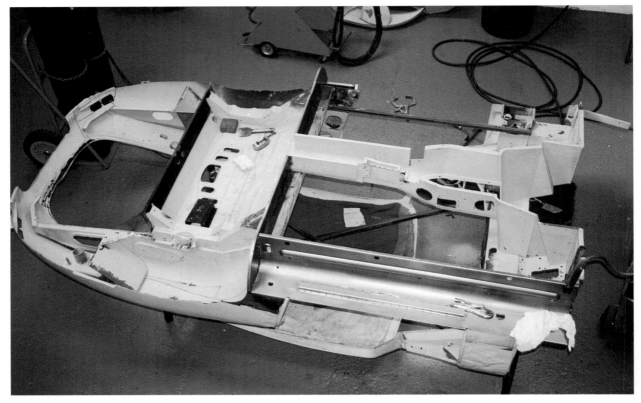

Though originality was important, safety was obviously even more crucial. Consequently, it was deemed prudent to replace certain structural members. Here we can see the new inner sills being fitted. When new panels were formed, they were made as faithful copies, incorporating any features unique to this car.

panels. On reflection, this is not so surprizing as only Roadsters and the *pavé* FHC had been built when 9600 HP was put together. The jig-built floors were then lowered on to the inverted shell and tacked in place. The shell was righted and fitted on to the main E-type jig.

Tim then turned his attention to the doors. Andrew was uncharacteristically generous with his comments! 'Tim's doing really well. I'm dead chuffed. The doors would normally be scrap, we'd just throw them away.' With a series of minor but highly skilled repairs, Tim managed to save the original doors, which was more good news. Without the door skin refitted, the skeletons were bolted to the hinges to set the gaps approximately. All fitting of panels revolves around the doors with the one proviso that the shell is square. 'We built the floor on the jig so we are perfectly happy with that. That is dead square. The doorskin is the final adjustment – we can

The new floors were fabricated using the old, heavily corroded floors as patterns and built on a jig to ensure dimensional integrity. Here, from left to right, we see panel beater Tim Griffin, Carlton presenter Emily Childs, cameraman Phil and CMC Technical Director Andrew Tart. Tim and Andrew are being filmed lowering the new floor section into place.

make the skin a little bit smaller or a little bit bigger.' Seven months to go!

One thing that became apparent was that the car had, at some time, had an accident on the left-hand side, though no one has yet admitted to it!

As Autumn approached, I started visiting people and boosting British Telecom's profits. It was a particular pleasure to build a rapport with Molly Carstairs. I went to see Peter and Anne Riley, and after telling me the story of their trip to Switzerland in 1961, they suggested I contact Peter Garnier. I then visited dear old Jack Fairman at the BEN – Motor & Allied Trades Benevolent Fund – home near Coventry. As we pulled up at Jack's local pub for lunch, my phone rang and it was Andrew. He wanted a decision about camshafts. He was very concerned about achieving the performance figures on standard cams and felt they must have been D-type cams originally. I agreed. Meanwhile Jack was getting hungry.

After lunch I went to see Pat Smart, who recalled registering the car in February 1961. Next day I wrote to Peter Garnier and Ron Easton, and emailed Ted Eves, all formerly of *The Autocar*. I had been in occasional email contact with Eves, who had retired to Portugal. It is likely that the trio who went to Geneva on behalf of the magazine were Maurice Smith, Harry Mundy and Ted. The first two died many years ago. A couple of days later I read that Eves had died.

That Monday Andrew phoned to say that colleague Simon Prytherch had been studying Haddock! This is a reference to an American gentleman who wrote an exciting little volume devoted to E-type authenticity. 'Haddock says that early cars had a reverse gear engagement warning light above the heater controls.' Stunned by this revelation, I immediately looked into it. Studying original photos yet again with a magnifying glass did indeed reveal a small warning light, or blanking stud.

On my next visit Andrew reported: 'A lot of parts are now back from cadmium plating. Very important to sort them out as soon as they come back because it's so easy to get them confused.' He believes in laying everything out logically – 'You can instantly see if you've got two of everything.

'To me these bits and pieces are important and you can't buy them. I'm now screwing bits together just so we know we've got them. We may not necessarily use the original screws, but we have the option. This is the steering column dust cover. These always break but this one's great. There's a little crack underneath where it's been slightly over-tightened, but it is lovely.' The enthusiasm was infectious.

To avoid polluting the water sewers, plating companies had to change over to zinc some time ago. However, they do have a few vats of cadmium which they can still use because these are now a minute proportion of the whole. Normally, CMC would zinc plate the parts when restoring E-types of the period, but on this car they have gone the extra mile. 'Cad looks nicer than zinc and is a better protection,' states Andrew.

'The triangular space frame that carries the bonnet hinges is very different to later models.' Following its accident a later type had been fitted but a rare early one was located. A genuine period item was coming from Richard Smith, who just called in to look at the car. So many people have been drawn into the fun and excitement, and

Smith was to prove a very keen and helpful adviser on authenticity.

Meanwhile the gearbox had been sent off to pre-eminent specialist Alan George, and the axle had departed to GKN for rebuilding. Alan found nothing unusual about the 'box but the first gear tooth was breaking up and the second gear synchro was worn out. Parts are now very hard to find and this proved quite a challenge. Eventually, he found a good second-hand set and fitted these and all new bearings. He warned me to treat first and reverse very gently. 'Always count to three!'

On the jig Andrew ground a groove in various positions along the centre. He then ran a fishing line down from one end to the other to measure from and check squareness/symmetry. 'The top of the scuttle has now been welded on. Bit of a compromise there, as you can't get behind it to planish it. So we have given it a quick linish and we will have to put some lead in there. That is a difficult area. We didn't want to put a complete new scuttle on it for obvious reasons.' Six months to go!

Peter Spackman, who originally set up the E-type Register in the seventies, 'phoned to say that he had traced Brian Playford, who worked on the car during Fairman's ownership. Also a contact of Peter's had visited the old site of Richardsons (the dealers) twice but had not, as yet, been able to trace anybody. By a coincidence Wednesday's post brought replies from both Garnier and Easton. I telephoned both and, though neither was at Geneva, they made helpful suggestions. I telephoned their former colleague Martin Lewis.

'Ah, yes! The alleged 150mph car. I recall they couldn't do it with two people in the car.' Though Lewis had only been with the magazine a few months, he still recalls the aura surrounding the car. 'I wasn't even allowed to sit in it! It was a fantastic car.' He confirmed who would have been at Geneva and made suggestions as to the photographer. 'I remember Peter Riviere was rather suspicious about some marks on the head. It might have had a D-type wide-angle head – it certainly wasn't a production car.' Lewis went on to say that Riviere had related the story to him some years later and all was not as it appeared. He then came out with the devastating fact that Peter Riviere had died many years ago. Another sad cul-de-sac.

Garnier had suggested I phone Ron 'Steady' Barker, one of the motoring world's great characters. 'I remember all the fuss,' said 'Steady'. 'I think the figures were fiddled. There was a lot of discussion about using stop watches, because the fifth wheel wouldn't go up to 150mph. Harry Mundy was completely ethical. I remember when he went to Jaguar, he discovered that all the road test Jaguars had been fitted with loose engines and larger valves.' With Smith and Mundy dead, he suggested the man I needed to speak to was Riviere. I said that I had just, some half-an-hour earlier, learnt that he had died.

'I don't think so. I'd be very surprised. *A* Peter Riviere died and that confused a lot of people. He became a Professor of Anthropology.'

'At Cambridge,' I interjected, remembering what Smith had told me 12 years previously.

'No! At Oxford.' 'Steady' was convinced that Riviere was still with us and living near the new Vintage Sports Car Club offices. Being a member, I knew they had recently moved to an old Post Office in Chipping Norton. I rather feverishly telephoned the VSCC offices and asked if they would very kindly scour a local telephone book. They did but found nothing. 'Have you tried Directory Enquiries?' I felt rather stupid saying that I hadn't but really, I thought to myself, I could not see much point. Oh well, it was worth a final try.

'What name?'

'Riviere, please,' and I spelt it. 'Peter.'

'A business is it?'

'No!'

'What address?'

'Well, I don't know.' I was feeling stupid again. 'Could you try Oxford, please?'

'I think I'll need more information than that.' A short pause. 'Sorry, I have nothing listed'.

'Could you try Chipping Norton?' I said forlornly.

Another short pause. Then she said, 'Hold the line' and a computer voice spoke to me.

'The number you require is...' I was amazed and cautiously elated. Could this be the right gentleman? Surely, it was too much of a coincidence? Of course, I dialed immediately - and got an answerphone. I left a message and wondered what the next step would be.

'Steady' also mentioned in passing that they used to call Bob Berry 'Fangio'. Lyons was famously careful about money and this may have explained 'Steady's' other comment about Berry. 'He never had transport or money.' He recalls that members of the press used to give him lifts from event to event.

Old friend John Pearson phoned a few minutes later. He had been searching, as requested by Andrew, for some period D-type cam covers but had not had any luck as yet. John then recalled being driven around the Silverstone area in the car by Jack Fairman on a couple of occasions when Jack owned it.

At twenty past nine that evening the phone rang. I answered and the voice at the other said, 'I am the Peter Riviere you are looking for.' Wonderful. I arranged to visit him. That Oxford was not sufficient for Directory Enquiries when Riviere's village was a mere five miles away, and yet Chipping Norton, which is a small town around 20 miles north of the famous university city, yielded his details is odd to say the least. The mysteries of British Telecom!

Back at CMC, the body had been taken off the jig, the sub-frames fitted, and Andrew had begun building the bonnet. He decided on a novel approach. Rather than build it as a unit, separate from the car, and then offer it up, modifying as necessary, he decided to assemble it on the car. As anyone who has tried to fit an E-type bonnet in recent years knows only too well, it is not just a matter of bolting the assembly on. Fitting will usually involve cutting metal, adding metal and even some reshaping. This was to be very much the case with 9600 HP.

The bonnet hinges are attached to the front valence and so he started by fitting this

While the guys at CMC were working hard on the restoration, I was feverishly following many leads as I endeavoured to piece together every aspect of 9600 HP's life. The original 150mph runs by Peter Riviere, who then worked for *The Autocar*, were one of the most important aspects of this whole story. I was delighted to track him down and find that he was very much alive in spite of reports to the contrary!

panel. Having satisfied himself that this was mounted square and level, he offered up the centre section and adjusted it to suit by means of shims on the hinges in the usual way. This large, flexible panel was then given some rigidity by gluing in the various ducting and strengthening panels. Gluing steel panels together was an innovation introduced on the E-type, according to Jones and Crouch.

Andrew then took himself off the body to concentrate on his first love, the engine, and Baz Cope joined Tim. Baz, who is another expert panel beater and builds racing cars as a hobby, concentrated on completing the bonnet. This was a complex and difficult job. Baz spent many hours unpicking the wired wing edges on the replacement wings, welding on new metal, profiling, trimming and re-wiring.

'The best way is to scribe a mark where you're going to bend it, cut the waste material off and then with some smooth-jawed pliers, bend it through 90 degrees, then planish at 90 degrees, then bend it even more, so you can just squeeze in the wire and then finish it off with a hammer and dolly. It's one of those jobs where you think, "How on earth do you do that?" but it's a lot easier than you would think. Once you have a go, you think, "I can do this!" It's really quite fun.'

Similarly the centre section had to be altered to achieve satisfactory gaps where it meets the scuttle, and the scuttle top had to be leaded to suit the profile of the centre section. Additionally, at the rear of the right-hand wing where the panel curves down to meet the sill, this section was short by about ⅛ inch. This does not sound much, but there is no way of stretching the metal to fit as it has a wired edge. Thus a further metal section had to be shaped, wired and welded to the wing to achieve the correct gap. It was found that the external bonnet lock catches, by which early E-types can be identified, are slightly further forward on 9600 HP and this necessitated further modifications.

Tricky areas are the headlamp apertures which are half-and-half, wing panel and centre section. Inevitably the flanging did not correspond where the panels join, and the profile and depth of the flanges varied. It is essential to try-fit such items as the headlamp rims before the body is painted, as it is quite usual that they do not fit! On 9600 HP they failed to fit in three ways: the round apertures did not match up, they did not sit evenly and the flanges on the centre section and wings did not match one another – otherwise they were perfect! The answer was a mixture of re-shaping the panelwork, cutting out and adding metal. These problems are good examples of why proper, reputable restoration takes so long, requires so much skill and costs so much. Baz himself found it hard to believe the time this work was taking, and Tim must have been thinking he would spend the rest of his life on the car. 'On a job like this,' said Cope, 'getting the last 20 per cent costs you 50–55 per cent in time.' Five months to go!

By now the restoration work on the barn, after six months' skilled work by our superb, sympathetic builders, was 95 per cent complete and, after a few days' frantic decorating, we moved our offices out of the house to the new first floor.

Following the visit from former Jaguar engineers Tom Jones and Cyril Crouch, we learnt that the boot floor and rear quarters had been made in one piece on this car. This area of the car was missing because the previous owner had started to fit a replacement which was later 'borrowed' by an E-type specialist as a pattern and never returned. Thus a new floor manufactured by Martin Robey Ltd was modified and butt-welded to new quarters, making one 'seamless' assembly. This was offered up to the repaired rear body structure and a new number-plate panel and associated bracketry fabricated. A few simple words do not do justice to this highly skilled piece of workmanship which took weeks of toil.

Next challenge for Tim Griffin was the tailgate. We know that the original *Autocar* road test was delayed when the tailgate sprung open at high speed while the car was being tested by Norman Dewis. Tim actually found evidence of the original damage done and the hasty repairs.

As stated, the tailgate is aluminium and the hinges and surrounding areas are all

One of the most challenging areas for Tim Griffin was at the rear end. The boot floor area was missing, having been removed when Punters started some repair work in 1976. Tom Jones and Cyril Crouch told us that the floor and quarter panels were originally made as one section on this car and Tim rose to the challenge. This work is normally difficult enough but the CMC guys gave themselves an even harder time by setting such demanding objectives. Their pride and satisfaction, though, were infectious.

different. Luckily the tailgate was in good condition and so local, but highly skilled, repairs were sufficient. However, sections of the guttering, which was originally hand-formed, rather than integrally pressed, had corroded. After unpicking the folded sections from the roof panel, the edges of this panel could be locally bead-blasted. Tim then made several new sections of guttering which sounds devilishly difficult. He describes the shaped double curvature guttering as having, 'Three turns, a curve and two folds!' Apart from coping with forming this complex fabrication, when fitting it in situ he had to guard against fixing it too high so it fouled the tailgate but with sufficient depth to house the rubber seal positioned correctly.

Talking of the tailgate, Tim reported, 'There were a lot of stress fractures in the aluminium but not much corrosion. The spot welds had split through corrosion. I've had to drill some of those through and Tig plug them to make sure they don't go again. Aluminium is a funny metal to spot weld. You can get away with it if you put a couple of pieces of spring steel either side of your spot weld arms.

'Apart from a few dents, we have not done much to the tailgate. To effect a

Tony Marshall, who had photographed the car when it was still highly secret, is seen shooting the restoration on behalf of *The Daily Telegraph* for whom he worked for over thirty years. By leaving the original tailgate guttering in place, Tim was able to make a rear closing panel to the correct profile to match the tailgate. The combination of double and treble curvatures was mind-boggling.

proper repair, I would have had to have annealed it, then taken the skin off the frame, then put the skin back on the frame and I don't think it would have survived. It's not in that bad a condition and it was better to leave it as it was, with all the factory bodyfiller that they had obviously put in round the hinges when it sprung open.' The roof and side gutters are normally all one pressing, but this car was found to have a separate guttering welded in.

'The tailgate latch will only fit in one position because of the way the holes have been drilled and Jaguar filed the latch to fit the drilled holes. Surprisingly, even after renewing all the metal, it is still in the right position. It is on all the original spacers.

'I would assume that when it burst open and bent the hinge, they would have put these spacers in the top hinge. There are two oval bonnet washers that have been cut and slipped in to space it a bit more. I put them back and it actually puts the tailgate in the right position. Do you want us,' Tim asked me, 'to make up a proper shim or put those back in as they were?'

'Definitely as they were, please,' I immediately responded. This original hurried solution is another little bit of history. Only four months to go!

Meanwhile, Andrew Tart had started stripping the engine. We know that the car has only done around 51,000 miles from new, as this is corroborated by the last MOT certificates. He was pleasantly surprised and certain that it had never been taken apart before.

'The condition of the engine was lovely, it was really good. Obviously it had been standing for twenty-odd years. It wasn't quite seized. You could rotate the engine a little way, but one of the pistons had gone very tight. I left some very thin oil in the bores and it eventually freed off. The original pistons are almost usable. They are in really good condition. Obviously the rings are rusted and stuck into the pistons but we can flick those out. We have cleaned them up and there is barely any wear on them. They are Brico pistons which were used by Jaguar in the early E-type days. It is just a standard Brico. They have the Jaguar part number, not a Brico part on it, so I think

Production cars were built with adjustment for the tailgate hinges but this had not been thought of when 9600 HP was built. Hence the adjustment was achieved on this car by the simple expedient of adding washers to the hinge bracket where it was attached to the tailgate rim. We retained them of course! Very historic washers.

they are definitely the pistons that were fitted at Jaguar. Similarly, we wouldn't entertain using the shell bearings again but they could almost be re-used.'

Following stripping, the block was sent away to Coventry Boring and the head to well-known specialists Chesman's. Various parts was crack-detected and this showed up one unfortunate problem. The crankshaft had a small crack in it and so another identical crank had to be found, which was not easy. 'The pistons and rods' continued Andrew, 'are balanced here statically and the crank, flywheel and clutch assembly will be dynamically balanced in Halesowen by Wilkinson Balancing.'

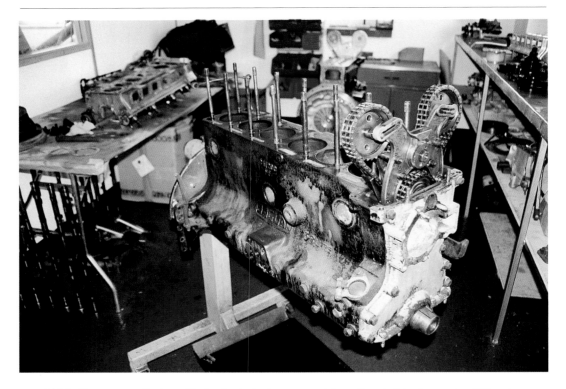

While Tim was continuing with the body, Andrew moved from the shell to the engine. When he stripped it, he was very pleasantly surprised. The condition was extremely good and entirely commensurate with the mileage.

Meanwhile, Neil Hussey and colleagues at principal parts suppliers, SNG Barratt were keeping the CMC guys fed with parts as everybody pulled together to meet the deadline of Geneva 2000 in March.

In late November I visited legendary *Motor Sport* Editor Bill Boddy and had a long and delightful chat. A few days later I drove to the Oxford area to finally meet the elusive Mr Riviere, the man who had actually achieved the 150mph for *The Autocar*. He confirmed that this speed had definitely not been fudged. I have a couple of period photos of 9600 HP with an unidentified gent. In one he is standing by the car in his hat and overcoat. In the other he is sitting in the car with his trilby perched on top of the roof, presumably his way of highlighting the lowness of the car. For years I had wondered who he was. I happened to show the photos to Peter, merely to remind him of the car, and he vaguely recognized him as a member of the management at *The Autocar*.

We then talked about the identity of Maurice Smith's unnamed companion on the way out to Antwerp. Riviere speculated that the lady in question was 'Elizabeth Hussey, who was Maurice's secretary. Now Elizabeth Hussey's family came from the firm that makes all the leather, Connollys. If it was a female person, my guess is that it was Elizabeth Hussey because, casting my mind back, I think Elizabeth did ski.' Excellent!

The front tubular sub-frames which carry the engine and front suspension were found to be the originals and displayed merely the patina of age. After delicate repairs, the door shells were refitted to the tub before the skins were fitted.

On my return I telephoned Anthony Hussey, whom I've known for years, at Connollys and he not only confirmed that the lady in question was his sister, but actually remembered Smith arriving at their parents' house in 9600 HP. I phoned Elizabeth Hussey, who could not have been more charming. 'Do come round and stay for whatever meal's appropriate.'

Remembering that Fairman's advert mentioned work being done on the car by Rowe's of Chichester, I determined to follow up that one. Who did I know in the Chichester area? Charles Fripp specializes in XKs and is based nearby. I phoned him. He knew the name and would investigate.

At this stage, the CMC guys were behind schedule and getting concerned. The areas around the screen pillar and 'A' post structure had consumed a lot more time than expected as the repairs were difficult and intricate. Also the boot floor area took longer than estimated because of their strict principles of doing everything as it had been rather than taking an easier route.

Andrew Tart: 'The boot floors are difficult at the best of times, and we just added to our problems by building it as one panel.'

Baz had now finished the bonnet but was on related work as it is imperative to check things at this stage to avoid nasty shocks later. 'We were fitting the heater the other day. You have to fit the heater to make sure the splash guards line up.

After extensive skilled work, the rear end was transformed from a selection of gaping holes, corroded and dented panels into the beautiful sculptural form that Jaguar created originally. The unique aluminium tailgate was luckily in excellent condition and needed little work. With the completion of the rear end, the bodywork was largely finished.

Everything has to be fitted to make sure the bonnet will close. So we offered up the heater and found that there were three holes, one of which is out of line on the bulkhead, and the three brackets that hold the heater on are all bent. So obviously at one point or other, they fixed the heater in, put the bonnet down when they were building the car and the bonnet fouled the heater. So they basically shoved the heater across and bent the brackets! There were only three bolts holding it instead of four and we've left it exactly as it was. So we have the original heater with the original Jaguar-bent brackets that hold it in place.'

The nearside bonnet locking plate was missing, so Baz has faithfully copied the offside one. 'The outer part of the bracket has three spot welds that have been drilled out. They obviously mounted the bracket there with a pin in, and then moved it down and put three more spot welds in. So we've done the same. I'm trying to copy Jaguar's apprentice riveting!

'The original Jaguar bonnet shut line was about an inch lower down and they modified the sill end by making a new top piece, spotwelding a plate on the back and then spotwelding the whole thing to the original and then leading over the front. We've done that on both sides. Again, we've replicated Jaguar's cock-up!' Just three short months to go!

CHAPTER TWELVE

The Pressure Builds

A TV crew from Carlton had been regularly visiting CMC to capture every major stage of the project. On the second day of December I joined the TV crew at CMC to watch Andrew assemble the engine in a day. That in itself was an interesting experience but what impressed us most was the almost fanatical lengths to which Tart went to ensure every component was spotlessly clean. We were all huddled into his little engine room, which already appears clinically clean. But every time he touched a component he wiped it down, applied some oil, wiped it again, looked at it, wiped it again and fitted the item. It is just as well the cleaning paper is recycled, or he would be responsible for destroying entire forests single-handed. Emily Childs, the presenter, who had been very enthusiastically following the project since the launch on 1 April, was not a happy bunny because she was being moved on from her motoring role – though it was excellent promotion.

'I think the engine is, in effect, a late 150 engine,' said Andrew as he worked. 'The timing gear intermediate twin sprocket is made in two pieces which I think I have only ever seen on XK engines, never on E-type engines. In the block itself, around the oil filter housing, it has some plugs – almost like core plugs – fitted, which I think is very unusual for an E-type engine. It hasn't got a rope seal at the back of the engine, which is normal for early E-types, but highlights that it's an early car. We've saved all the bits and pieces, even the spring washers. On one side only of the spring washers, they are serrated – some more pronounced than others. You can't buy those nowadays. They are used with the bolts that hold the sump on. I am going to have to re-black them and use them again.'

Rather than use replacements, 'The head nuts will be re-chromed; same with the cam cover nuts. It is only an ordinary 3.8 cylinder block, but the unusual thing is that the engine number has been ground off and re-stamped at some stage, which is very strange, but this number still appears on the cylinder head. The number on the cylinder head has not been changed.'

'It is not,' I suggested, 'as though somebody has faked it because they would do it correctly.'

'If I was going to fake it,' replied Andrew, 'I'd make a better job of it. So that was definitely done at the factory.' I suggested it would be interesting to X-ray this area. Subsequently we would learn, in the maze of research, that the first engine had been renumbered, and all this started to make sense!

'I think,' continued Tart, addressing his remarks to Emily and chuckling, 'that all E-types have a rope seal on the crank, but this one doesn't, so you will have an oil leak! I rather like that because when Philip says, "It's leaking oil," I can say, "Yes, they do!"'

'The con rods have had new small end bushes and been re-sized. I nearly didn't bother re-sizing them and they were nearly OK, but we want to be able to drive it really hard and we don't want to worry that it is not quite right. We have put new big end bolts and nuts in.

'The head is obviously the original head. I am putting some D-type specification cams in. It has been ported and polished and we'll match it to the inlet manifolds. These are all things that certainly would have been done if Jaguar were trying to

Following stripping, machining, balancing and various preparation work, Andrew Tart virtually built up the engine in a day for the TV cameras. He has a separate engine room at the CMC workshops and it is kept spotlessly clean. In spite of the time pressure, Andrew took immense care at each stage to check and clean all parts as he went along. We had decided the engine would be rebuilt with big valves and hotter cams with the 150mph target in mind.

produce extra horsepower. The bucket guides that sit on top of the valves wear and, although these weren't bad on the inlet side, on the exhaust side we have replaced them. Nowadays we just bore them out and put an oversize bucket in but I didn't want to do that as I wanted to keep it standard. So we have put new guides in and retained the standard buckets.'

In early December Andrew phoned to say that he had just heard from David Morris of Four Oaks Fuels who does their carburettor rebuilds. All SUs are stamped with a letter and number, which denote the date they were originally built. The carbs from 9600 HP were stamped with an 'S', which equates to 1959 and a '9' which indicated September. Also, he spotted that the throttle linkage was hand-crafted. A few days later Andrew phoned again to say the engine was now running and sounding sweet. It was excellent news and another milestone.

While Tim was finishing off the rear, Baz tackled the bumpers. We had decided we wished to rebuild the car in its ultimate road test form, both mechanically and visually. This meant having no overriders on the front. It was not, though, just a matter of leaving them off. Baz had to make some 'extended beaks. It was a devil's own job because the chromers stripped the chrome off but didn't strip the copper off. I'd

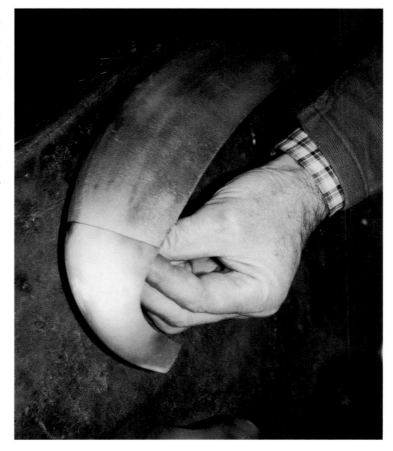

Meanwhile Baz Cope, who owns these fingers, was skilfully adapting the bumpers as we decided not to have overriders or motif bar. Our thinking was to recreate the car in its ultimate road test form. The car is also more distinctive in this guise and emphasises the individuality of this particular E-type.

never come across it before, but you can't weld anything that's contaminated with copper. I've been welding for years and I'd never come across that. You weld and then if you move the metal slightly, it just cracks. So we ended up with some braze on it to stop it cracking. They took quite a while to get right. A huge amount of work – I think it was close on three days.

'This we believe is the original bumper blade as it came from the offside and it has a definitely more pronounced edge under the sidelight – a sharper profile. This is the N/S one, which clearly couldn't be original, due to the accident, so I have chased a sharper edge into that one to replicate the O/S one. These are off to the chromers now.'

It is normal to finish off the work on the body by using traditional plumbers' lead to fill where necessary and create the correct profiles. Famously Jaguar used 'a ton of lead' on many models, or at least this phrase is part of Jaguar folklore now. Because the chaps at CMC had worked to such a high standard, only a minimal amount of lead was needed. Tim did notice that lead had been used in some unusual places, such as the door shut faces. 'And there isn't lead on this car where the production cars are usually leaded. The production cars are usually leaded down the "A" post on the reinforcing joint which supports the scuttle. I've got to consult the

Baz Cope (right) had the challenge of altering the new front wings to make them fit properly and maintain the high standards throughout the car. Here we see Tim and Baz completing the bodyshell by filling with traditional plumbers, lead. Because they had done such a superlative job, very little lead was needed, in stark contrast to how many Jaguars were built originally.

photographs, but I don't think this was leaded.' Two-and-a-half months remaining!

With the leading completed, the shell was transported to the House of Kolor in Belbroughton. Over the years Steve Molineux has done a lot of specialist work, including painting show cars for motor manufacturers and design studios. We all felt that cellulose paint should be used, as was used in the period, even though it is nowhere near as durable as modern two-pack paints. Steve's first and biggest challenge was finding a source today.

With the shell lead loaded, it was transported to the specialist paintshop some fifteen miles away. I always think it is a tragedy for the panel beaters that most of their hard work is never seen. It is the paintwork that everyone sees and so clearly this had to be of the highest quality finish. There is no substitute for preparation and sheer hard work. To maintain originality, cellulose paint was used even though it is less practical. Back at CMC, the fitting-up stage could begin.

As a result of the high quality of work from Tim and Baz, the preparation required was kept to a minimum. The only filler used was a small amount of aluminium filler on the tailgate. The body was given three coats of primer, two coats of epoxy primer and two coats of colour. Steve feels that the older primers, even if you could now obtain them, were so dreadful it would be a crime to have used them. So the car has the advantage of modern base coats for durability. With time so short, the main shell returned to Bridgnorth, while Steve and colleagues Ian Hutchins and Matt Gillard completed the bonnet and doors.

I asked Andrew Tart about colour matching. 'We have just taken a panel from inside the car that hadn't been affected by the sun and matched to that.' Steve explained the process to me. 'The exact colour was achieved by getting some material [paint] which was a formulation made up for the original colour. We then did spray-outs to see how closely it actually matched the original. It wasn't exactly right so we tinted it to match. You can vary the amounts of metallic you use. The more you add the more the sparkle effect but also it can change the colour completely.' The car was due to go back to House of Kolor over the Christmas period for the next stage.

On 14 December I went up to CMC to view another milestone, namely, the fitting of the engine into the car. As ever, Carlton TV were there. As they began to film Andrew moving the engine over to the car, a door directly behind opened and in walked Father Christmas. The filming had to halt for several minutes due to the jangling of his trousers.

With the car back at Bridgnorth, the fitting-up had started. This was the responsibility of Colin Howell, who had carefully stripped the car. A very quiet, shy man, he is highly respected by his colleagues and also has an infectious enthusiasm for the car. As the pressure was really on, and the fitting-up stage is so complex that it

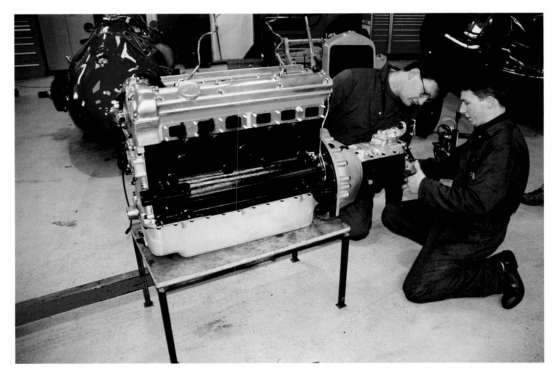

With the engine completed and the rebuilt gearbox fitted, the unit was ready to be re-united with the car. Andrew Turvey (right) would do much of the fitting up work, alongside Colin Howell. Here Turvey assists Andrew Tart with various details a few moments before taking the engine over to the car.

always takes longer than anybody predicts, Colin was joined by mechanic Andrew Turvey. They started by building up the braking system, including the infamous bellows-type servo, and fitting the front suspension.

Younger Andrew was very relaxed considering his wife was due to give birth that day. 'Now I know why Jaguar cut that hole out!' he suddenly exclaimed. He was looking at the side of the prop shaft tunnel where there are three large holes hacked out. 'It's to remove the speedo drive from the gearbox. There's a little bit of damage on the thread so I'm just going to take it out and dress the thread, but I can't get it out in situ. I've got to remove the [access] panel that Jaguar have very kindly provided.' Andrew Tart then chipped in with the suggestion that Jaguar would have needed access here to change the speedo drive pinion whenever they changed the back axle ratio.

Later that day, I had a chat with the mobile trimmers, Tom and Dan Hampton, and Andrew Tart. We huddled round a table, poring over the period photos, trying to deduce what we could. The heavy grain on the sill material has always been very obvious, and Paul Skilleter had mentioned it when checking that the car was genuine back in 1977. Tom, who used to manage a large trimming company and also taught the subject before deciding he preferred to concentrate purely on the art of trimming,

Andrew Tart does not believe in fitting an E-type engine from above. It is a tight fit and there is always the danger of damaging the paintwork. His method is to lift the front of the car, slide the engine underneath on rollers, lower the body and then raise the engine to its final resting place. Within minutes it was in and the auxiliaries could now be fitted.

dropped a bombshell. Looking at a photo showing the dashboard, he pointed out the reflection of an instrument in the facia panel to the left. The left- and right-hand facia panels are normally trimmed, but it would be impossible to see a reflection on material. On this car these parts of the dash must have been painted. Discussion ensued and the collective decision was that we would go that route.

I asked Tom if he had had any difficulties. 'Sourcing has been the main problem, particularly the heavily grained material. The original vinyl they used was the same as used on the later 150s. We have found it now but that was a concern.' The dash top, he felt, would have been a metal panel with foam on top and material over that. 'They wouldn't have kitted up to do vacuum forming at this stage. I reckon that's where the sharpness comes from. It's really sharp round the bottom.' Another oddity was the covered trim panels that attach behind the 'B' posts, which are steel, as opposed to Millboard for production cars.

A year or two previously, I had mentioned to Stirling Moss about him driving 9600 HP through the car wash but he did not remember it. I happened to mention it at Goodwood to his wife Susie. She suggested I showed him a video of the newsreel footage to jog his memory. Accordingly, in late December, I faxed Moss asking if I could visit him at home, armed with a video and a bottle of something to his taste. I suggested early January when I would be in London for the Sherlock Holmes Society Dinner.

I then telephoned John Paddy Carstairs' one surviving brother and he kindly invited me round to view some of his brother's paintings and for a chat. A few minutes later I received a faxed reply from Moss. 'Sorry, but I have to leave for the States on 26th and am not due back until January 24th. Can you keep the Chardonnay cold until then? If so, give me a few days to sort through my mail and we could fix it. Regards, Stirling.'

I then telephoned Brian Playford to fix a visit and Moss phoned and we arranged a date. Later I was in the bath, with cordless inevitably at my side (well almost), when Charles Fripp phoned to say he had done some research on Rowe's of Chichester. They still existed and he gave me a name and number to try.

Next day I wrote a begging letter to Bernard Cahier, who had driven the car prelaunch. Mark Hughes, who had been writing up the project in *Classic & Sports Car*, had given me an address and phone number in France, which he thought might be a combined fax number. I tried it and M. Cahier answered, 'Allo, Allo.' He then realized it was *un fax* and let forth an almighty bellow to someone, presumably elsewhere in the building, 'Fax, fax, fax!' A little later, he replied to say that he had photos and he would be pleased to send me some when he visited his archives in mid-January. It was great news and the perfect Christmas present.

Bill Boddy had suggested I should speak to Michael Tee, his co-driver on their prelaunch run. My old friend at *Motor Sport*, Gordon Cruickshank, provided the number. Poor Gordon was going to act as a specialist Directory Enquiries several times over the next weeks as my research hotted up.

I wrote and followed up with a phonecall. Mr Tee mentioned he always kept a notebook during his many years with *Motor Sport*. Whenever he had driven a car, he would always jot down a few salient words to act as an aidé-mémoire. When he had received my letter, he had had a good look for the notebook but had been unable to find it. As we chatted, he had another idea as to where it might be. I held my breath. The search proved fruitless. Shame. We chatted on and then, suddenly, he had another idea, looked and, 'I've got it!' Within seconds, he was reading out the relevant passage to me.

'"Demo. Jaguar E-type GT 1961. 155 miles in 2 hours. 155mph. 12 miles in 5 mins on M1."'

The two-hour run was done, rather obviously, at an average of 77.5mph and the five-minute average was no less than 144mph. He mentioned that they timed the top speed, and this is surely excellent proof of the maximum for there is nothing better than timing. It avoids all such variables as tyre size and growth, instrument inaccuracy and suchlike.

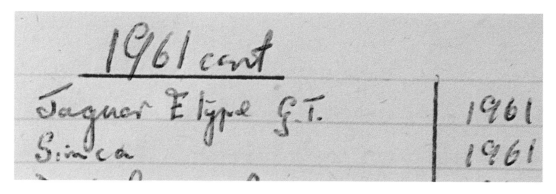

This is Michael Tees original notebook in which he wrote his one line aide memoire after driving 9600 HP pre-launch for *Motor Sport*. Note that he claims a top speed of 155mph.

I telephoned former Jaguar engine man, Frank Philpott, and arranged to meet in the New Year. He mentioned that engines had a top end variation of ten per cent and that could make quite a difference. A phone conversation with Stuart Bladon was very helpful as he told me the story of his involvement with the original *Autocar* road test. Here and there, I took a few hours off over Christmas and went to the odd party and dinner. What staggered me was that people I had never met before, even people not interested in cars, knew about the 9600 HP project.

My old pal Gil stayed with us after Christmas and we visited the painters on 30 December. The shining paintwork had been rubbed down with fine abrasive paper and taken back to a matt finish. When we arrived, it was being masked up ready for final painting. 'There has been about 200 hours work put into it already,' stated Steve. 'We will now apply three coats of colour. Start with the roof, work our way down the tailgate, down the rear quarters, down the sides and then on to the

Though the paintwork looked finished, the car was taken back to the House of Kolor over the Christmas period for the gloss finish to be rubbed down and flatted prior to the final coats of cellulose and varnish. Using traditional materials brought fresh challenges. With the car now semi-built up, it was imperative to carefully mask various areas.

bonnet. Then, after a flash-off time, another coat of the same. The final one will be a cross-coat which will even up the colour. Then we will lacquer it with two coats of clear. Then it will be ready for a cut and polish when that's dried.

'When applying cellulose every coat has to be even. You have to be more careful with cellulose. The metallic content in cellulose settles a lot quicker. Normally we paint a car in stages but in this case you just couldn't. It would be too much of a risk.' Because of the danger of the paint changing colour during the process, Steve and Ian were going to tackle it together. I asked Steve how they avoided painting each other! 'In stages I'll paint from the outside edge into the middle of the roof and he'll carry on from the middle to his outside edge. This is the first time I've used cellulose in 15 years and this is about the most difficult colour. Grey metallics are notoriously difficult. We will use about ten litres of colour, which is more colour than usual because cellulose just evaporates, and about seven litres of lacquer.' These traditional materials take much longer to cure and cannot be force-dried in an oven.

Cellulose is infamously impractical. 'Cellulose will fade, like the original did, so it will be authentic in that respect!' Final polishing would take place when the fitting-up was complete.

With the car back at Bridgnorth, the final countdown was beginning with a month-and-a-half to go. The pressure was on Colin and younger Andrew. They fitted the rebuilt carburettors, which were now looking magnificent, assembled the clutch controls and fitted the dynamo, starter motor, coil and distributor to the engine. Colin is principally a superb auto-electrician and, rather than throw away the old wiring loom, which is normally a no-brains decision on any restoration, because the 9600 HP restoration was so different, he had thoroughly checked out the old loom, made some minor repairs and rebraided it. So the car even has its original wiring, which is splendid. At the rear the fuel pump, rebuilt from several pumps including a couple I had on my shelves, and fuel tank went in, and the handbrake controls were built up.

The rear suspension unit had already been rebuilt, to save time at this stage, and this was now fitted, as were the wiper motor, heater, prop shaft and steering column.

The rear suspension unit was, of course, totally rebuilt with all wearing parts replaced. Otherwise, the unit was very original with even the old discs skimmed and retained. A few differences were noted from production car practice. Notably, the radius arms were made of thicker gauge steel. The diff. unit was rebuilt by GKN.

A number of holes had to be tapped to remove paint, and all the cavities were wax-injected. Jaguar paid no heed to corrosion originally, but we were keen for 9600 HP to last rather better second time around. CMC were getting close now and my research was really hotting up as well.

I mentioned to Tart my conversation with Michael Tee. He deduced from the speedo reading low, when *Motor Sport* tested it, that the car had been specially fitted with a higher back axle ratio. This would, of course, give a higher top speed but cause the speedometer to read slow. On the track of Rowe's of Chichester, I phoned Richard Woolley and he told me that the old Rowe's of Chichester was 'defunct'. He suggested I have a word with his colleague, Karrigan Enser. Mr. Enser could not help as he joined in '69 but suggested Roger Halsey who was now retired but had been Manager at the time. By various means, I tracked down Mr Halsey but he did not remember the car. I decided I had gone as far as I could on that one. Ah well, you can't win 'em all.

I then sent a photo of 9600 HP at Geneva and some text for publication in the monthly newsletter of the Guild of Motoring Writers', to which I have belonged for many years, in the hope that some of our elder members might be able to help with recollections. A few days later, I was thrilled to receive a fax from veteran BBC personality Raymond Baxter and a phonecall from Alistair Milne, who recalled his testing of the 7-ton lorry at MIRA and having a ride with Dewis in 9600 HP.

On the evening of 4 January, in preparation for the next day's interviews, I went through piles of paperwork again and found some testing records for the second engine. These covered a number of bench tests and showed that it had been fitted with petrol injection. That day I had faxed Bob Monkhouse, Sir Norman Wisdom, Leslie Phillips, Tommy Steele and David Jacobs, seeking more background on John Paddy Carstairs. The next day I spent successively with Bob Berry, Frank Philpott, Kate Sayer and back to Berry again. This was a good day and I made big strides.

Poor Bob Berry. I grilled him for several hours for every minutest detail, and later returned to subject him to more of the same. He remained charming and utterly helpful throughout the ordeal. Frank told me he had arranged to go to Jaguar to look up the information on the relevant engines. Having some knowledge of Jaguar's archives, I was very surprised to hear that such paperwork still existed. Frank was now on the case and would prove an energetic ally. He had already been in contact with former colleagues and I found his enthusiasm very touching.

'I also spoke to Dick Cresswell [a later Chief Tester] and his first comment was, "It wouldn't have been done [the 150mph runs] on standard tyres and you'd have gone much better on racing tyres". I spoke to another colleague, Jim Eastick, after Christmas and he said, "Ah, we had that engine in and put a new head on it between tests." He didn't know why it was done but we presume it was because we had heads about that we knew the performance of. So it may very well have done some of that work with an engine which we had not actually had as one unit on the bed. But we will be able to find that out if the records are there.'

For some while Andrew Tart had been concerned about how the car achieved the speed without the rev. counter going off the clock. The necessary revs, he reckoned, would be well above peak power. I put Andrew's point to Frank. 'If you compute tyre size, back axle ratio and revs, at 5750rpm, you will only have, say, 140mph.'

'Absolutely right.'

'So how did it do 150?'

At this point Frank chuckled heartily and put on a silly voice. 'This we don't know! Andrew's absolutely right. The rolling radius of the tyre could've made the difference. You've got to look for a change in the gearing. It's either the axle or the tyres.'

I suggested that perhaps the engine was more powerful.

'You've got to have a lot more power to extend the power band. I think I shall find that with the standard head we got close on 250 horsepower. Mr Heynes used to say he was not so much interested in what we were going to give the customers, but had we got the gross power? That meant with open intakes, no air cleaner and no exhaust. So he knew that if we only had 240 hp, we were probably going to get 220 in the car. So he used to say, "Get the power first."

'So we used to get the power and it was on standard components. The airflow on the heads was a very important thing with us and with Heynes at the time. We'd get that absolutely right and match the ports and match the manifold, make sure everything was right, put it all together and we'd test. Dick Cresswell said, "A sort of blue-printed engine" and that's right.

'If you ran an XK engine with the sump up to the Full mark, you'd lose a couple of horsepower or more. You'd not just lose power but you'd churn the oil and so you'd lose the lubrication due to aeration. So if we ever went for a maximum power run, I said to my people, "Make sure the oil level is on the bottom edge of the dipstick".'

Derek Brant, from whom I bought the car in 1977, has never shown the slightest hint of regret yet still has great enthusiasm for the car. His pleasure in the car being rebuilt is as great as anybody's and I will always be immensely grateful to him for selling the various E-types to me. In this photo he is looking at his original letter to Paul Skilleter, which played an important part in the story.

On 7 January I visited Derek Brant in Esher to hear how he originally acquired the cars and his moving story of how he made the decision to sell them. I then called on Miss Elizabeth Hussey in Kingston who had said she would identify her house by putting her skis in the front garden! Elizabeth was able to put a name to the gent in the photo that Riviere had vaguely recognized and also found her diaries, which gave us a date for the outward journey to Antwerp. Then it was off to the British Film Institute to spend a few hours researching Carstairs. Next morning I called on his charming brother in Chiswick.

Four days later, I got up at 3.30am and drove to an airfield near Chester to meet up with Peter Neumark. With his pilot Geoffrey at the controls, we took off in Peter's Citation jet at seven and landed at Geneva at 10am local time. Within minutes Eric Biass had joined us and we set off in his very swift Series I XJ6 for a day of exploration.

We drove first to the Parc des Eaux Vives. It was quite an emotional experience, I found, to see the name on the gates and drive up the winding road to the old restaurant. I had studied the pho-

Like everyone associated with the car, either intimately or tenuously, Elizabeth Hussey was both charming and enthusiastic. For me it has been fascinating and most enjoyable tracking down everyone and following every possible lead, even though many inevitably led up cul-de-sacs. 9600 HP seemed to touch the lives of so many interesting people and vice versa.

tographs so many times and often written about the events of 39 years before, but to visit this E-type 'shrine' at last was quite eerie. To our delight the surroundings seemed largely unchanged. The restaurant building precisely matched the period photos, though the roof and interior had been damaged by fire within the last couple of years and the whole was now scaffolded. Remarkably, most of the trees remained and were recognizable and very few additional ones had forced their way into the picture.

Next we made our way to the old test course and by means of elimination worked out the route. It is not heavily built up but there is a fair scattering of dwellings now, and it was not easy to imagine E-types and Ferraris thundering round these tiny roads at unmentionable speeds. The hairpin must have been exciting, though!

Leaving the lakeside area behind us Eric drove back into the centre in search of the old exhibition building. As we approached, Sky News telephoned to ask me about the F-type Concept car which had been unveiled at Detroit that morning. In concentrating on the call, I was disappointed to miss this landmark. Then Eric and Peter broke it to me. It had been flattened!

The original dealership, Garage Place Claparède, which was owned by Marcel Fleury, closed down some years ago and there are now two very smart Jaguar dealerships in Geneva. We visited both but neither could help. However, an elder salesman at one was able to find out where the original premises had been. We drove there and it is now just a humble workshop.

The F-type Concept press release was waiting for me when I got back. Under the heading of Jaguar Roadsters, there were a series of bullet points. After one mentioning E2A, the next read. 'Nine months later, in 1961, Jaguar created a sensation at the Geneva Motor Show with the E-type, powered by the 3.8-litre 'S' version of the XK engine, with a top speed approaching 150 mph'. Not, I think, a Roadster that caused the sensation at Geneva. Interesting to note the phrase 'approaching 150 mph'!

I was delighted to receive a hand-written fax from Bob Monkhouse at his house on Barbados. Bridgnorth was a little cooler, but things were hotting up at CMC.

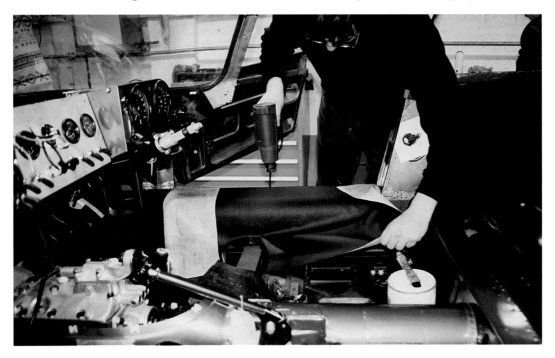

Back at CMC the car had reached the stage where the trimmers, Tom and Dan Hampton, could make a start. One of the first jobs was fitting the new sill coverings. Like everyone else, Tom and Dan entered wholeheartedly into the spirit of the job and put a lot of effort into obtaining all the right materials. Period photos show that Jaguar originally used a very heavily grained material and this took some obtaining in 2000.

Items being fitted included the exhaust system, various sound deadening pads, windscreen, chrome trims, the door glass, rear lights and bumpers. As the rebuilt instrument panel was being installed, the gearbox cover and dash top were fitted. The bonnet was built up with wiring, lights and bumpers, but no overriders or motif bar in the mouth. Meanwhile an extra ashtray was being made up for the centre console, as one appears in early shots of the car. Also the radio console was unique to this car. Luckily, Barratts persevered and managed to obtain some of the original-type textured aluminium sheeting from which these items could be fabricated. The bonnet catch 'T' bar would uniquely be clipped to the right-hand 'A' post, and a curious pocket, which had been on the passenger's door, was added.

Trevor Crisp, who had joined Jaguar in 1954 and specialized in engines all his career, had recently been promoted to head up Cosworth. He wrote saying he had been delayed in replying by their preparations for the Monte Carlo Rally and Formula One testing.

'You are really taxing my memory on 9600 HP. I do indeed remember the car appearing in the Experimental Department where I was working and can still see it in my mind as it looked so dramatically attractive compared with the prototype Roadster with which I was familiar.

'As far as the engine is concerned, I really do not know and I'm sure George Buck and Frank Philpott would be better informed. I know it ran on racing tyres for the main speed tests and I heard rumours that it had slightly oversize valves and modified cams.'

Remembering Berry's comments about the Geneva launch being organized by the Society of Motor Manufacturers and Traders, I spoke to Jonathan Wood to seek his advice on who to contact at the SMMT. Jonathan is a respected motoring historian and I reminded him of the day that we met in 1977 before I went off to view the E-types. Paul had been photographing cars in front of a house for the cover of Jonathan's first book. He told me that, by a strange coincidence, in 1984 he married Rosemary Wilson, who had lived in that very house.

It seems that the SMMT has indulged in ageist cleansing in recent years and there was no one left from the sixties. Jonathan suggested a gentleman who might be able to help, even though his subject was statistics. I phoned what Jonathan believed to be his direct line and a young man answered. He told me that the other fellow was not available and asked why I wanted him. I was unwise enough to tell him. He said I was in luck as he himself was the person to speak to because he was in the Press Office and the other fellow was in Statistics. He would look into it and phone me back. Sounded encouraging.

That afternoon he duly phoned and he said he had had little luck. All he could tell me was that the E-type had a 3.8-litre engine when it was launched and some time later this was replaced with a 4.2. He had been advised that the best person to speak to was someone called Philip Porter. I was not impressed but he retorted – and here he made it sound like an exceptional gesture – that he had taken the trouble to phone me back. In this day and age what should be basic manners and profession-alism is considered exceptional.

However, I was not going to give up as easily as that and asked this cocky youth to put me through to the fellow I had originally requested. To put the fear of God into him (some hope!) I said that I wished to cover the SMMT's role, or lack of role, in this story. He said he would pass on the message. Of course, I never heard another squeak.

I then telephoned Patrick Mennem, who in 1961 was Motoring Correspondent of the *Daily Mirror*. He was at Geneva for the launch in the Parc and told me about the 'gasp' as the car was unveiled. Then I phoned photographer friend Tony Marshall for Susanne Dryden's phone number. Susanne is the widow of the late Colin Dryden, who was Motoring Correspondent alongside John Langley at the *Telegraph*. Re. SMMT, Susanne helpfully suggested Dougie Armstrong, Anne Hope, Gerry Kunz (son of Charlie of jazz fame) and others. Meanwhile I faxed 'Jabby' Crombac, of *Autosport* during 'our' period, and old friend Nick Georgano, of *Encyclopaedia of Motor Cars* fame, about the Gordano car. Nick phoned immediately with sugges-tions of whom to talk to.

On 24 January, I telephoned the Driver & Vehicle Licensing Authority (DVLA) at Swansea to see if they could help with the missing link in the chain of ownership. Unfortunately, their information started when the computer records were first set up in 1980 and the only information which they had was provided at that time by a fel-low named Porter.

During the day Peter Neumark had something of a shock. He received a phonecall from Jaguar PR in response to his final, final letter about the project.

Throughout this time I had been in regular email contact with Paul Skilleter, try-ing to jog his memory about his original contacts with Derek Brant. Paul's magazine *Jaguar World* had been running my regular reports of the progress but he was amazed at how well CMC were doing. 'I am astonished that the Geneva re-run is to be this year! An astounding achievement by all concerned if it happens. What port are you intending to leave from? I would like to see you and the car off. I will con-tinue to look for other 9600 bits and pieces. Who knows what we may find? Maybe a receipt from D. Brant to me proving that I really bought the car!'

On 23 January Sir Stirling Moss accepted the title of Patron of our XK Club and two days later I was in London for the glitzy Jaguar Formula One launch at Lords' Cricket Ground. There I had a chat with Jackie Stewart and Johnny Herbert about E-types, and bumped into Bernard Cahier, one of the members of the Pre-Geneva Drivers' Club. I quickly asked him about the launch. 'No, no, no. I am sure it was not in the restaurant. It would not go in.' Spotted Mike Cross, Jaguar's Chief Test Driver today, and sought his advice about the 150mph runs we were aiming to do. Michael Bowler, formerly of *Motor* and founding Editor of *Classic Cars*, suggested I should try Dick Benstead-Smith, who might have been at Geneva. Then took a taxi to my pub-lishers and had the pleasure of being entertained by a proper old London cabbie. He wanted to know what I did. 'Should I know you?' I had to disappoint him!

Back at work in the barn, David Jacobs, of *Juke Box Jury* fame and very much a part of the sixties scene, phoned. He only knew Carstairs slightly but bought one of his paintings of the South of France. He did recall his first ever run in an E-type as 'an extraordinary experience. It was the first time I had ever done 100mph.' 'Jabby' Crombac faxed to say, 'I wasn't at Geneva in '61. Autosport needed me only at the Paris show, mainly to organize entertaining! I know Charrier is still alive, but he lives in a strange place like Denmark. He is an artist. There is hate between Bardot and himself so don't ask her where he is!'

On 1 February I was in London for Alan Clark's memorial service, as he had been our previous XK Club Patron and loyal supporter. After lunch in the Commons with my old pal Sir Sydney Chapman, who had helped in 1986 to obtain the foreword by the then Prime Minister, I dashed, after another meeting, to the Newspaper Library at Colindale in North London. I was in search of the advert in *The Sunday Times* which Derek Brant had spotted. I arrived at 4.00 to the cheerful greeting that they shut at 4.45. I obtained several reels of microfiche, repaired to a viewer and started whizzing through the pages. I decided to begin in January 1976, as we knew Derek owned the car by June 1976 when he wrote to Skilleter. Gradually I got the hang of where the classified ads fell in the paper each week. I got faster. I was checking the ads under the headings, 'Collectors Cars' and 'Jaguar and Daimler'. In true Holmesian style – but this was no affectation – I had to use my magnifying glass as the text was small and indistinct. I finished the first reel. So, unless I had missed it, the ad did not appear in January or February. Time was racing on. Feverishly I rewound the first reel and started the next one. It was 4.40, lights were starting to go out. Living 100 miles from London, it would be a disaster to have to return another day just on the off-chance of finding an ad that might even have been a figment of Derek's imagination. My eyes were streaming as the text blurred passed in front of me as I screamed through, anxiously trying to squeeze every last second out of my visit. It was 4.43. Suddenly – what's this? 'First FHC E-type Jaguar...' Got it. Well done, Derek. Another piece of the jigsaw puzzle.

On my return I tried phoning the two Manchester phone numbers. The bemused person on the other end of the first number stated he had only lived there seven years. Dead end. No reply from the other one but later, the phone rang and it was someone asking if I had recently been phoning him. He had dialled 1471. Unfortunately, he had only been there since 1986.

On the same tack, I phoned my old pal 'Phil the Fuzz'. Though retired from the police force, he was still working for them as a civilian. He thought there was a good chance he could help. Currently he was working closely with BT Communications – sounded hopeful. He would speak to his contacts and come back to me.

At CMC things were getting very close. Tom and Dan Hampton, the trimmers, had found that the seats were in very good condition. 'The seats have been stripped down,' Tom told me, 'painted up and put back together again. Everything inside is good – the leather's good, the foam's good, it's all in really good condition. They'll come up really well again.' That was certainly a bonus to know the original seats had survived so well. I had taken the precaution of storing them carefully, but without realizing they are not a matching pair!

Fitting the headlining was quite tense, for it is glued in. A quick-drying impact glue is applied to both surfaces. So, while Dan was lying in the car spraying the underside of the roof panel, Tom was coating the material. With a minute or so to complete the operation, and get it right first time, Tom loosely folded the square and ran over to the car. He joined his brother as, lying on their backs, they carefully lined up and committed themselves. Spot on!

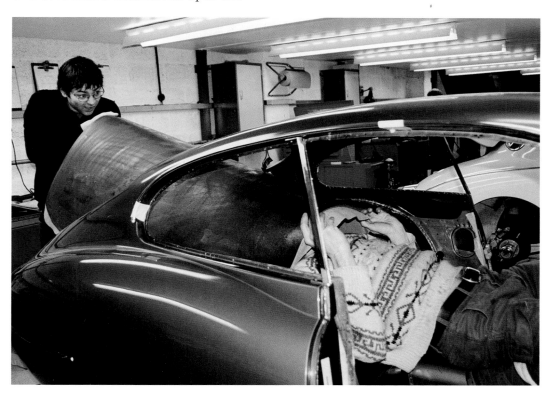

Fitting the glued-in headlining was a team effort. While Dan (right) had been spraying the roof with glue, Tom had been doing the same to the new headlining. With less than two minutes available before the glue went off, Tom dashed over to the car with the headlining, fed it in (as we see) and then also climbed in to fit it, with Dan assisting. It was a tense, but amusing moment, with two bodies athletically writhing around as they had to get it right first time. They did!

Colin and Andrew Turvey had been making fantastic progress with the fitting-up and clawed the project back on schedule, but they had hit a major problem with the cooling system. The early E-types had aluminium radiators, few of which have survived. The original 9600 HP one was long gone and so the hunt had been on for a

With the front suspension on, engine in, Cambridge Motorsport aluminium radiator *in situ* and many details completed, Colin Howell and colleagues were nearly there. Colin had stripped the car with Andrew Tart originally and had the satisfaction of being involved at the beginning and end. His principal skill is as an auto-electrician and it was splendid that he managed to save and re-use the original wiring loom.

replacement. Several were tracked down but all bar one were too far gone for rehabilitation. The skilled guys at CMC tried all they knew to rescue the half-reasonable one, but finally even they had to admit defeat. A good radiator is, to say the least, important on an E-type.

I therefore made a swift call to Richard Galvani who co-owns Cambridge Motorsport. One of their specialities is aluminium radiators and awhile back I had purchased one for the XK120 FHC. Their E-type rads are not 100 per cent identical to the originals, and authenticity was imperative. Time, though, was running out. A scrap original was despatched urgently to Cambridge Motorsport and, like everyone, they rose to the challenge and a week later we had a superb, exact reproduction.

Replacement rear overriders were needed, but luckily Barratts managed to locate some at their US branch. They discovered that the late Peter Gould, who owned British Auto USA until his untimely death, had managed to find a small quantity. With the tailgate built up and seals applied to this and the doors, the car was put on a ramp and every nut and bolt checked for tightness. On 16 February Nick Goldthorp phoned to say that the car would be having its first run later in the day for Carlton TV. The tragedy was that, due to pressure of work, I just could not drop everything and rush up there. But, I gather, all went well. Quite rightly, the honour of the first drive fell to Andrew Tart. It was another milestone.

I was ecstatic when Bernard Cahier's photos arrived. In one he is seen talking to Harry Mundy and former Grand Prix driver Tony Brooks. Telephoned Brooks but whilst charming he could not remember ever having driven the car or being photographed with it. He suggested I send him a copy, which I duly did.

I was intrigued by Sayer's reference in his CV to having designed GP bodies for Moss and his entrant Rob Walker, and having improved bodies for Brabham and Cooper. I telephoned Rob Walker, who racked his brains but could not recall the name. Said he would not necessarily have known of Sayer's involvement and that he might have liaised with [Moss's mechanic] Alf Francis without his knowledge. As we chatted, he said, 'We did do our own body on the Lotus 18, changing it from a cigar box to a proper-looking racing car. We got the Lotus 18 in 1960, so it would have been 1961.' He thought there was a good chance that Ken Gregory would know and that I should try him. It would also be worth speaking to Tony Robinson, Stirling's mechanic.

Phoned the long-suffering Gordon Cruickshank at Motor Sport for various phone numbers and he suggested trying Robert Edwards who wrote an excellent book on Archie Scott-Brown.

Richard Hassan phoned and we chatted about 9600 HP, which he had viewed on several occasions at CMC. He said that the chap we really needed to talk to was a fellow apprentice at the time, Barry Wood, who subsequently became a senior man at AC Delco. According to Richard, Barry would have done a lot of the work on the car originally and he would contact him and aim for a meeting the next week. 'Barry would know the car inside out. When I had the green overalls, he had the brown overalls.'

Robert Edwards phoned back and made countless suggestions. I faxed Duncan Rabagliati about Gordanos and Iotas, and he proved to be most helpful. Richard Hassan phoned again to say that Barry Wood was in California until April!

Telephoned Ken Gregory about Sayer. Gregory, who was Moss's manager, tried to help. He remembered Stirling being very impressed by Sayer's C-type. He didn't remember him being involved with any single seaters. Suggested contacting Tony Robinson and checking Alf Francis's book. Sayer, he said, was not involved with BRP. As to the Lotus 18, he 'thought that was designed by "Chunkie" [Colin Chapman].' That night I checked Francis's book – which I last read as a child – but no mention of Sayer.

Remembering Susanne Dryden's suggestion, I phoned journalist Anne Hope. She said she would be at the Geneva Show, which started at the end of February and had various contacts there. She suggested I email some questions to her. Anne then proceeded to bombard me with emails, making copious very helpful suggestions. She was another who was hooked and well and truly on the case now. Phoned Douglas

Armstrong and he recalled that Lyons gave Berry a rocket for being late. 'He was a hard taskmaster.' He felt the rooms in the restaurant were too small to get a vehicle in and over many years of attending launches in the Parc he could never remember anybody having a car inside. He reckons the cars were always outside. He also mentioned that the main entrance was up some steps. He suggested trying Gordon Wilkins. I had spoken to Wilkins, who used to introduce the BBC *Wheelbase* programme, in Belgium the year before, but he did not recall the launch.

When Brant owned the car he had taken it to a West London firm called Punters, and Skilleter photographed it there. I phoned but nobody could remember the car being there. The workshop was in New Road, Hillingdon. In the late 1960s it was a Jaguar breakers and then a repair business that tended to keep up the Jaguar connection.

I then had the idea of asking the Geneva Press Office to put up a sign and period photos in the Press Room at the 2000 Show. I duly sent a pack, receiving an email from M. Lambelet saying they would be pleased to help, and armed Anne Hope with a similar pack.

On another London trip I called on Brian Playford and chatted about the work they had done during Fairman's ownership. Next day I saw Sir Stirling and we viewed the *Pathé News* sequence. The next weekend my two-page article on the restoration appeared in the *Telegraph* and this yielded more interesting and helpful communications. I had an email from Geoff Linssen, erstwhile Manager of Richardsons, and Alan Currie, who was at Jaguar and a close friend of Sayer's. Linssen was particularly enthusiastic – 'It is part of our history, part of English history' – and Currie kindly provided more information on Sayer.

Meanwhile, I snatched a few odd moments to read a slim volume entitled *How to trace the History of Your Car* by Philip Riden. As a consequence, I faxed The Museum of British Road Transport in Coventry to see if they held any vehicle licensing documents for the car. They telephoned to say they did not, but suggested I try the City Archives. I faxed them and they came straight back and said, 'Sorry'.

Frank Philpott reported that he had been into Jaguar twice, once to the Engineering Centre at Whitley, where he had had no luck, and once to the Jaguar Daimler Heritage Trust archives at Browns Lane. He said he would be going again the following Monday. Recalling that Berry thought 9600 HP might have been the course car at Shelsley Walsh hill-climb, I telephoned old friend, former MAC Secretary and now Archivist, Mark Joseland. Mark said he would check the old programmes and photo archives over the weekend. Telephoned David Benson, as suggested by Anne Hope. He was not with *The Motor* until 1964 but recalled that when they road tested a 4.2 E-type, they could not get more than about 148mph. 'Bill Lyons said, "You can't publish that" and Jaguar had the car back to see if they could get more out of it.'

In search of photographers at Geneva, I phoned Maurice Rowe (of *The Motor*, who had not been at Geneva but made helpful suggestions), Peter Cramer

Sir Stirling Moss, newly knighted, consults his diary for 1961 to remind himself of the day he drove 9600 HP. I do not mind admitting he has been one of my heroes since I was a very small enthusiast and it is a great thrill for me that he drove the car, albeit only very briefly.

(of *Autocar*, ditto) and Charles Pocklington (not there). I mentioned to Charles the slight variations in journalists' Geneva recollections. 'They would write their copy and have to make a good story and then that's what they remember!' Ted Loades, of Abbey Panels fame, phoned from the Isle of Man and told me about building E-type bodies. Then, coincidentally, another senior inhabitant of that island phoned. I was particularly delighted to hear that Sir Norman Wisdom remembered being driven in 9600 HP, and it was a genuinely very funny conversation.

Still keeping BT afloat, I phoned Mark Joseland re. Shelsley. He had kindly done a lot of research in the Midland Automobile Club archives. He had found that the hill-climb in June 1961 was opened by the President, Sammy Newsome (Coventry Jaguar dealer and theatre owner), and top hill-climber David Boshier-Jones in an E-type but, as there was no photo, we cannot be sure whether it was 9600 HP or not.

Next I phoned John Pearson, from whom I had bought my XK140 Roadster back in 1973 and who had ridden in 9600 HP several times in the 1960's. Incredibly enthusiastic, knowledgeable and helpful as ever, John made copious suggestions during our 1 hour 39 minutes chat. Above all, he recalled the anecdote about 'Lofty' driving 9600 HP after Mike Parkes had stuffed Lofty's car into a hedge.

Nick phoned from CMC. Andrew Turvey had taken 9600 HP up to Shrewsbury to tax it. As he pulled up, someone walked over. 'Oy mate. Isn't that the car that's being restored?' He was amazed it was completed. Andrew was very chuffed.

Next morning Pearson phoned. He had been digging through his extensive archives the night before and found various very good stuff on the Experimental engine. I was then stunned to receive a fax from a total stranger which read, 'I have been following the story of 9600 HP's reincarnation... It was a great surprise and pleasure to see the car yesterday, on the road, heading for Bridgnorth from the Shrewsbury direction.... I was going about my employer's business in the repmobile when I saw the distinctive E-type nose heading towards me and then saw the number on the bonnet. So, just a quick line to let you know how splendid the car looked and sounded and to congratulate you and the team at CMC for achieving such a splendid result. The sight and sound brightened up my day considerably. Kind regards, Mike Rigby.'

A few minutes later the irrepressible Pearson was on the phone again with more good suggestions and more fascinating engine information. 'I'm into it – can't give up now.' The copies he sent me revealed that the first engine had been renumbered and thus the first and third engines were really one and the same. We appeared to have engine number R1001-9 – the very first E-type engine.

At the suggestion of Jaguar automobilia specialist Ian Cooling, I had faxed Roger Gloor of the Swiss magazine *Automobil Revue*. In an earlier life Ian had been a diplomat stationed at the British embassy in Switzerland and met M. Gloor. I briefly explained the 'Geneva Conundrum' and asked for his thoughts. He looked in their archives and, excellent news, found some photos of 9600 HP in the Parc with Sir William and the Show car – in the restaurant. He confirmed that this took place on Wednesday, 15 March. I felt we had definitely cracked it. The Show car must have been in the restaurant while 9600 HP was outside.

Admittedly, we still do not know why there was the extreme urgency to get 9600 HP there on time and why Lyons was so angry. Presumably it was felt that one static car crammed into a small room was far from adequate and not ideal for photography. It seems 9600 HP was there for photography and to show that the E-type was more than just a pretty face.

While I was following up John Pearson's many suggestions, Dick Benstead-Smith phoned. He was not at Geneva, so regretted he could not assist. George Hodge, formerly in the Service Department at Jaguar and then one of the most respected XK engine specialists, remembered the car being used by his boss 'Lofty' England quite a lot and being regularly in and out of the Department.

I then broke off the research and writing for a few hours for an important meeting with Stuart Dyble, the new PR Director at Jaguar. We had frank discussions and forged what I hope will prove to be a good relationship. He was very positive about 9600 HP and we talked about the F-type. We planned to work together. At last, and just in time, we seemed to have a new spirit and an enthusiasm on the part of Jaguar for 9600 HP. Many people had expressed their dismay at Jaguar's apathy and lack of co-operation.

Saturday morning Ron Beaty phoned. Another long-standing engine specialist, Ron worked in Experimental during the 9600 HP period and remembered seeing the car around. I asked him the million-dollar questions about how modified the road test engine was. 'It had lower radial pressure rings, a big valve head, gas-flowed head and manifolds, probably polished rods and crank, which was an option, and gave about 20/25 horsepower more than a standard engine.' This was strong stuff. I challenged him. 'Are you really sure about the big valves?' I asked. 'Yes, definitely,' was the unequivocal answer. 'Frank Windridge, who died long ago, did the gas-flowing. It was built in the old Experimental shop. Oil consumption was diabolical on the lower radial pressure rings.'

I mentioned Frank Philpott's point about keeping oil in the engine to a minimum for maximum power. Ron agreed and said that having more than the minimum was 'disastrous on power, getting hot and throwing oil out'. Frank then phoned. He was very angry and alleged that his research in the archives was being blocked. So perhaps we will never know the full, definitive specification of the road test engine. Intriguing, though, is it not?

Duncan Rabagliati faxed from a hotel in Singapore, my fax having been forwarded, and kindly clarified more Gordano and Iota points. John Cooper phoned to say he remembered Sayer but could not specifically remember him doing any work for them. I phoned Tony Brooks, who remembered driving the car thanks to his wife! The ever helpful Anne Hope returned from Geneva having spoken to more than forty people. I instantly followed up several leads, including telephoning a former Emile Frey employee in Switzerland, but without any success. In the very last paragraph of her long email to me she wrote, 'I didn't see Fred van der Vrugt at Geneva, but in 1961 he was editing the Dutch magazine *Autovisie*.' With my deadline literally two days away, it was worth one last try, so I faxed this gentleman. Next day he replied.

'My goodness, almost forty years ago! What do I still remember? ... I went to the attic room to look for the 1961 volume of *Autovisie*. Look what I found: "Despite the presence of the world-media at the Geneva press-day, Jaguar acted very mysteriously and did not show the new car on the stand. The official press introduction took place in the well-known restaurant of the Parc des Eaux Vives, but even there the car was hidden in a sort of cardboard coffin. Talk about chauvinism, the first driving impressions were reserved for British motoring journalists."'

So, there we have it – final, contemporary proof. The anonymous show car was *in* the restaurant but it was probably some feat getting it in and out. 9600 HP was there to be seen in a real environment, to be photographed with Sir William Lyons and for driving, and thus demonstrating what a truly stunning car the E-type really was. They shared the honours.

Meanwhile, the restoration story was coming to an end. It had been a Herculean task. The bare facts are that some 3500 hours had been expended in 11 months, at an average of 73 hours a week. But such statistics, whilst interesting, tell only a small part of the story. The team had, without exception, done a truly magnificent job, with great enthusiasm and in complete harmony. Now their work was going to be put to the test.

With the exception of Peter Neumark, this is the full CMC team, plus the proud owner. This shot was taken just before we departed for Geneva, exactly 39 years to the day after Bob Berry had left Browns Lane, Coventry. The team deserve the most enormous credit for one of the greatest restorations in the history of old cars.

CHAPTER THIRTEEN

On the Road Again

The emotions were many as I pressed the starter button for the first time. Visions of the car's eminent past and the many great names who had also pressed this same starter button flashed before me. I thought of the many years I had had to wait for this moment. I thought of all the heroic effort which had gone into its resurrection.

As the engine burst into life, my feelings were a mixture of boyish excitement and a sense of awesome responsibility. But as I drove off and started to experience the car, the overriding emotion was one of sheer pleasure. I soon became aware that the chaps at CMC had done a superb job. Examples of the same model of car can vary enormously and people, even respected journalists, have sometimes based their judgement on a poorly restored or very tired E-type. There is a world of difference.

But what is 9600 HP, a creation of the last century, like to drive today? The simple answer is that a good E-type is still a tremendously exciting and impressive car, even though it was conceived as long ago as the 1950s. All of the journalists who have driven 9600 HP since it was completed, and there have been quite a few, have been genuinely surprised and generous with their praise.

To someone who has only driven modern cars, the E-type will feel dated, though not as much as most journalists expected. Once you become accustomed to that, the E-type will be more rewarding and much more fun than almost any modern machine. If you want a car with air-conditioning, cruise control and glued-to-the-road cornering ability, an older car will disappoint. If, however, you prefer a greater involvement in driving, and you consider driving an art, then a good E-type is a wonderfully satisfying and exciting experience.

As you feed yourself into the low car, the aura of the E-type immediately becomes apparent. The view down the long curvaceous bonnet is one of life's great experiences. But the first thing you notice, as you drive away, is the docility of the car. The

Previous pages: The finished car is seen in front of the finished barn. Both had been transformed in less than a year. The old weather-boarding on the exterior of the barn masks a good deal of major work, yet over 90 per cent was still original. In similar vein, the shining 9600 HP paintwork hid three-and-a-half thousand hours of painstaking work.

The interior is once more pristine. It looks right and it smells right. Remarkably, quite a lot of the interior is still original, including the radio console vinyl, the embossed aluminium panels, the steering wheel, the instruments, the facia panels and, most pleasingly, the seats. By re-using such items as the (non-matching) seats, the interior looks smart but not overtly restored and new.

excellent torque means great flexibility, which is just as well because the gearbox on the 3.8 is one of its few shortcomings. Without synchromesh on first and with slow changes between the other gears, it can be tedious. It is vital to adopt a more patient approach to selecting a gear to avoid heart-rending crunches.

The steering is direct, precise and a sheer joy. As to the suspension, the ride was exceptional in the period for a sports car and is still very acceptable by today's standards. It combines relative comfort with excellent roadholding. The suspension and steering transmit consistent messages and allow you to press on with a good margin of safety. If you wish to indulge in more enthusiastic driving when conditions permit, then the car is very controllable at, and over, the limit. The tail can be hung out or the whole car chucked sideways, and because it all happens at a lower speed than today's performance cars on their wide, low-profile tyres, you do not need reactions in the Formula One class.

On the open road, the E-type comes into its own. On fast country roads, the pleasure is immeasurable. Coming up behind a slower car, you accelerate, the fabulous bonnet comes up and you quickly gobble up the car in front. Dip down into third and the acceleration is even more vivid. Heeling and toeing makes everything smoother and even more satisfying. As you settle into your stride, you realize this is very much a driver's car, a car that rewards good driving and above all is an incredibly tactile machine.

But the E-type does not have to be driven fast to be satisfying. It is quite happy pottering along in town or traffic. It will not exhibit any ill-mannered tendencies like other high-performance motor cars of the period. The E-type knows how to behave! But it is relaxing to know that when that opportunity to overtake finally presents itself, you have the necessary power under your right foot to do the job to devastating affect.

Apart from the gearbox, the only other main shortcomings of the early E-types are the brakes and the seats. The brakes, if properly set up, are not as bad as many claim. Those on 9600 HP seem more than adequate. Very often, as I have said, people are basing their judgement on a car with worn parts or one that has not been properly maintained. The seats were criticized at the time and still are. Personally, I have no problem with them even after several hours at the wheel, but we are all built differently. Some people feel the embossed aluminium panels on the dash and centre console on the 3.8s are rather inferior, whereas others like the style. The array of switches on the centre dash panel is the total opposite of an ergonomic design, which is sufficient reason to love them! It is another example of the E-type being designed by individuals for individuals. It was a product of the days before computers took over and made everything so near to perfection that all the character is lost.

Of course the E-type is dynamically dated today but, as someone once wrote, anyone can drive a tram. Compare it with its period rivals, and there is little comparison. Compare it with today's superlative but characterless creations, and it exudes personality.

Within days of the car being finished, BBC's *Top Gear* were on the phone wanting to borrow the car for their next programme. They used a helicopter to film 9600 HP running up and down a runway and the pilot complained the car was too fast for him!

Right: Quentin Willson, the Top Gear presenter, never seems lost for words and is always eloquent about E-types, having owned several in his formative years. He actually remembered 9600 HP from his boyhood and was all too aware of the recent transformation having seen the car in the barn some years before. In the passenger seat is fellow presenter and former racer Tiff Needell.

But all the above comments apply to any good example of a 3.8 E-type, which will always be the classic model. What of 9600 HP after its fanatical restoration? I am biased on many counts, so I was keen to hear the comments of others whom I respect, people like Mark Hughes, the former Editor of *Autosport* and *Classic & Sports Car*, Christian Frost of *Bil Magasinet* and Mark Bos, television motoring presenter and producer. All are highly experienced and not easily impressed. Yet all had a reverence for this car, both before and after driving it. The quality of the workmanship is somehow so apparent. It just looks so right. The body shape and all the gaps are spot-on. We know that under the skin there is great craftsmanship and so much history has been retained. The paintwork is just right. The car looks stunning yet is not over-restored. The interior drew many favourable comments – the quality of the work, the unique features, the lovely feel and the right smells!

It is all a little crazy. How many people are proud of the fact that their car seats do not match? I am! Others rejoiced in the fact. The asylum awaits us all.

Within days of the car being completed, we had an urgent call from the BBC *Top Gear* programme. They were doing a piece on British sports cars and would like to feature 9600 HP. Presenter Quentin Willson has always been a great E-type enthusiast. He was very excited about the car and, having driven it, *by* the car. I asked what it meant to him.

'It is important generally to the world because it is the first E-type that all those millions and millions and millions of people saw back in March 1961 when they came down from their beds to their breakfast tables, opened their newspapers and there it was. It was the most sensational-looking, the most sensational-performing and the most affordable supercar people had ever been able to get near. It had such an influence. The world took one look at this and just sighed in disbelief.

'For me it is just remarkable because I was one of those people who came down one morning as a small boy and was shown this car by my father, and having been associated with it over all these years, having seen it in your barn, with flat tyres and cobwebs, looking so sorry for itself, and now sitting in it in this absolute state of pristinity, if I can coin a word, it's amazing. This car has survived and that's the most important thing. It is probably *the* most significant – significant in terms of influence – *the* most significant car in the world.'

Two days later Andrew Tart took the car to a rolling road to set up the engine and check the power output. This was found to be 243bhp, which is very probably about the same as the car produced in its original road test form, and rather more than a standard production car.

Three days later, on 14 March, after more regional TV coverage, our small party set off from Bridgnorth bound for Geneva. Accompanied by Mark Hughes and photographer Tony Baker from *Classic & Sports Car*, Peter Neumark and Andrew Turvey from CMC, Mark Bos and TV crew and my old friend and distinguished photographer David Parmiter, we headed first for Jaguar Cars. There we were greeted by Stuart Dyble, the PR Director, and various colleagues. To my surprise they

En route to Geneva, we called at Jaguar's famous Browns Lane factory in Coventry where 9600 HP had originally been built in the Experimental Department. The first was joined by the last as Jaguar brought out the last V12 to be photographed alongside the old prototype. Peter Neumark (rear), Andrew Turvey (middle) and I pose for the cameras in front of the Jaguar Daimler Heritage Trust Museum.

produced an album of photographs of the event in Geneva and on one page there was an original invitation.

This invitation was a personal one from Sir William Lyons to attend at four-thirty in the afternoon. Whilst fascinating, this timing appeared to throw a large spanner into all that I have written in earlier chapters. I speculated whether it could have been a separate, private function. Bob Berry, who is probably the only person alive who could throw any light on this, had departed for the States a few days after we met in January and was not due back until early April.

I had to put this to the back of my mind as we had a schedule to keep to. We bade our farewells at Browns Lane and headed for Dover. On this occasion it was not possible to faithfully recreate the entire route in detail and so we went round London and boarded a six-thirty ferry. We were told the crossing took ninety minutes which, with the hour difference, meant we were due to dock at nine. I telephoned the Château de Cocove, where we were staying and which is 15 minutes from Calais, to be told they stopped serving dinner at the hour we were due to dock. Some 30 minutes into our 90 minute crossing we thus decided to dine on board. We ordered and, as our starters arrived, we tentatively enquired whether that was the French coast-line we could see lit up in what appeared to be rather close proximity. We were assured it was indeed France. We tucked in, but the waiter quickly returned with a worried expression. We were half-an-hour ahead of schedule and docking in a few minutes. They would not be able to serve our main courses! We made it to the hotel just in time for a fine three-course dinner!

We rendezvoued at the Château with Christian and Katrine Frost (of *Bil Magasinet*) from Denmark. Next morning we all motored towards Reims, Dijon and, rather than taking the direct route over the mountains, headed for Bourg and then drove due east as Berry had done 39 years before. Even this route is surprisingly mountainous and extremely twisty, which emphasized the challenge he had to over-come. Though we were treating the engine with care, this was real fun and 9600 HP was in her element, sweeping through the faster bends, going up and down through the 'box and accelerating between the hairpins. This was worth waiting 23 years for.

We arrived in Geneva that evening and met up with Eric Biass. Next morning we proceeded to the Parc des Eaux Vives, and once again it gave a thrill to drive through the gates – this time in the old girl herself. A large ad hoc committee then formed itself and decided upon the precise positions in which to place the car to recreate the original shots. Lacking extras in period dress, holding elderly cameras, we made do with our party and various local enthusiasts. With many shots taken, we set off for the hill course and I chucked 9600 HP through the hairpin with a tad of opposite lock for the cameras. Then it was time to head home. Leaving Geneva around mid-day, we arrived in Worcestershire at three-thirty next morning, the car having per-formed faultlessly and superbly. Full marks to the chaps at CMC, plus suppliers SNG Barratt, Cambridge Motorsport and the rest of the team.

The Geneva trip was just the first of a series of events which are planned or to which 9600 HP has been invited. Mark Bos has created a superb video and there is talk of television programmes. Indeed, we plan to make a programme about visiting all those who played a part in this story and faithfully recreating various events. Already the car has a film-star diary, but in spite of all the pressure, it is time to reflect for a moment.

It is understandable that I should be excited by the whole project. It is not too sur-prising that the guys at CMC were very motivated, but it has not ceased to amaze me how enthralled many others have become. Carlton TV presenter Emily Childs is a good example.

'The E-type is probably *the* car of the century. It is a very evocative car. Everyone knows them when they see them on the road and when we heard the very first E-type was about to be restored, we thought, "Yes! We've got to jump on it. It's a perfect story."

'It is something we can follow through and something our viewers would be very interested in, and I don't think it's just motoring enthusiasts either. It is a car being brought back to life, so the story is there, the characters are going to be there – peo-ple like Stirling Moss, Sir William – the great man at Jaguar. They all had big

Though the engine was still running-in, the drive down to Geneva was an opportunity to finally sample the delights of 9600 HP after 23 years of waiting. She did not disappoint. I was reminded of just how superb an E-type feels even today and how absolutely fantastic it must have felt in 1961. My co-driver on the Geneva trip was Mark Hughes who was writing it up for *Classic & Sports Car* magazine. As a former Editor of the magazine, he has vast experience and was seriously impressed.

Following pages: The return to Geneva and the *Parc des Eaux Vives* was an emotive one. So little has changed that we were able to recognise exactly where the car had been positioned all those years before when history was made. Compare this shot with the original on pages 92 – 93.

With smiles on everybody's faces, we were a happy bunch. Most of those present for our little pilgrimage had played a part in the recent story, whether it be filming, photographing, writing, researching in Geneva or working on the car. Personally, I was exhausted but elated beyond words. Note the restaurant in the background, as seen in the shot on page 90.

influences on this car and I think that's something that needs to be said. And the best way to do that is to film and show this being brought back to life.'

In Denmark Christian Frost has written several articles in *Bil Magasinet*. This magazine is a glossy, stylish journal which majors on modern cars. Every year they conduct a readership survey to determine readers' favourite articles. Christian's articles on 9600 HP came out top!

After eleven long months, how do they feel at CMC now? 'We were excited at the beginning,' says Nick Goldthorp, 'but now that the car's finished, the excitement is growing. For me, on the business side, having got the car completed in quite a tight time schedule has been an achievement. Before Christmas, I was quite concerned whether it would be finished on time. The body seemed to take forever. I remember adding the hours up each week and thinking, "Oh, bloody hell!" Everything else on the car has been very smooth and quite planned and has all come together as we imagined. Everyone in the company knew this was a unique opportunity for them. It has created a really good team effort and everybody's contributed to the car in some shape or form. Everybody's enjoyed it.'

Andrew Tart: 'For years and years, for as long as I've been involved with E-types, I've always hankered after restoring this car. It is just the ultimate car. I like challenges. It's a wonderful challenge. It's fun to try to find out the history and what's happened to it. That's what it is all about. It can be a vintage Alfa or any other car, but if you can go into the history and find individual problems that other people had

After the posing, a little action. This is the hairpin on the old test course and I did not need asking twice when somebody suggested I do a Bob Berry for the cameras. Whilst I will do all in my power to look after this most historic car for posterity, I am not going to wrap it in cotton wool. It has had an exciting life and I hope its second life will continue in like manner.

Previous pages: The Roadster was completed some years ago and, to my surprise and pleasure, I discovered it had been used in the late sixties in the film *The Italian Job*. By the time 9600 HP was completed, I had owned the cars 23 years and the house and barns 22 years. By a mixture of unrelenting hard work, plenty of luck, the assistance of several key people including Andrew Tart and Peter Neumark, and dogged blinkered determination, I had eventually achieved several of my long-term goals.

with the car and what happened during its history, that's fun. That's as much fun as the restoration. As we pulled the car apart, it was a lot of fun learning how bits and pieces were put together.

'You pick up a Jaguar book – not just one of yours – and 9600 HP is in there. With Ferraris or Alfa Romeos, people don't talk about an individual car. But if you talk about E-types, this is the one. There are very few marques that have an icon as this is. So this is *the* E-type.

'We all pride ourselves in our work and without exception we all enjoy what we do, that's why we do it. I have tried to restore it in such a way that when it's restored again in, let's say, another 40 years, the restorer will be just as enthusiastic and understand what we did. Now it is finished I am dead chuffed. The car looks like an old E-type, not like a re-manufactured E-type as so many do. You can look at the original photographs and it's the same car. It sits in the same way and it gives the same impressions. It'll be nice to drive it quickly.'

I am often asked what makes the E-type so special. I believe it is the intoxicating combination of driving pleasure and the beautiful, sensuous body that is a stunning, timeless piece of pure automotive sculpture. Today we live in a nanny state, but the E-type was a rebel, and handsome rebels often become romantic idols. It is a reminder of a freer, less regulated age. It is thrilling to think that 9600 HP led the way, both in style and performance.

On *Top Gear* Quentin was in his element, eulogizing away. 'British sports cars aren't what they were. But 39 years ago the King Kong of British sports cars was born. In 1961 for around two thousand pounds you could buy a missile that would do almost 150 and make the nearest female bite the back of her hand – the Jaguar E-type. And there isn't a car in the entire world, and I include all your Ferraris, that has been as pretty as this. So, what's so special about this E-type? Well, 9600 HP is the oldest surviving example, but more than that, this was the car that everyone saw splashed all over their newspapers in March '61, the car that reached 150, the car that was so perfect for the sixties.

'The last time I saw this car was, I don't know, about ten years ago in a barn – flat tyres, cobwebs, mossy, rusty – and it is just fantastic to see it now, completely restored after three thousand hours of very, very hard work back to its original immaculate condition. But has the old girl still got it, can she still make headlines?' He wound up 9600 HP down a two-and-a-half mile runway and we saw the speedo on 140 and, moments later, Quentin exclaim '150'!

In the mid sixties, an American journalist Henry Manney III famously summed up the E-type as 'The Greatest Crumpet Catcher Known to Man'. He wrote, '…I have driven many cars here, there and everywhere, getting more than my fair share of appraising looks, and as I am an ugly and hairy old man I have never taken them for my benefit. Conducting the E-type roadster I got enough dark looks to curl my hair; two birds actually tried to pick me up, and fur-faced Jenkinson (owner of a red coupé) even claims that girls smile at *him*. The Jaguar advertising boys have been barking up the wrong tree with their grice, spice and pice. All they need to point out is … "If You Want to Get Laid, Buy a Jaguar". Then all Sir William would need to do is take over BMC's factories and turn out Es like bread rolls.' The irony is that, in 1966, BMC took over Jaguar. Clearly Jaguar had not listened to Manney's advice. The added irony is that by early 2000 it looked as though Jaguar production would soon overtake that of the combined total of the old BMC companies.

Just as I was completing this chapter, I heard that Bob Berry had returned from the USA earlier than planned. To my intense relief, he confirmed that it was indeed just before midday that he had arrived in Geneva in 1961. He agreed that the invitation referred to a separate function for Sir William's special friends, something he was wont to do.

This happy-looking gentleman is Peter Neumark, caught by David Parmiter's camera as Peter took the wheel for a stint *en route* to Geneva. Without Peter's enthusiasm, this amazing restoration would never have happened and the last three chapters could not have been written.

That 9600 HP is once more able to take the stage is a tribute to Peter, Andrew, Nick, Tim, Baz, Colin, younger Andrew, trimmers Tom and Dan, painters Steve, Ian and Matt, plus many others behind the scenes, the parts suppliers, the sub-contractors and the support team at CMC. They all deserve enormous credit.

Without my father's support, I would never have become the owner (I prefer *custodian*) of 9600 HP. Without Andrew Tart's burning ambition, the restoration would never have happened in this way. Without Peter Neumark's business success, enthusiasm for the car and drive, it never *could* have happened in this way. To me, the final twist in this convoluted tale is the realization that if 9600 HP had not sat in my old barn for 22 years, it would never have been restored to this extraordinary standard. It is only very recently that the conservation approach has been adopted. Just proves, it does not pay to rush into these things!

The story of 9600 HP is ongoing, with new adventures ahead. Looking back, it almost seems like a fairy tale and too good to be true. I am a very lucky chap. Above all, 9600 HP lives again.

If you think the Jaguar script badge on the tailgate is crooked, it is. It was originally. It is part of the character of this car, a car which seems to make friends wherever it goes. As the very lucky custodian of 9600 HP, I look forward to sharing the car with as many friends as possible in the years to come.

First published in hardback in 2000 by Orion Media
an imprint of Orion Books Ltd
Orion House, 5 Upper St Martin's Lane, London WC2H 9EA

Copyright © First published in paperback in 2002 Philip Porter 2000

Philip Porter hereby asserts his moral right to be identified as the author of *The Most Famous Car in the World*. All rights reserved. No part of this publication may be reproduced, stored in a retrieval system, or transmitted, in any form or by any means, electronic, mechanical, photocopying , recording or otherwise, without the prior permission of the copyright holder.

A CIP catalogue record for this book is available from the British Library.

ISBN 0 75283 182 8

Designed by Staziker Jones, Cardiff

Printed in Italy Printer Trento S.r.l.

PICTURE CREDITS

Tony Alden: 121. Tim Andrew: Front cover, endpapers, ii, 160, 226, 228, 240, 245. BP: 9. Bob Blake: 34. Derek Brant: 156. Bernard Cahier: 68, 74, 77, 80. Norman Dewis: 19, 50, 52. Express Newspapers: 96. Arthur Foster: 168, 170. Christian Frost: 5 (lower). Geneva Motor Show: 83. Julian Ghosh: 29 (upper). Nigel Harniman: Back cover. Haymarket/LAT: 99, 118. Hulton Getty: 111. Jaguar Daimler Heritage Trust: 3, 17, 45, 54, 57, 59, 90, 91, 92, 108, 115, 117, 123. John Langley: 81. Peter Lockhart Smith: 139, 141 Peter Murray: 29 (lower). David Parmiter: 4, 5 (upper), 172, 224, 233, 235, 236, 238, 239, 243. John Pearson: 16. Philip Porter: iv, vi, 38, 136, 177, 178, 179, 180, 181, 182, 183, 185, 186, 187, 191, 193, 194, 195, 196, 197, 198, 200, 201, 202, 203, 204, 205, 208, 209, 211, 212, 213, 217, 218, 221, 230, 231. Kate Sayer: 25, 31. Paul Skilleter: 122, 145. Michael Tee: 207.